# Introducing Sociological Theory

## DARREN O'BYRNE
Roehampton University

**Longman**
is an imprint of

Harlow, England • London • New York • Boston • San Francisco • Toronto
Sydney • Tokyo • Singapore • Hong Kong • Seoul • Taipei • New Delhi
Cape Town • Madrid • Mexico City • Amsterdam • Munich • Paris • Milan

**Pearson Education Limited**
Edinburgh Gate
Harlow
Essex CM20 2JE
England

and Associated Companies throughout the world

*Visit us on the World Wide Web at:*
www.pearsoned.co.uk

First published 2011

© Pearson Education Limited 2011

ISBN: 978-1-4082-0388-0

**British Library Cataloguing-in-Publication Data**
A catalogue record for this book is available from the British Library

**Library of Congress Cataloging-in-Publication Data**
O'Byrne, Darren.
 Introducing sociological theory/Darren O'Byrne. – 1st ed.
   p.  cm.
 Includes bibliographical references and index.
 ISBN 978-1-4082-0388-0 (pbk.)
1. Sociology.  I. Title.
 HM585.0297  2011
 301–dc22

                                        2011010533

10 9 8 7 6 5 4 3 2 1
14 13 12 11

Typeset in 10.5/14.5pt Sabon by 35
Printed and bound in Great Britain by Henry Ling Ltd.,
at the Dorset Press, Dorchester, Dorset

# Contents

Contents

# Acknowledgements

## Author's acknowledgements

Over the years, I have enjoyed teaching sociological theory alongside a variety of colleagues, whose distinctive approaches have helped to inform my own. These include: Sarah Cant; Steven Groarke; Alex Hensby; Christopher Jackman; David Woodman. My personal love affair with this subject matter, though, was probably shaped during my undergraduate years at Sheffield University, and for that, I owe a huge debt of gratitude to Maurice Roche, a quietly inspiring and always supportive tutor. I must also thank Andrew Taylor at Pearson, who first encouraged me to undertake this project and who has been supportive throughout its execution. Finally, I would like to thank the many students who have had to endure my classes on sociological theory, for doing so politely and with good humour!

## Publisher's Acknowledgements

The publishers would like to thank the many reviewers who have commented upon, and helped improve, the original idea, and the draft chapters, for this book.

We also thank Darren O'Byrne for the dedication, skill and commitment to teaching sociological theory he put into writing the book.

The publisher would also like to thank the following for their kind permission to reproduce their material:

Tables

Table 9.3 from *Theorising Global Studies* Palgrave (O'Byrne, D. and Hensby, A. 2011), reproduced with permission of Palgrave Macmillan.

## Acknowledgements

Picture Credits

(Key: b-bottom; c-centre; l-left; r-right; t-top)

Alamy Images: INTERFOTO 48, The Art Gallery Collection 25; American Sociological Association: 119tl, 150tl; Columbia University Archives: 37; Corbis: Bettmann 93tc, Swim Ink 71; Getty Images: AFP 50, 196tl, Time & Life Pictures 51, 125bl, Harvard University Archives: 31; **PARIS MATCH/SCOOP:** IZIS 198tl; TopFoto: The Granger Collection, New York 102bl, 145bl.

All other images © Pearson Education

Every effort has been made to trace the copyright holders and we apologise in advance for any unintentional omissions. We would be pleased to insert the appropriate acknowledgement in any subsequent edition of this publication.

# 1 | Introduction: The history of sociological theory

## What is sociology?

Yes, this is another book about sociological theory. And no, this is not the only book about sociological theory that you will need if you want to fully understand the history of and complex debates within that field of inquiry. It is intended to be a first step along the journey to achieving that understanding, nothing more. There are plenty of good books out there which cover sociological theory and go into considerable detail about the many perspectives contained within our discipline of sociology. But one problem I have consistently encountered in all the years I have been teaching theory classes to sociology students is that however good and well written such a book is, it falls on deaf ears if it presumes too much background knowledge. A chapter on functionalism may contain the most elaborate explanation of **Talcott Parsons**'s famous AGIL scheme but this is pointless if the reader is not yet equipped to understand what functionalism even is. A chapter on Marxism may contain a fantastic introduction to **Karl Marx**'s surplus theory of value but such knowledge is lost on a reader who is not yet clear on what a Marxist approach actually involves. And so on, and so forth . . .

It was during the course of a conversation about precisely this problem that an astute commissioning editor uttered those ominous words to me: *Why don't you write the book that solves this problem?* This book, the final product of that conversation, is an attempt to *introduce* sociological theory without all the detail about complicated ideas, major studies, lots of names, but rather through an engagement with eight major traditions and perspectives in the discipline, eight distinctive ways of seeing the world sociologically. Yes, it will introduce you to names. Yes, it will introduce you to a selection of studies. And yes, it will highlight some of those complex ideas. But its purpose is not to provide the

1

definitive account of them – for that, you should consult one of the other, larger texts or, even better, when you feel ready to, check out the original source – but to use them as illustrative of what each perspective actually means, to see how those contributions reflect and form part of a wider tradition or perspective. You, the reader, the student of sociology, are invited to put yourself in the place of an exponent of each of these perspectives, to imagine how they see the world, to *do* sociology as they would do it. What does it involve to see the world as a Marxist, feminist or interactionist? What tools and concepts are used to make sense of the world?

Sociology is the study of society – and society is comprised of people and the institutions they create to best manage their lives. These institutions include government and politics, the economy, religion, the family, education, work, culture and media, business and organisations, sport and leisure. Each of these institutions serves a purpose in the lives of 'ordinary' people, but each of them, like society itself, is driven by inequalities inherent in the social **structure** – inequalities based on class, status, 'race' and ethnicity, gender, age, sexuality, physicality. Sociologists are interested in all of these institutions and inequalities, and their intersections. All of this seems clear enough, surely, but for some commentators, sociology lacks credibility as a discipline. Why should this be the case? Other disciplines, such as biology, psychology and history, don't seem to suffer from this problem. This is partly, no doubt, because its scope is so broad that it has lost its focus, become nothing more than an unnecessary vocabulary which, along with sibling disciplines and fields such as social anthropology and cultural studies, merely serves to over-complicate common sense. Or so the argument goes. It's certainly an argument I have heard time and time again, when I have described myself to people as a sociologist.

There can be no doubt that 'common sense' provides the intellectual breeding ground for sociological insight. But this is equally true of other disciplines. We can all be amateur historians. Like biologists, we all have bodies, so we know about them, in one capacity or another. Even hard science is to some extent driven by common sense – how many scientific miracles have been first imagined by writers of science fiction? Sociology suffers most because it provides opinions on the things that we live through and in as people, every day of our lives. But the academic study of society is not the same as the everyday understanding of it, any more than the academic study of the body is the same as the physical reality of living with it. Sociology answers to a broad set of questions about how society works, how it evolves, what its constituent parts are and how they relate to one another, and what part people play in its constitution.

To understand the meaning of sociology as a discipline, one first has to understand what is meant by its subject matter, society, the social. When we talk of a social event, we tend to mean one attended by friends bound by something not related to work, but to friendship or family, or perhaps it does involve work colleagues, but it is not in itself a work event. People meet socially. Alternatively, politicians and their constituents talk about social security, or social services. What unites drunken parties and welfare policies? The answer is surprisingly simple. Former British prime minister Margaret Thatcher famously declared that there is 'no such thing as society'. To her credit, the then Conservative leader used the term 'society' appropriately – she wanted to make the point that you, the voter, the individual, the citizen, the consumer, have no responsibility towards others, even those less fortunate than you, no duty to protect anyone other than yourself, and no expectation of support from other people, or from the government. It is down to you to make your way in this world. Thatcher's dismissal of society is reminiscent of, if ideologically opposed to, an equally accurate theorisation of 'society' – the French philosopher Jean-Paul Sartre's famous suggestion that Hell is others. Living in a world with other people is difficult. It means we cannot get away with what we really want to get away with; we cannot exercise total freedom. We are bound by the fact that we live in a world with other people, and we have to take them into consideration whenever we act. Society is about other people. Sociology is the study of how we live in a world with other people.

Some sociologists limit themselves to the study of particular components of society. Thus, there are sociologists of religion, of education, of the family, and so on. Others try to provide bold theoretical frameworks for the dynamics of nothing less than society itself. Others still make modest comments about human action and behaviour, and grow to be treated as exponents of broader concerns. Sociologists are interested in all of these concerns. They ask 'grand-scale' questions about the emergence of societies and the state, and analyse historical social change and large-scale processes such as industrialisation, **capitalism**, and, more recently, **globalisation**. But they also ask questions about identity, human **agency** and the self. They are concerned with culture, our norms and values, what it is produced by and how it impacts on our lives, and how it may carry a particular bias, in the form of **ideology**. They ask how individuals interact with one another, and how social networks and kinship systems operate. They look at the multiple forms of inequality, social stratification, that exist in societies, including hierarchies of class, gender, ethnicity, and so on. They ask how **social order** is maintained and who exercises power in societies.

If sociology is about all of these, what makes it distinct? To answer that question, we can turn to one of its most vociferous champions, the nineteenth-century French sociologist **Emile Durkheim**. Durkheim wrote a famous book in which he compared the suicide rates in different countries. He wanted to show that suicides could be caused by factors external to the individual, factors to do with the norms and values of those societies and the individual's relationship to them. He was trying to prove a point, that although suicide is one of the most intimate and personal things you could look at, to fully understand it we need to look beyond psychology, the science of the individual mind, and analyse it sociologically. A sociological theory thus looks for factors outside the human mind to explain phenomena like suicide, or educational achievement, or gender inequalities, or kinship systems.

Since Durkheim's famous defence of sociology as a discipline not reducible to psychology, sociologists have been comfortable with the knowledge that their discipline is in every sense legitimate. *Social* theory, however, is broader in scope than *sociological* theory. Consider three disciplines – sociology, psychology and biology. A sociologist and a psychologist may be interested in the same object of study, such as suicide rates. What distinguishes them, as Durkheim rightly claimed, is their choice of explanatory factors. Similarly, psychologists and biologists have often been interested in seeking to explain the same phenomena, such as mental illness, but have done so using quite different methods. It is not inconceivable for biologists and sociologists to overlap as well – both may be interested in the causes of crime (as might the psychologist). But such overlaps are less common. For the most part, sociologists may have engaged in active debates with psychologists, but have left biologists alone. Why, after all, should a sociologist try to explain how the human heart works, or how plants receive their nourishment? Sociology – like any other discipline – has never promised to explain everything! Similarly, why should biologists, whose discipline is equally legitimate and equally modest, seek to understand the reasons for the significance of religion in people's lives, or the relationship between class and educational achievement?

However, the relationship between the two disciplines is not, actually, so egalitarian. Sociology simply does not have the tools to even try to explain how the heart pumps blood around the body. Biologists, though, do have the tools with which to try to explain, should they feel the need, almost every aspect of human life, even religious meaning or educational achievement. From crude physiological studies of criminality to contemporary popular ideas emerging from the study of genetics, biologists are (at least hypothetically) capable of providing a plausible *biological* explanation of a *social* phenomenon. Biology can, then, give us a social – if not a sociological – theory. During the early days of sociology as a discipline, many of its practitioners were doing just this, using biology as a basis for their pseudo-sociology. Back in the nineteenth century, the French physician Paul Broca linked brain size to intelligence in order to show that men are naturally more intelligent than women. An Italian prison doctor, Cesar Lombroso, then claimed he could identify certain physical markings, such as small craniums and pinned-back ears, that distinguished criminals from non-criminals. Examples like this may seem ludicrous to us now, and rightly so, but they do at least serve to highlight the distinctiveness of a sociological approach. Gender inequalities and criminal behaviour are entirely appropriate objects of study for sociologists, but the sociologist would not seek to explain them in terms of such physical characteristics, but rather in the broader institutions, norms and values of wider society. It is not the *question* which gives sociology its distinctiveness, but the *answer*.

All of which leaves one question still unanswered. Is sociology a science? Certainly, as we will see, some of its founders certainly thought so. But others, especially more recently, have resisted making such claims. We frequently refer to sociology as a *social science*, as if this

## EXERCISE 1.1  Sociology, psychology and biology

Throughout this book I will be setting you little exercises to try to follow through on the points I want to introduce in the text. In this case, I want you to think about the differences between a sociological, psychological and biological explanation for something. Try to think of one example of each kind of explanation for the five problems listed. I've already provided you with some starters in the text above.

| | Sociology | Psychology | Biology |
|---|---|---|---|
| 1 Why might some people commit crimes? | | | |
| 2 Why might some people do better at school than others? | | | |
| 3 Why do some people have more political power than others? | | | |
| 4 Why might some people commit suicide? | | | |
| 5 Why might some people believe in religion? | | | |

carves out a space for it between the 'real' sciences and the humanities, but this is perhaps just a way of dodging the question. The truth is, it *can* be a science, but it doesn't have to be. For something to be a 'science' has nothing to do with how academic subjects are arranged in convenient groups, like faculties at universities. It depends on what the point of the specific research is. If you are studying something with a view to uncovering general laws, to *explain*, then you are conducting a science. But if you wish to *interpret* an event, document it, without trying to generalise, then your research fits better under the banner of the 'humanities'. If you intend for your work to uncover not laws but *problems*, to serve as a critique of the way things are and inspire change, then it clearly has a more practical, political, activist focus. Over the years, sociology has been all of these things.

## A brief history of sociological theory

If this is how we can define sociology, then there is some truth to the suggestion that is often made that the discipline was being practised long before it found itself named and formalised as an academic subject. Many classical philosophers, theologians and political theorists were effectively doing some form of sociology. However, for the sake of this brief introduction, it is probably wise to skip through them and concentrate on the formal origins of the discipline. It was a nineteenth-century Frenchman, **Auguste Comte**, who first named sociology as a discipline in its own right. Comte set himself the task of establishing a *positive science* of society. That is to say, he believed it was possible to treat the social world in much the same was as a scientist treats the natural world – to uncover the universal laws that *explain* why it is as it is. You should note here that Comte's **positivism** was very different from those kinds of approach to social behaviour which merely sought to extend existing ways of explaining things to accommodate social action. Someone who, for example, uses biological explanations to tell us why a person commits crimes is hardly doing any sociology! They are trying to explain social phenomena biologically. Comte by contrast wanted to establish sociology as a distinctive science to take its place next to the likes of physics, chemistry and biology. Like them it would utilise scientific *method*, the use of experimental methods and the development of generalisable laws to explain things, but these would be its own laws. Comte took the idea of society to be a thing in its own right, an object of study capable of being explained in this fashion. It is hardly surprising that, in these early days of the discipline, so much emphasis was placed on establishing sociology as a science – it was a means of legitimising it. Although the pioneering British sociologist **Herbert Spencer** approached his subject matter in a way radically different from Comte, he also sought to foreground its scientific credentials by utilising developments in evolutionary biological theory and applying them to the question of social change.

Comte and Spencer were responsible for getting sociology off to a start, but the key contributors to its development in the nineteenth century

7

were Karl Marx, Emile Durkheim and **Max Weber** – the so-called 'holy trinity' of founding fathers. These three classical writers differed greatly in so many important ways, and thus effectively paving the foundations for the eclectic range of different sociological schools of thought which were to emerge in the twentieth century, but in a sense, they were all united by a single shared curiosity. Each of them was aware that around them, the world was changing rapidly. The nineteenth century in Europe was the time of the Industrial Revolution. Factories were being established to accommodate the new system of production made possible by new technologies. People were flocking from the villages to where these factories were located, and new urban areas, cities, were emerging as a result. Life in these cities was qualitatively different from life in smaller rural communities: people related to one another in different ways, more specific roles were being developed. Entire ways of life were being transformed – community bonds giving way to more formalised networks of association, extended family structures breaking up and being replaced by more immediate nuclear family structures. There were changes, too, in how goods were bought and sold, with the onset of the new capitalist economy. Entire hierarchies of power were being transformed. The old 'feudal' model of the landed gentry, the aristocracy, enjoying the luxuries of life solely by virtue of having been born into it while the 'peasants' worked the land under the patronage of their lords, with no opportunity to ever be on a par with them, was being brushed aside. Capitalism transferred power to a new 'middle class' comprised of those among the former lower class, the serfs, who had enterprisingly taken advantage of the new factory technologies. Suddenly, power and status were not things one had because they were ascribed to them at birth, but rather things that were achieved through work, investment and the capacity to exploit the new system. The entire political landscape was changing – as the new middle classes enjoyed more and more economic power, so did they demand more political power. Political power was relocated from the local communities to the cities, and especially to the capitals. Arbitrary local decision-making surrendered to the more formalised rule of law. Control over the 'means of violence' – the right to exercise punishment and carry out 'justice' – was wrested from the hands of individuals and communities and given over to the law courts, the police, the army, all agencies of the state. The modern centralised nation state, with absolute authority for the maintenance of social order within its recognised territorial boundaries, was born.

These were sweeping transformations. Naturally, they did not happen overnight, but such was their impact that the greatest minds of the time were understandably inspired to ask the simplest of questions: *what, precisely, is the cause of all of this?* This is the intellectual curiosity that drove Marx, Durkheim and Weber, and more besides, to develop their complex and brilliant accounts of the social world. Each of them, metaphorically, looked out of his window and felt compelled to investigate the things that were happening around him. They were, each of them, looking at the same world, aware of the same transformations, even if Weber was in Germany, Durkheim in France, and Marx, writing a generation before the other two, was a German who spent much of his life in England. Precisely how they proceeded to explain those same transformations is what makes them so remarkably distinct, and it is from these distinctions that modern sociology really does emerge. Marx insisted that the driving force behind all this change was the transformation from a feudal 'mode of production' to a capitalist one. By 'mode of production', he merely meant a system for organising the economy, the production of material goods necessary for survival. Marx's account, which we come to in greater detail in Chapter 4, was a fundamentally *materialist* one, and his core concern was that if the feudal system had been defined by an exploitative power relationship between the aristocracy and the serfs, the new capitalist system had merely replaced that with an even more exploitative relationship between the *bourgeoisie*, the owners of the factories and the like, and the *proletariat*, who worked for them. These were the new **social classes**, defined objectively by how their members relate to the means of production (either as owner or as worker). Humans are naturally creative animals, but this capacity to work and to create is inherently stifled in capitalism, where those who do the work do not benefit directly from it (he called this **alienation**). Capitalism, in Marx's mind, was based entirely on one group of people benefiting from the labour of another, and this, by its very definition, constituted exploitation. He set about describing this unequal system in vivid detail and predicting the inevitable fall of capitalism and its replacement with a new *communist* mode of production in which those who work retain control over and benefit from their labour.

9

Durkheim and Weber both entered into an implicit dialogue with Marx. Durkheim did not believe that the shift from feudalism to capitalism was unimportant, but felt instead that the primary factor in the transformations in society was not changing economic relations so much as changing sociocultural ones. A professional sociologist and anthropologist (unlike Marx who was a writer and an activist more than anything), Durkheim was most fascinated by the transformation from one way of life to another – from a set of social arrangements characterised by strong community bonds and flexible roles, which he called 'mechanical solidarity', to one characterised by greater individuality and a more rigid division of labour with more specialised and formalised social roles, which he called 'organic solidarity'. It was Durkheim who gave us the idea of the *conscience collective*, the shared value system which unites people into a single societal community. The weakening of those collective bonds, and detachment from the wider value system, results in a condition of normlessness, or *anomie*. Like Comte, then, he saw society as a thing in itself, *sui generis*, and is often described in similar fashion as a sociological positivist, committed to uncovering laws and to studying social *facts*.

Weber undertook a more direct engagement with Marx's ideas, and effectively inverted much of the emphasis Marx had placed on forms of economic organisation as being the engine of society. Weber wanted to show, *contra* Marx, that the capitalist form of economic organisation was itself a reflection of a changing *world view*. Being a materialist, Marx had argued that matter predates ideas. Weber disagreed. He saw the real issue at the heart of these great transformations as being the emergence of a new form of *rationality*. He argued that it was a new way of seeing the world, linked to Protestantism and emphasising individualism and competitiveness, that had made capitalism possible. Weber also differed from Marx and Durkheim by placing far greater emphasis on the duty of the sociologist to try to understand the world as it is experienced by people in it – on **interpretation**, or, to use the German word, *verstehen*. According to Weber, this process of rationalisation was ushering in a dominant way of seeing the world heavily committed to finding answers to questions, solutions to problems, means to ends. It was manifesting itself not only in the guise of capitalism but in the emerging institutions of social control and regulation, attached to the modern nation state. More so than either of the other two 'founding fathers', Weber's was a pessimistic sociology, describing as it did an increasingly regulated world in which freedom was being eroded, and power transferred from people to impersonal systems.

We can see, then, that each of the three was attempting to understand the driving forces behind this massive process of social change going on around them – the transition from 'tradition' to 'modernity'. Clearly, for Marx, that motor was an economic one, the transition essentially being the change from a feudal to a capitalist economy, with everything else a direct result of that. For Durkheim, the motor was sociocultural, consisting of changing norms and values. For Weber, the motor was political, in so far as it was about a new way of seeing, ordering and regulating the world. Table 1.1 gives us a snapshot of how these three approached similar questions with quite different answers.

So, the classical sociological theorists – Marx, Durkheim, Weber, and also Comte, Spencer, and many others – developed their ideas in an effort to understand the sweeping social, economic, cultural and political transformations brought about by the Industrial Revolution in Europe. As a body of knowledge, their combined works contributed to the professionalisation of sociology as an academic discipline. Another important pioneer of sociology during this classical phase – who is often relegated to the margins of the discipline because he did not have the direct impact on the later emergence of sociological schools that the others did – was **Georg Simmel**. Simmel's kind of sociology was distinctive because he paid far more attention to the *forms* of social interaction, the different ways people related to one another. He was still interested in comparing old with new, though, just like Marx, Durkheim and Weber. For him, new forms of sociality had emerged which had exposed the individual to more dispersed networks or 'webs' of interaction. Simmel's greatest contribution was his insistence that we need to understand the micro-dynamics of interaction in order to better understand the macro-dynamics of power and social change.

It is worth noting at this stage that this potted history of the early days of sociology excludes a number of important names. Not only could much be said, space permitting, about the contributions of others,

Table 1.1 Comparing and contrasting Marx, Durkheim and Weber

|  | Marx | Durkheim | Weber |
|---|---|---|---|
| *What type of activity forms the social base?* | Economic activity (work, labour, production) | Sociocultural activity (norms, values, ways of life) | Political activity (rationalisation, ways of ordering and regulating) |
| *What characterises the transformation from traditional to modern society?* | Feudalism to capitalism (i.e. different modes of production) | Mechanical to organic solidarity (i.e. different patterns of social relationship) | Tradition and value-based rationality to instrumental rationality (i.e. different forms of action) |
| *What forms the basis of the division of labour in society?* | Social class (i.e. different economic positions, relationships to the means of production) | Differentiation and specialisation (i.e. different roles in society) | Class, status and party as distinctions derived from economic, social and political positions |
| *What characterises the type of estrangement prevalent in modern society?* | Alienation (i.e. estrangement from the product of labour and the process of production) | Anomie (i.e. estrangement from the value system of wider society) | Disenchantment (i.e. estrangement from the machinery of government, the 'red tape' of bureaucracy) |
| *What provides the basis for collectivism in modern society?* | Shared class consciousness (i.e. realisation of mutual economic position) | Conscience collective (i.e. realisation of shared norms and values) | The state (i.e. shared sense of identity within a political territory) |
| *Humans are social animals because . . .* | . . . they have the capacity for consciousness (*homo sapiens*) and for creativity (*homo faber*) | . . . they live in a world of shared norms and values; they live in communities, and sociality is constructed | . . . they have the capacity for meaningful social action as opposed to just behavioural action |
| *The sociologist should look at . . .* | . . . the dialectical relationship between structure and agency | . . . the way structure shapes agency | . . . the way agency shapes structure |

but the list itself is entirely white, Western and male. Even so, it is a fair list of the most important individual contributors to the discipline, in so far as their contributions have been acknowledged to have created a discernible legacy. This is not to say that sociology was not being done by non-Westerners, people of colour, or women – far from it. It is just to recognise, to our collective shame, that such contributions were largely downplayed or ignored. It is commonplace now for sociological theory books to seek to correct this retrospectively, at least to some degree. For example, while books on classical sociological theory cannot exclude Marx, Durkheim and Weber, many add one or another pioneering feminist scholar to the list (Harriet Martineau, Harriet Taylor Mill and **Charlotte Perkins-Gilman** appear to be among the most popular selections). The truth of the matter is that in most cases such pioneers did not exert as much influence over the discipline as they should have done, and their rediscovery and promotion to the high table is a matter of contemporary sensibility rather than historical accuracy.

Although its pioneers were largely European, it was in the United States of America that the academic study of sociology took off in the early twentieth century. In particular, it was in universities across the Midwest, and most importantly at the University of Chicago, that modern sociology took shape. Chicago was the home to a number of extraordinary social researchers and theorists – **Robert Ezra Park**, Ernest Burgess, Jane Addams, Albion Small, **George Herbert Mead**, to name just a few. Park, for instance, had worked as a journalist and as secretary to the civil rights activist Booker T. Washington, and while he appreciated the need for theory, having studied under Simmel, he was particularly committed to the practical side of sociology, famously telling his students to go out into the world and 'get their hands dirty'. Park and his colleague Burgess were particularly fascinated by the influence of the environment upon behaviour. Chicago was a thriving metropolis, full of energy but at the same time riddled with social problems such as crime and unemployment. Members of the 'Chicago school' linked these to the expansion of the city. Burgess famously mapped the city according to its socio-economic arrangement (see Figure 1.1), as members of the school 'got their hands dirty' carrying out research using **ethnographic methods** into life in the more run-down parts of the city, the 'zone of transition'. Park's dedication to the ethnographic study of everyday life, echoed by his colleagues in the Chicago school, then merged with the social psychology of Mead and others, to gave rise to what was probably the first great sociological tradition – symbolic interactionism (which we discuss in detail in Chapter 7).

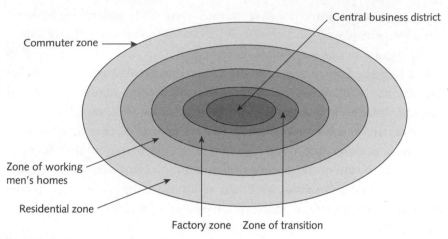

**Figure 1.1** Burgess's model of concentric urban zones

The Chicago dominance eventually waned out, and after the Second World War, the focus of sociological activity shifted eastwards, to the genteel Ivy League surroundings of Harvard University, where a young sociologist named Talcott Parsons was attracting considerable interest. Parsons had also studied in Europe, and had encountered the ideas of Weber and Durkheim, among others. In his first book, he constructed a theoretical framework, known as the *voluntaristic theory of action*, drawing heavily on Weber. In his second major work, Parsons shifted away from action theory towards a more structurally oriented, holistic view of the world. This theoretical approach, which saw society as a kind of *system* comprised of interrelated parts, became known as structural functionalism, and in the hands of Parsons and his students and colleagues, especially **Robert Merton**, Kingsley Davis and Wilbert E. Moore, it dominated sociological thought during the 1950s. Indeed, functionalism as a framework for conceptualising society was so absolutely dominant at this time that as many commentators have pointed out, to do *sociology* was effectively to do *functionalism*. If you get the chance to pick up any student-focused sociology text book from the time, you will see what I mean. Whereas today we have numerous books like this one outlining many of the alternative frameworks available to you, many such books from the 1950s had no space and no need for introducing and contrasting such alternatives, as it was taken for granted that the functionalist framework was *the* framework for doing sociology. We will be examining this framework in greater depth in Chapter 2.

Of course, it was never the case that functionalism enjoyed a total monopoly in the discipline. There were always significant dissenting voices, of which the name of **C. Wright Mills** comes first and foremost to mind. Critics were rightly pointing out that the functionalist framework was far from universal in its reach. It was very much a reflection of its time and place. In the United States and Great Britain in the 1950s, it was a time of relative social and economic prosperity, of post-war political consensus, and of nation-building. From the wealthy, white, Western, male perspective of Harvard, the world must indeed have seemed like a relatively stable and harmonious place. Outbreaks of conflict, dissent, inequality, could have very easily been dismissed as mere blips, problems which could be sorted out, rather than anything more endemic. Functionalism quickly established itself as the dominant paradigm not only for understanding the social world 'at home' in Britain and the US, but it also presented itself as an exemplary framework for development and nation-building worldwide. Its implicit advocacy of Western liberal, democratic, capitalist values, its inherent conservatism, its inability to deal with social change, conflict and difference, soon became all too obvious. Issues easily dismissed as 'blips' in the 1950s had by the 1960s become major concerns, such that they could no longer be ignored or downplayed, even from the ivory towers of Harvard. Against a backdrop of the Vietnam War, the civil rights struggle, women's liberation, anti-colonial independence struggles, political corruption, and numerous other signs of conflict in society worldwide, younger scholars turned away from functionalism towards more critical approaches. In Europe, **Ralf Dahrendorf**, **John Rex**, John Goldthorpe and David Lockwood, and others were constructing an alternative approach, inspired largely by Weber, which foregrounded the role of conflict in modern societies (which we cover in Chapter 3). Feminist activists, such as **Kate Millett** and **Shulamith Firestone**, were developing more radical projects in opposition to issues of male power (discussed in Chapter 5). There was also a rediscovery of Marx, and a growing significance of some major neo-Marxist theorists of the twentieth century, including

**Antonio Gramsci**, the Frankfurt School of critical theory, and **Louis Althusser** (all of which are discussed in Chapter 4). Around the world, Andre Gunder Frank and others were successfully shifting the focus of attention away from simple 'development' towards complex issues of power relations, juxtaposing the economic, social and political power of the Western countries with the relative powerlessness of those in Latin America, Africa and parts of Asia.

Various other sociological approaches emerged which contributed to the assault on functionalism from entirely different angles. **George Homans**, a friend and colleague of Parsons at Harvard, launched an attack on Parsonian functionalism for being abstract, overly holistic, and ignorant of the most important thing about all societies – the people living in them! His 'exchange theory' was an attempt to bring the individual actor back into sociology (and is the subject matter of Chapter 6). Interactionist sociology also experienced a renaissance, thanks to **Howard Becker**'s 'labelling theory' and the dramaturgical approach of **Erving Goffman**, and from it sprang **Harold Garfinkel**'s 'ethnomethodology', an audacious new paradigm which challenged nothing less than the foundations of sociology itself (see Chapter 8). Structuralist thinking, which was long since established in social anthropology and other disciplines, began to exert an influence on sociology (see Chapter 9). Sociological theory was rife with a plurality of alternative approaches.

During the 1980s, the direction of sociological thinking changed dramatically yet again. The world was changing fast – the Cold War, for instance, was coming to an end, while the revolution in communications technology was beginning. The grand political projects popularised during the turbulent 1960s had clearly failed to bear fruit after the events of May 1968, and the consequences of this were beginning to be felt by a younger generation of scholars. Many turned away from these grand plans – Marxism, feminism, structuralism and so on – and found inspiration instead in new theories of discourse and identity politics as developed by the writings of the French theorist **Michel Foucault**, and 'post-structuralism' was born. From this came a fresh look at the issue of social change. Just as classical sociological theory had emerged out of a desire to understand the transformations from pre-industrial society to industrial society, and feudalism to capitalism, here was a new wave of interest in transformations of apparently equivalent historical significance: new forms of production beyond the old factory system associated with a 'post-industrial' phase, huge technological developments in media and communications, new forms of transnational capitalism, and the apparent decline of the influence of the nation state in the world. Out of post-structuralism emerged '**post-modern**' theory, derived from the belief held by some that we were living in an entirely new historical phase, freed from the shackles of those grand and all-encompassing attempts to 'explain' the world. Against this, **Jürgen Habermas**, arguably the leading social theorist in the world today, breathed new life into the neo-Marxist tradition of critical theory and used it to defend the possibility of building a better world against the apparent nihilism of the post-modernists and post-structuralists. Other contributions emerged which were decidedly eclectic in their make-up, such as **Pierre Bourdieu**'s 'theory of practice' which fused ideas from Marx, Durkheim and Weber. In Britain, **Anthony Giddens** developed his theory of 'structuration', possibly the most ambitious attempt to devise a 'grand theory' since Parsons himself. There was even a re-interest in Parsons and functionalism, thanks largely to the efforts of Jeffrey Alexander and Niklas Luhmann who gave us 'neo-functionalism' and 'systems theory' respectively.

Today, we teach the history of sociological theory with a special emphasis on the founding fathers – Marx, Durkheim and Weber. Beyond this 'classical' phase, in which the discipline was finding its feet, we move into the second phase of sociology, during the twentieth century, when sociological perspectives like the ones we discuss in this book emerged. Towards the end of that century, the age of sociological schools passed, and in its place came a third age of individuals carving out distinctive sociological theories of their own, all liberally blending elements of what had gone before. In theory classes of the future, many of these will be rightly considered 'classics': Habermas, Foucault, Giddens, Bourdieu. There are already those who happily operate within the frameworks inspired by these theorists. Perhaps those theory classes of the future will need to compare and contrast the new schools of thought which might emerge from their inspirational ideas. At present, it remains the case that much of the history of sociological theory since the 'founding fathers' can be contained within the eight broad, distinctive perspectives outlined in this book.

## Eight traditions and perspectives in sociology

As I have already said, the purpose of this book is to simplify sociological theory for those new to it. Sociological theory is rife with contradictions and contraventions, and not easily reduced to broad, generic classifications. Apart from the Introduction and Conclusion this book, then, is divided into eight main chapters (Chapters 2–9). Each chapter represents a broad starting vision of the world, full of these internal disputes which are lumped together for the sake of convenience because they at least share this starting vision. The starting vision is, in effect, a perspective, a view of the world as seen through a particular set of spectacles. Imagine this scenario: You wake up in the morning, and are about to look outside the window. The world outside is the same, but you have eight pairs of spectacles to see it through, and each guides you to a different emphasis. Some give you a clear perspective on the whole picture. Others focus in on the small things that make up that big picture. Some introduce you to the inequalities and struggles inherent in that world.

The arrangement of these chapters is not chronological, but rather designed to unfold like a story. We begin with functionalism. Although it became dominant in Western sociology only in the 1950s, and fell away shortly afterwards under the weight of the attack from other perspectives, it is a good place to start, because by doing so we can read the subsequent chapters as engaging in a dialogue with functionalism. In many respects the limitations of functionalism are what give these other perspectives their ammunition. These limitations can be divided into two camps: those connected to its consensus-oriented view of society, and those connected to its overly structural view of society.

The next three chapters deal with perspectives that focus largely on aspects of conflict, difference, inequality and power relations in the world. Conflict theory is dealt with first because it is the least radical, the closest to functionalism. We follow that up with Marxism. Marxism is a good illustration of what I meant, when I said you should treat these chapters as representing extremely *broad* perspectives. There is no single Marxist sociology. It is an umbrella which incorporates rigid, scientific, 'structural' Marxists, more humanistic 'critical theorists', internationally focused 'world-systems theorists', and a variety of neo-Marxists keen to update Marx's own ideas about the world to make them more applicable to the conditions we find ourselves in today. What *unites* these quite disparate voices is that they all, to varying degrees, take their lead from Marx's own insistence that societies are primarily driven and structured by economic factors, resulting in inequalities between those who 'have' and those who 'have not'. Marxism as a broad perspective – the Marxist spectacles, so to speak – directs us to these economic inequalities. Feminism is an equally broad umbrella perspective. There are multiple forms of feminist theory, ranging from the liberal feminists who highlight gender inequalities in society, to the radical feminists who focus instead on **patriarchy,** the system of male power over women, and many more besides. Again, for our purpose, what unites these into a single perspective is that they highlight, in different ways, the issue of gender relations.

In Chapter 6 we turn our attention to the other kind of assault upon functionalism – that which sought to shift the focus of sociological attention away from big social 'systems' (the 'macro-sociology' of the functionalists) towards the actions of individuals (micro-sociology). In that chapter we discuss exchange theory, a perspective in sociology which owes an unqualified debt to psychology. Then, in Chapter 7, we address another kind of micro-sociology – interactionism. Interactionism represents a decidedly *anti-positivist* kind of sociology. It makes no pretence to being a science of any kind, firmly distancing itself from Comte's original mission for sociology. For interactionists, as we will see, sociology cannot *explain*, but it can *document*, rather like a theoretically sophisticated form of journalism. In Chapter 8, we find ourselves taking the interactionist mission to its extreme and logical conclusion when we look at ethnomethodology.

With ethnomethodology we appear to have come full circle from our starting point in functionalism (for reasons that I won't try to explain here, but will hopefully become clear once you have read the chapter). In fact, though, there is one more chapter left to go before we do come full circle. Chapter 9 introduces us to structuralism, a perspective which, like interactionism, seeks not so much to explain as to reveal *meaning*, and which, like ethnomethodology, is interested in the way our understanding of the world is shaped by *language*, but which, like functionalism, owes a huge debt to the legacy of Durkheim. Then, finally, in

Chapter 10, the Conclusion, we look at some of the more important debates which have inspired more contemporary sociological theories: attempts to reconcile issues of structure and agency (whether we produce or are produced by the world around us), and attempts to make sense of the more recent transformations in society, especially debates around post-modernity and globalisation.

I hope this book not only serves as a usual first step towards understanding sociological theory, but actually helps to nurture your own sociological imagination. Remember two things about theory: first, it isn't something you can learn about only in your designated theory class – it is there in *all* your sociology classes, because it is the blood that runs through the whole discipline of sociology and brings it alive; second, it isn't something you just learn *about*, something that *other people* do – it is what *you* do, when you exercise your own sociological imagination, when you take a look outside *your* window and ask what's going on out there.

## Key terms

*Definitions for the key terms listed below can be found in the Glossary on page 227.*

- Agency
- Alienation
- Capitalism
- Ethnographic methods
- Globalisation
- Ideology
- Interpretation

- Patriarchy
- Positivism
- Post-modernism
- Social classes
- Social order
- Structure

# Biographies

*Short biographical descriptions for the names listed below can be found on page 240.*

- Louis Althusser
- Howard Becker
- Pierre Bourdieu
- Auguste Comte
- Ralf Dahrendorf
- Emile Durkheim
- Shulamith Firestone
- Michel Foucault
- Harold Garfinkel
- Anthony Giddens
- Erving Goffman
- Antonio Gramsci
- Jürgen Habermas

- George Homans
- Karl Marx
- George Herbert Mead
- Robert Merton
- Kate Millett
- C. Wright Mills
- Robert Ezra Park
- Talcott Parsons
- Charlotte Perkins-Gilman
- John Rex
- Georg Simmel
- Herbert Spencer
- Max Weber

# 2 | Functionalism

In this chapter we will be:

- introducing a theoretical perspective in sociology known as functionalism, and pointing out that this was the dominant perspective in Western sociology in the 1950s;

- looking at the distinctive characteristic of functionalism, namely, its description of society as a 'system', and defining what a 'system' is;

- looking at how functionalism presumes the existence of a shared set of values across society, and identifies conflicts of values as problems needing to be solved;

- looking at how functionalists have taken the system metaphor to its natural extension, and portrayed changes in societies across time as akin to evolution, as part of the process of 'modernisation';

- suggesting a number of reasons why functionalism fell from grace, not least its perceived inability to deal with the realities of conflict, diversity and change.

## The rise and fall of functionalism

The purpose of this book is to introduce you to eight broad perspectives in sociology, eight ways of answering the question: What *is* society? With that in mind, it makes a lot of sense to start with functionalism. There are a number of reasons for that, although one of them is not that functionalism 'came first'. It didn't – it burst onto the sociological scene in the middle of the twentieth century, although functionalist *ideas* had been present in the writings of a number of the nineteenth-century 'founders' of sociology we discussed in Chapter 1. However, while it may not have come first chronologically, it does provide a useful starting point for the narrative of this book, partly because at one level it presents a relatively straightforward answer to our question, a fairly clear model of society, and partly because the model it gives us, which for so many years dominated the scene, has been subjected to so many criticisms that it is fair to describe other perspectives as emerging or re-emerging *in response to* the perceived shortcomings of functionalism.

In its simplest terms, a functionalist perspective on society begins with a metaphor – that society is a *system*. We will discuss what this means in greater depth below. Suffice to say at this point that a system is a whole which is comprised of various parts but more than just the sum of them. To study society as a functionalist would, then, is to see it in its entirety, as a 'thing in itself', but also to see how its various component parts work (how they 'function') in relation to this greater whole. This way of looking at society owes much to the natural sciences, and in particular to biology. Consider the way one might approach studying the human body. It is a complex thing which is comprised of multiple organs and the like, and each of these has its own role to play to help keep the body 'healthy'. So, one needs to understand its *structure* – how it is constituted as a whole – and also the particular *functions* performed by its component parts.

Comparing society with a body is useful as a way of introducing the idea of the **social system**, but it is more than just a casual analogy, because it is crucial to the history of functionalism as a perspective. If you think about this idea of a 'healthy' body, you get some idea of the relationship between biological theory and medical practice: the 'medical model' suggests that if we know how the body works, then we are better placed to keep it 'healthy', to 'fix' any problems which might emerge, by locating the cause of the problem. To some extent, that is precisely how functionalism approaches society. It begins with the assumption that there is a healthy state, and looks to correct problems by 'fixing' the bits that aren't working properly. Stop and think about this for a while, and carry out the little exercise below – which we will return to later in the chapter.

The biological metaphor for society is most closely associated with the nineteenth-century English sociologist, **Herbert Spencer**. It was Spencer who made the core distinction between *structure* and *function* as objects of sociological enquiry, which he likened to the distinction within medical science between anatomy and physiology – anatomists

## EXERCISE 2.1 The medical model

1 Make a list of five medical conditions or illnesses which a doctor might try to cure. Now, thinking about the body as a system, identify the part of the body which might need to be 'fixed' in order to cure the condition.

2 Now make a list of five 'social problems' – things which might be called illnesses in society. Again, try to identify the parts of society which might need fixing if these problems are to be solved.

3 Once you have done this, take a look back at your lists. Ask yourself whether you think the two are generally comparable. In order to list illnesses you first needed to have an idea in your head of a 'healthy' body. Can you think of any examples where having such an idea might be controversial? Now turn to your other list. What were the features of the 'healthy society' you were imagining when you identified the five social problems you chose? Again, can you think of anything possibly controversial about this?

tell you how the body is composed, physiologists tell you how the parts operate together to make it work. Spencer made this his core idea for understanding the way the social world works. It was Spencer who first explicitly treated society, as an object of study, as a *system*, comprised of interrelated parts.

If Spencer provided the nuts and bolts of what would later become the functionalist movement, the real theoretical substance of the perspective derived from a later nineteenth-century writer, the great French sociologist **Emile Durkheim**. Despite what you may have read elsewhere, it isn't entirely correct to refer to Durkheim as a functionalist himself, partly because there was no such movement at the time, but mainly because like so many of his peers Durkheim was a prolific writer whose ideas developed over the years. But what is most certainly fair to say is that in his earlier writings, and particularly in his most famous text, *The Division of Labour in Society*, Durkheim sowed the seeds of what would later become the functionalist approach to society. There are two major contributions from Durkheim which need especially to be singled out here, and which we will discuss in greater length later in the chapter. First, there is his idea of the *conscience collective* – that there exists a kind of collective consciousness among people in a given society of shared norms and values, which provides the glue that binds us all

Source: Alamy Images/The Art Gallery Collection

Emile Durkheim

together within that society. From this emerges one of the key functionalist assumptions – that the natural state of a society is one of cultural *consensus*. Second, there is his concept of **differentiation**. This is a theory of how societies change, adapt, evolve to become more specialised. It is how roles in society become more clearly defined, but, read in a very functionalist sense following Spencer, it is really about how these roles correspond to the functions that are needed to keep the broader system ticking over.

Neither of these writers were functionalists *per se*, though. Before it entered sociology, the term 'functionalism' was used in the related discipline of social anthropology to refer to the contributions of early twentieth-century intellectuals such as Bronislaw Malinowski and A.R. Radcliffe-Brown. In sociology, functionalist accounts of social problems – accounts which explicitly looked at their subject matter in terms of the functions they perform for the greater whole that is society – were being produced in the inter-war years by American sociologists such as Kingsley Davis and Wilbert E. Moore. However, it was the Harvard professor **Talcott Parsons** who crystallised these ideas into a coherent sociological theory, in his definitive (and complex) book *The Social System*. In fact, Parsons's earlier work had been more in the tradition of **Max Weber** (especially his massive book *The Structure of Social Action*, which sought to blend together the insights of four major European writers – Weber, Durkheim, Vilfredo Pareto and Alfred Marshall). But it is as the guru of sociological functionalism that Parsons is best remembered, the grand theorist who provided the definitive model of society as a system, how it works and how all its parts link together. From the beginning, Parsons had been interested in the grandest of all questions, the question which was most famously asked by the seventeenth-century English political philosopher Thomas Hobbes and which is there in the works of Durkheim, Sigmund Freud and many others: how is social *order* – the kind of stability we take for granted when we get up in the morning and head out to work or school – even *possible* (Parsons, 1937)? Much of Parsons's subsequent career was spent answering that question. In fact, much of sociology as a discipline has been.

What Parsons did was really a revolution in sociology. He provided a theoretical framework for understanding society that became so widely accepted, so dominant, that for a while in the 1950s the entire discipline of sociology was largely synonymous with working within the functionalist framework. This should seem strange to us now, because we should take it for granted that any academic discipline is defined by a competing range of theoretical approaches. Of course, even at the time there were significant dissenting voices, but the sheer scale of the dominance of functionalism and the assumptions contained therein should not be downplayed. Centred largely around Harvard University, Parsons and various colleagues, students and ex-students including Davis, Moore, Robert Merton, Marion Levy, Albert Cohen, Robert Bales, Neil Smelser and Edward Shils, extended the functionalist theory of society, society as a system bound together by a cultural consensus, into specific areas of sociological enquiry: the sociology of crime and deviance, the sociology of education, the sociology of the family, the sociology of class and stratification, the sociology of religion, the sociology of work, and so on. If Parsons had provided the framework, the 'grand theory', a sequence of research publications from these and other writers added the detail. Their approach to sociology was deceptively simple: if you start with the assumption that society is a system which in its 'healthy' state exists as a consensus of norms and values, then what specific functions do the various institutions within society perform, and to what extent can social problems be explained in terms of the breakdown of that healthy system?

So, given this position of dominance, what are the shortcomings which produced such criticisms from other, rival perspectives? There are many but they can be conveniently gathered into two broad concerns. One is that functionalism concentrates solely at the level of society, or social *structure*, and thus has little to say about *people*. This is a fair criticism: many functionalists, not least Parsons, seemed to see people as the products rather than the producers of society. Reacting against this structural bias, or to put it more bluntly this structural *determinism*, in different ways were the exchange theorists, the interactionists, and some feminists and Marxists.

The second is that functionalism is inherently *conservative*. When I say 'conservative' here, I am not referring to an explicit political position, in the way that the term is often used. Some functionalists might have had conservative views, but Parsons was more of a political liberal, and the other great functionalist writer, **Robert Merton**, was quite radical in his quest to highlight inequalities in society. Instead, I mean 'conservative' in that as a perspective, functionalism takes for granted that there is a 'natural' and 'healthy' state of society, and that as a result it cannot deal with difference, or with change. It was very much a product of the relative prosperity and stability people seemed to enjoy in Western societies in the 1950s, especially from the privileged perspective of primarily white, male, Western academics sitting in the ivory towers of elite universities, but by the 1960s social unrest, turbulence and conflict were much more apparent, so sociologists turned instead to conflict theory, Marxism and feminism, among others.

By the 1970s, then, functionalism was all but extinct. Some have tried to breathe new life into it – recent examples include Niklas Luhmann, a German who studied under Parsons, who has developed a complex approach called 'systems theory', and Jeffrey Alexander, an American who started the 'neo-functionalist' movement. However, these are too specific to be included here. But as students of sociology we should not ignore the importance of sociology to our discipline, or the contributions it has made. If we are to better understand sociological theory in all its forms, we could do worse than to begin with the functionalist model.

## The social system

Let us take a step back for a while and return to this metaphor of society as a system, which is crucial to any functionalist approach in sociology. Make sure you are clear on what we mean by a system. Systems are defined as consisting of component parts which are intended to work together to help the broader system operate smoothly, although each part has a designated role or function to perform to that end. The example we have already used is that of the body. In order for the body to perform to its maximum capacity, to be in a fully 'healthy' state, the heart, the liver, the brain, the arms and legs and so on all need to be doing their jobs properly. If one of these component parts is faulty, the body is deemed to be less than fully healthy. Of course, some of these are more important than others. The heart, for example, is charged with the task of pumping blood around the body. If it stops doing that, the entire system breaks down. Failures elsewhere do not have such a critical role to play; there is therefore a natural hierarchy of component parts. The same can be said for all other systems. A computer is a system, a structure that is more than the sum of its parts, which include the hard drive, the monitor, the keyboard and the mouse. If the hard drive crashes, the damage done to my computer as a whole is far more significant than if my mouse is faulty. A car is also a system. For it to perform its task properly, the engine needs to be running smoothly, the wheels need to be turning, the steering wheel and brakes need to be operational, and so on.

So, to what extent can we describe *society* as a system? Logically, this would mean adopting a *holistic* approach, treating society as a 'thing in itself' (*sui generis*) which is reliant for its survival, its successful maintenance and reproduction, on the smooth running of its constituent parts. Within society, these constituent parts – the social equivalents of the heart and the liver and the lungs – include the major social institutions, such as the education system, the family, the political system, religion, the legal system, the media, the economy, and so on. A functionalist would therefore study each of these institutions in terms of the functions they perform for the benefit of wider society. She or he would recognise the existence of a hierarchy of these institutions which, in Talcott Parsons's terms, are *subsystems*. Before we go any further into the complexities of how the social system *works*, according to Parsons, let us take a quick breather, and occupy our time with another exercise.

---

**EXERCISE 2.2 The functions of social institutions and practices**

Identify one or two positive functions performed by each of the following social institutions and practices for the benefit of wider society:

- The family
- Education
- Religion
- Law
- Crime and deviance

---

There is little doubt that Parsons (1951) has provided us with the most elaborate model of the constitution of the social system, in what has come to be known as the AGIL scheme. This stands for the four basic and universal **functional prerequisites** which, according to Parsons, all systems must satisfy, namely:

1 *adaptation* to the external environment;
2 *goal attainment*, successful accomplishment of its core demands;
3 system *integration*, which involves minimising conflict so that all the component parts are working in harmony with one another;
4 pattern maintenance, or *latency*, which involves the maintenance of a commitment to certain values.

How does this scheme relate to the social system? This is where Parsons's theory gets a bit complicated, because it really does contain everything including the proverbial kitchen sink, so bear with me. First, Parsons speaks about society in very general terms as a *system of social action*, which is divided into four parts: the *cultural system*, the *social system*, the *personality system* and the *biological organism* (the subject matters of anthropology, sociology, psychology and biology respectively). Each of these is charged with satisfying one of the functional prerequisites identified above. Specifically, the role of the social system is to ensure that the collective norms and values of the cultural system are transmitted into the personality system (see Figure 2.1).

|  |  |
|---|---|
| _L_ | _I_ |
| Cultural system | Social system |
| Behavioural organism | Personality system |
| _A_ | _G_ |

**Figure 2.1** Parsons's general action system

Parsons then divided up the social system into four distinct subsystems: the *economic system*, the *political system*, the *societal community* and the *fiduciary system* (are you starting to see a pattern emerging in how Parsons does things?). The first of these, the economic system, allows the social system to adapt. The second, the political system, allows it to achieve its required goals. The third, the societal community which includes our social networks, associations and organisations, performs the function of integration, while the fourth, the fiduciary system, including the family and educational establishments, satisfies the need for pattern maintenance, to keep things nice and ordered (see Figure 2.2).

|  |  |
|---|---|
| _L_ | _I_ |
| Fiduciary system | Societal community |
| Economic system | Political system |
| _A_ | _G_ |

**Figure 2.2** Parsons's subsystems of the social system

By now you are probably either baffled by the abstract nature of Parsons's scheme, bored by it, or won over by the simplicity of dividing everything into convenient compartments. It certainly does try to explain everything (I've only touched the surface here), and is considered to be

Source: Harvard University Archives

Talcott Parsons

a definitive example of what we call *grand theory*. But functionalism as a theory need not be so abstract – if Parsons provided the broad framework, most of his followers were content to prove it by carrying out more empirical studies of specific institutions, to see just how they carried out their alleged roles. Parsons's student, Robert Merton (1957), used the term 'middle-range theories' to talk about the more modest aims of this group, himself included. Functionalists of this ilk tended to be specialists, students of particular social institutions, such as education, the family or religion, and their job was to explain the functions these institutions provided for the wider social system.

So, let's look at some of these institutions, and you can cross-check what the 'experts' said against what you came up with in the last exercise. We can start with education. Few people would disagree that it is a positive thing. Durkheim argued that it was vital for the healthy transference of the norms and values of wider society, its heritage, history and sense of shared belonging, on to individuals. Schools also serve the function of preparing children for the world of work. The family serves similar needs, preparing children for later life, but, according to Parsons (1959), it also provides adults with a stable, warm and secure environment to escape into. George Peter Murdoch (1949) celebrated the reproductive, economic and educational functions played by the family unit. In addition to the family and the school, though, young people need spaces in which to exercise their individualities, even to rebel and

**31**

let lose their 'deviant' tendencies, so as to make the transition from childhood to adulthood as smooth as possible, and this function is provided by youth culture (Eisenstadt, 1956).

Let's take another example – religion. Durkheim drew attention to the way it maintains social solidarity, and Parsons saw it as crucial in shaping the moral core of the shared value system. Parsons and Malinowski both suggested in addition that it comforts people in times of difficulty. Malinowski (1954) in particular showed how religious ceremonies and rituals often accompany those moments which seem to threaten the social equilibrium, bringing people together and reminding us all of our common norms and values. This isn't just the case with 'proper' religion, it also applies to what we call 'civil religion'. One thinks, for example, of how Americans are brought together through a shared allegiance to flag and country, or how people come out in collective mourning after the death of a national favourite, perhaps a British royal. These are rituals of nation-building as well as the healing of wounds.

Of course, once the nation is 'built', it needs to be maintained. That's where the law comes in. Durkheim himself said that it serves as a reflection of the *conscience collective*, the shared value system. So, punishment must reflect the retributive demands of society – justice seen to be done (Conrad, 1981), while the law itself must function to resolve conflicts (Llewellyn, 1960).

The positive contributions made by education, the family, youth culture, law, and religion are perhaps easy to understand. But how does a functionalist approach the subject of something more controversial, like, say, crime, or social inequality? Surely these provide no functions for society? In fact, functionalists have rather controversially found positives even in these 'social problems'. Durkheim had told us that crime is healthy because it prevents societies from becoming stagnant, and allows for social change. For example, Albert Cohen (1966) said that deviance prevents radical upheaval by providing a means of expressing anger or uncertainty, and that it highlights possible malfunctions elsewhere in the system. Kingsley Davis (1937) went further when he drew attention to how prostitution assisted men in releasing their sexual energies in a non-aggressive way outside the family (slightly problematic, for sure). Together with Wilbert Moore, Davis also (1945) showed how social stratification is functional because it allows for the most important social roles to be allocated to the most suitable and able of candidates.

So far so good, but it isn't just about each institution in society serving a particular function. They also have to work together, complement each other, so as to serve the interests of the broader system. It's no good if the family reproduces a set of values that conflict with the education system, after all! And these two subsystems don't only need to work in harmony with one another, they also serve the interests of another subsystem, the economy. Keeping all these subsystems together is what Parsons means by *system integration*. This is essential for the smooth running of the wider system. So, Davis and Moore (1945) point out that the school serves as a kind of 'selection process' which reproduces the hierarchies of real society and, so to speak, separates the proverbial wheat from the chaff, thus benefiting the broader economic system, the world of work.

---

**EXERCISE 2.3  An exercise in system integration**

For this exercise, I want you to choose one of the three following pairings of social institutions, and write a 500-word piece on how they complement each other in terms of their contributions to the wider social system: (1) Family/education; (2) Family/work; (3) Education/work.

---

So far, we have concentrated on the rather obvious functions provided by each of the institutions we have discussed, following Parsons's scheme. But as Robert Merton (1957) pointed out, not all functions are obvious. Some are hidden and even unintended. Merton distinguished between *manifest and latent functions*. Let us use education as an example: if the functions of transmitting knowledge and preparing for work are obvious, *manifest*, then the way the school itself operates as a miniature society, and thus prepares children for the complex, hierarchical and rule-bound world outside, is more of a *latent* function.

We have also highlighted what some functionalists hail as the positive functions of rather negative things, like crime and social inequality. Merton was not happy about this aspect of functionalist theory so he introduced the concepts of *dysfunctions* and *non-functions*. He suggested that some institutions may have positive consequences for certain parts of society, but negative ones for others, and some may serve no apparent functions at all! These are not easy to accommodate within Parsons's own scheme, but Merton claimed it was possible to adapt functionalism to incorporate these different levels of functional analysis. So, one can identify the positive contributions something makes at the level of the social system (which Parsons was interested in), while accepting that it is also dysfunctional at a more local level. Equally, something which appears wholly beneficial at a local level may be dysfunctional at the level of the social system. For example, a dysfunctional child within the family unit might be functional for the parents, and even for wider society, but not for the child in question (Vogel and Bell, 1968). Much the same could be said for Davis's prostitutes.

## Shared values and social integration

The attention paid by Parsons and others to system integration is a natural development of the system model of society pioneered by Spencer. However, though the foundations for functionalism may have begun, by and large, with Spencer, he paid little or no attention to cultural factors which were to become the definitive feature of the tradition in the hands of Parsons, Merton and the like. Functionalism is a definitively *normative* perspective, interested in ideas and values, and this emphasis on the role of culture was inherited from Durkheim. It was Durkheim, more so than any other classical social theorist, who prioritised cultural transformation and cultural integration, and who posited shared norms and values – the *conscience collective* – as the 'glue' which binds society together.

Parsons's contributions, then, are a direct continuation of Durkheim's interest in what functionalists refer to as **social integration**. As we have already said, Parsons began his exploration into the history of sociological theory with the fundamental question originally posed by the English philosopher Hobbes: What is it that binds society together in a state of order rather than chaos (Parsons, 1937)? The answer, drawn directly from Durkheim, is the presence of a shared value system. In particular, Parsons's work provides a strident critique of the utilitarian tradition, which sees society as merely the aggregate sum of numerous self-interested individuals (for more on which, see Chapter 6). For Parsons, as for Durkheim, social action can never be explained solely in terms of individual self-interest. It is motivated by values and orientations which are external to the individual, grounded in the belief system of society itself. Remember Durkheim's study of suicide rates, which we discussed in the Introduction?

Actually, although Durkheim provides the inspiration, the actual explanation adopted by Parsons for how people become integrated into society comes from another source – the psychoanalysis of Sigmund Freud. For Freud, as for Durkheim, individuals are in a natural state driven by biological impulses, and society is what makes them keep those urges in check. **Socialisation**, or in Parsons's sense social integration, serves to repress the basic human tendencies towards violence. It does so by introducing the child to the moral code present in the society. Thus, the social system, via such institutions as the family, provides the medium through which individuals internalise these norms present in the cultural system.

At this point, you may have identified a problem. The entire scheme developed by Parsons appears to assume that all individuals are neatly integrated into the wider system through this process, an assumption which has led one critic, Dennis Wrong, to criticise Parsons for adopting an 'overly socialised' concept of the person. But what happens if the individuals are somehow *not* fully integrated into this wider set of values, this *conscience collective*? What happens when the process of social integration is incomplete? This is a question which preoccupied both Durkheim and Merton. In his famous study of *Suicide*, Durkheim showed how systemic imbalances might occur as a result of some flaw in the social structure, with severe implications for the actors involved. Durkheim's four types of suicide – the extreme response to these imbalances – are displayed in diagrammatic form in Table 2.1. One such imbalance is a condition of normlessness, wherein individuals feel detached from wider society because there is a lack of a shared consensus on these norms, values and goals. Durkheim termed this condition, which occurs where regulation of norms and values is weak, **anomie**. Where anomie exists, Durkheim argued, it is the fault of the social structure, the result of society's failure to provide a reasonable and attainable consensus on values and expectations.

**Table 2.1** Durkheim's four types of suicide, as responses to structural imbalance

|            | Integration | Regulation |
|------------|-------------|------------|
| *Too strong* | Altruistic  | Fatalistic |
| *Too weak*   | Egoistic    | Anomic     |

The concept of anomie was further refined by Merton (1938), who paid particular attention to the relationship between the goals themselves and the means made available to achieve those goals. In a balanced society, Merton argued, there needs to be an equal emphasis on the goals and the acceptable means. If the goals are seen as more important than the means, rules can be discarded, and anomie can occur. For example, if one cannot achieve these social expectations within the formal structure of society, one may turn to illegal means to do so. The so-called 'American Dream' is a good example of a set of goals which are supposed to be shared by all Americans. Because the United States does not have a formalised system of social stratification as found in many European countries, this set of values – material wealth and possessions, success at work – is presented as the desirable achievement of all Americans, and not just members of a particular social class. At the same time, though, there is an understanding that only some means of attaining these goals are socially acceptable – a good education, hard work, talent, ambition. The relationship between goals and acceptable means is a fragile one. The careful balance which holds together the social system can be upset if social actors are detached from either the 'shared' goals, or the 'acceptable' means. Merton listed five possible outcomes, the first of which is 'accepted', the other four of which are, in some way or another, 'deviant' (see Table 2.2).

**Table 2.2** Merton's five types of means–end relationship

| Acceptance of approved means | Acceptance of 'shared' cultural goals | Outcome |
|------------------------------|----------------------------------------|---------|
| Yes      | Yes      | Conformity |
| No       | Yes      | Innovation |
| Yes      | No       | Ritualism  |
| No       | No       | Retreatism |
| Replaces | Replaces | Rebellion  |

Merton thus inverted Durkheim's suggestion that lack of regulation leads to greater aspirations. He argued instead that a wider set of aspirations results in deregulation which leads, in turn, to greater levels of deviance. This, Merton said, is the 'strain to anomie'. Even though the majority of people actually *do* conform, nevertheless the strain to anomie is powerful. One possible response to a lack of integration into the 'accepted' norms of wider society is the establishment of subcultures. Albert Cohen (1955) agreed that deviation occurs when there is conflict between structural and cultural norms. Because not everyone has equal access to structurally acceptable means, subcultures develop which borrow from the wider culture, but redesign whatever is borrowed so that it is accessible to all members of the group. So, the 'delinquents' studied by Cohen actually develop their own set of norms and values which set them apart from 'mainstream' society. *But,* even though writers like Merton and Cohen accept that society is full of such different 'subcultures', they remain identifiably functionalist, because they *begin* with the assumption that a single dominant set of values exist and treat these subcultures as *reactions against* this dominant system. You should

*Source:* Columbia University Archives

Robert Merton

compare this to the approach adopted by Walter Miller, which we discuss in the next chapter. Another example of a 'social problem' being explained by the tension between shared goals and the realistic means to achieve them causing a rupture in the social system is Dadrian's (1974–5) account of the causes of genocide, which he says is most likely to occur when forces from outside upset the social cohesion of a given society. Again, compare this example with the alternative account of the same problem given by Leo Kuper in the next chapter.

## The evolution of societies

I suggested earlier that a lot of people criticised functionalism for not being able to deal with *change*. They suggested that its model – society as a system – was too static, because it represented some absolute 'perfect state'. Of course, that's not entirely fair. Some systems, like bodies, *do* change, in so far as they *adapt* to their environments over time. We call this process *evolution*. In natural science, the theory of evolution is most associated with Jean-Baptiste Lamarck in the late eighteenth century and Charles Darwin in the nineteenth.

Not only did Herbert Spencer pioneer the use of the social system idea, he also championed the claim that society, like any other system, or indeed like any biological organism, experiences change according to natural evolutionary laws, adapting itself over time to satisfy new needs so as to survive. Spencer's 'evolutionism' (he can also be described as a consummate 'social Darwinist', although his ideas about social evolution actually predated Darwin by some six years) was rather controversial because even close supporters felt that his treatment of society as a kind of biological organism was problematic. However, one important aspect of it was the theory of differentiation, which was for many years taken for granted as the functionalist theory of change, a natural extension of its system metaphor. In biology, differentiation refers to that process through which parts of an organism develop specialised functions in order to help the organism adapt and evolve, so, when applied to society, it is the idea that specific social institutions (like the ones we have already mentioned) become separated from one another and perform increasingly specialised tasks necessary for the functioning of the wider system. In biological organisms and in society, differentiation occurs as systems become increasingly complex. For example, the human body is a more complex system than the amoeba (from which we no doubt evolved), so, necessarily, its component parts perform more specialised functions to accommodate this complexity. The same is true of social systems, said Spencer – *modern* societies of the nineteenth century, with their industrial production techniques and capitalist economies, are larger, and more complex, than *pre*-modern ones, with their feudal ways of life and militaristic power structures, and are therefore more highly differentiated. Table 2.3, which is adapted from Sztompka (1993: 103) summarises this comparison.

**Table 2.3** Spencer's contrast between 'military' and 'industrial' society

| Military society | Industrial society |
| --- | --- |
| Social structure based on the defence of its territories and expansion through conquest | Social structure based on peaceful co-operation, and the production and exchange of goods and services |
| Integration enforced through coercion and sanctions | Integration achieved through contract and voluntary participation |
| Citizens subservient to state; little freedom | State subservient to citizens; freedom |
| State monopoly in all spheres | Private organisations have autonomy in their fields |
| Autocratic and centralised political structure | Democratic and decentralised political structure |
| Ascribed status, low social mobility, 'closed' system of stratification | Achieved status, high social mobility, 'open' system of stratification |
| Protectionist economic policy; self-sufficient groups | Free market; interdependence in economic exchange |
| Emphasis on individual strength, courage, discipline, obedience, loyalty, patriotism | Emphasis on individual initiative, inventiveness, independence, honesty |

It's not Spencer, though, who is hailed as developing this insight into what would become the functionalist theory of change, but rather Emile Durkheim, in his first major work, *The Division of Labour in Society* (1947). Here, Durkheim recast Spencer's theory of evolution in the form of the social *division of labour* – who does what? In more 'simple' societies, said Durkheim, social roles do not need to be clearly defined, so there is little or no division of labour. Imagine some isolated village somewhere where everyone chips in to work the land and keep the streets clean and safe, and if someone does have a sufficiently specialised skill, perhaps the baker, then as well as baking the bread he might very well be a magistrate. But as societies become more complex, the division of labour gets more specialised, with specific roles being formalised and attached to individuals rather than shared among the community.

Now, there's something of the romantic in all of us, and from time to time we may all yearn for simpler days when there was a 'real' sense of community around here, everyone knew everyone and looked out for each other, and it was safe to leave your door unlocked (am I sounding like anyone you know?). For some nineteenth-century sociologists, such as the German Ferdinand Tönnies, this increasing differentiation associated with **modernisation** was a bad thing, a loss of tradition, but for Spencer, ever the liberal optimist and ardent advocate of capitalism, it was good because it represented 'progress'. Durkheim was neither pessimistic nor optimistic about it – it simply meant, he said, the replacing of one form of social bonding, based on *sameness* (what he called 'mechanical solidarity') with another based on *difference* ('organic solidarity'). These are, of course, 'ideal types' that Durkheim is talking about here, not sweeping changes that suggest the total replacement of one by the other, but dominant ways of life at the time, accepting that pockets of an earlier way of life continued (and continue) to exist during a later period. Table 2.4, again adapted from Sztompka (1993: 105) indicates some of the comparisons Durkheim made with regard to these two models.

Table 2.4 Durkheim's contrast between 'mechanical' and 'organic' solidarity

| Mechanical solidarity | Organic solidarity |
| --- | --- |
| Division of labour based on similarity of tasks | Highly differentiated and complex division of labour |
| Emphasis on community (collectivism) | Emphasis on individual (individualism) |
| Identity based on ascribed status | Identity based on achieved status |
| Strong collective conscience with shared moral and religious consensus | Differences of opinion required |
| Economy based on plurality of self-sufficient groups | Economy based on mutual dependence and exchange |
| Social control through repressive law directed at the punishment of 'deviants' | Social control through restitutive law directed at repairing social balance |

This contrast between 'traditional' and 'modern' societies is fundamental to the functionalist account of social change. The differences
identified by Spencer, Durkheim and others resurface in the later writings of Talcott Parsons and his followers. What Parsons and his colleagues (of whom Wilbert E. Moore, Schmuel Eisenstadt, Marion Levy,
Seymour Martin Lipset, Walt Rostow and Daniel Bell are among the
most prominent in this context) took from these earlier contributors
was that social change was *progressive*, because it followed a preset
route towards some 'better', more 'complete' future, a systemic state
better suited to its environment. This became known as the theory of
modernisation. In the 1950s this approach had a considerable influence
on international economic policies designed to 'help' economically
poorer countries 'develop', or rather, 'modernise'. One of the chief
architects of this idea was Rostow, whose *Stages of Economic Growth*
(1960) presented the blueprint for modernisation in the form of a five-
stage continuum from 'traditional' to 'modern', a kind of measured,
controlled process of change rather than a radical one happening overnight or a long-term evolutionary one. The argument for this kind of
regulated change pretty much went as follows:

1 It is in the interests of those countries to modernise, that is, to attain
  a particular level of social development.
2 This modernisation can be brought about by internal or external
  agents, and so foreign investment is one possible method.
3 It is possible for this modernisation to take place without causing any
  major imbalance in the world economy, so long as it is carefully regulated by the external agents of the modernisation process, namely the
  wealthier countries.

What, though, was *meant* by modernisation? Its major advocates
accepted that it had a far more specific set of meanings than merely
adapting the evolutionist models devised by Spencer or Durkheim, even
though most specific instances are clearly indebted to their general
observations. Part of the package, of course, meant embracing the qualities of 'modern' societies, such as free-market capitalism and political
democracy, which were implicitly considered superior to the pre-modern
alternatives. Moore suggested that it was nothing less than a 'total transformation' in respect of technology, economy, political structure and

social organisation (1963: 89). Smelser has listed the various structural transformations included within modernisation (1973: 747–8):

1 acceptance of scientific knowledge and technology;
2 shift from subsistence farming to commercial agriculture;
3 shift from human and animal power towards machinery and energy;
4 urbanisation and 'spatial concentration of the labour force';
5 democratisation of the political structure;
6 increasing emphasis on greater education, knowledge and training of skills;
7 secularisation in the religious sphere;
8 decline of traditional kinship structures and greater specialisation of family roles;
9 move from ascribed to achieved status, with greater chance for social mobility.

From the 'classical' evolutionism of Spencer and Durkheim to the more controlled and regulated 'modernisation theory' of Parsons and others, the functionalist approach to social change was always subject to two massive criticisms. First, that it tended to misuse the idea of 'evolution' – twentieth-century functionalist anthropologists such as Malinowski and Radcliffe-Brown were among the many who rejected attempts to turn a strategy for comparing societies into a *hierarchy*. Second, that it was too simplistic, perhaps even naive. It was born out of a heavily pro-Western set of assumptions, rarely questioning the idea that the transition to a Western way of life represented 'progress'. In a sense, both these criticisms link to the more general criticism of functionalism as a theory, namely, the 'medical model' that presumes there to be an 'ideal', 'healthy' state to which societies should aspire. It's an understandable step to take from this basic premise to the suggestion that 'progress' means moving towards that state, and, therefore, that history itself only travels in one direction. Even if some writers have tried to rescue the evolutionary roots of the functionalist theory of change (most notably Niklas Luhmann, who reminds us that evolution is never supposed to be one-directional and predictable), there is little doubt that the association of functionalist sociological theory with the naive, liberal policies of modernisation employed in the 1950s, was one important reason for its decreasing popularity in the subsequent decades.

## Summary and final thoughts

In this chapter, we have discussed the sociological perspective of functionalism, which was, for a while at least back in the 1950s, the single most important theory in the entire discipline. Although we have discussed some potentially complex ideas, like social integration and modernisation, as part of this broader theory, the best way for you to understand them is to hang them all on the single idea of the social system. If you are clear about what a system is, and then about what it might mean to think of society as a system, then the rest should fall into place. Social integration is, after all, nothing more than a way of saying how people fit into that social system, the process by which we all come to accept, and not challenge, those cultural values of society which glue the whole system together. Modernisation is nothing more than a way of saying that some social systems aren't as fully functional as others, so, rather than waiting for evolution to play its hand, we can actually control their growth, their progress to something 'better'. In both cases, whether it is you as an individual exhibiting deviant traits or an entire society not holding together, functionalists identify *problems* and, by extension, seek for *solutions*. This is the 'medical model' – identify the cause of the illness so as to cure it.

At the beginning of this chapter, I asked you to consider examples of medical 'problems' and equate them to social ones. I asked whether you could think of anything controversial about this. The point of this was to get you to address the issue of what constitutes a 'healthy' state *critically*. If you think back about the example of the human body, if you identified liver failure as a medical condition which impacted upon the healthy status of the body as a system and that needs fixing, you probably wouldn't feel too uncomfortable, but if you identified blindness as such a condition, do you think you might feel differently? Okay, maybe you would still want to stress that blindness is a *problem* which, if it can be 'cured', should be. But if you are a blind person reading this, how do you feel about the assumption that you are 'unhealthy', 'imperfect'? Now, let us take this a step further. There are those who feel that homosexuality is a biological imperfection, a medical condition which can be 'cured'.

The point of this little examination is that the definition of what constitutes the body in its so-called 'healthy' state is itself problematic. I'm sure we can all agree that this need not be the case for all systems – the computer and the car *are* built in such a way that there is a 'perfect' design to which all the mechanised parts are supposed to contribute. But it is morally problematic to ascribe such a status to the body, and perhaps even more so to society. The functionalist approach to social change, rendered in terms of modernisation, presumes that there is an 'ideal' state to which all evolving societies should aspire. But who defines this ideal state? Why is it that Western liberal democracies should be taken as the template for the ideal society?

This obviously raises a question about the accuracy of a typical functionalist theory of society, but it needn't signal the end of functionalist analysis as such. We can, after all, imagine the idea of a functional analysis of any system without any prior conception of its ideal state. Systems need not be static. Computers and cars do change, evolve. The body can take multiple forms without there being any presumption of the 'perfection' of any one of them. But the computer still needs the hard drive, and the body still needs the heart, or something equivalent to it. Functionalism can surely survive beyond its Western bias. This is precisely the challenge that the more recent writers influenced by Parsons, such as Alexander and Luhmann, have taken up, but as yet their ideas have not generated sufficient interest to make their way into most undergraduate curricula (although Luhmann's work is huge in the German-speaking world).

In summary, functionalism as a general theory provides its own way of describing and understanding the key objects of sociological enquiry, including the constitution of social structure, the nature of social institutions, the emergence of the division of labour, and even, despite its critics, the role of individual personality and self-identity, and the causes and dynamics of social change. Whether or not it provides *satisfactory* explanations for these is a judgement call. In the chapters that follow, we encounter a series of voices who state clearly that it does not.

## Key terms

*Definitions for the key terms listed below can be found in the Glossary on page 227.*

- Anomie
- Differentiation
- Functional prerequisites
- Modernisation

- Social integration
- Social system
- Socialisation

## Biographies

*Short biographical descriptions for the names listed below can be found on page 240.*

- Emile Durkheim
- Robert Merton
- Talcott Parsons

- Herbert Spencer
- Max Weber

# 3 | Conflict theory

In this chapter we will be:

- introducing the theory known as 'conflict theory' and seeing how it relates to the functionalist perspective we covered in Chapter 2;
- tracing the origins of this approach in the idea of 'cultural relativism';
- defining 'interest groups' and showing how they are central to the way conflict theorists see the world;
- discussing how conflict theorists present a relativist theory of social change in the form of a new 'historical sociology'.

## Conflict and consensus

One of the fundamental features of any sociological perspective is how it defines the 'natural' state of a society. Are societies inherently stable, held together by a consensus of shared values – which sometimes people lose sight of – and by smoothly integrated institutions – which sometimes malfunction? Or are they actually defined by competition and difference, occupied by a vast array of groups and communities with diverse cultures, values and interests, some of which are incompatible with one another?

Functionalists, who we discussed in the previous chapter, clearly subscribe to the former position. They begin, following Durkheim, with the assumption that there is a shared value system underpinning society, and that this forms part of the same project that binds together all the institutions within that society, a benign process of social reproduction and evolution. Disagreements, conflicts, violence – these are all the result of malfunctions, and malfunctions, like diseases, can be cured. Thus, the delinquent wants to follow the same goals as everyone else, but for

Source: Alamy Images/INTERFOTO

Max Weber

one's position in the state. Each of these produces some form of social inequality, and can result in social conflict between different actors, based on the inequalities that stem from them.

Conflict theory should also not be confused with the various sociological approaches focusing on self-interested individuals making 'rational choices', which we will cover in Chapter 6. For these perspectives, while conflict is a driving force in society, it derives from some inherent property of the individual. Our concern in this chapter is with a more structural kind of sociology, which looks at how conflict exists as a basic property of society, and forms the arena within which rival **interest groups** compete.

Functionalism was at its peak in the 1950s, during a period of post-war optimism and relative economic stability in much of the West. It spoke to and from the perspective of all that is 'good' about liberal democracy. But by the 1960s, the social, political and economic climate was far more turbulent. Demands for fair treatment and respect for civil rights from the African-American community in the United States, the women's movement, the gay liberation movement, and many more such

48

marginalised groups in society highlighted the extent to which the functionalist model of a social structure based on consensus and shared values was based on a façade, that in reality the wealth, prosperity and social luxuries enjoyed by middle-class, white, Western men was largely at the expense of others. Similarly, anti-war protests highlighted significant discontent on political matters. For many social scientists, the functionalist explanation for these forms of social conflict was quite simply no longer good enough. Conflict was not simply an anomaly, it was rife in society at large and sociologists began to recognise their duty to treat it as such. As functionalism declined, its near-fatal wounds brought about by its obvious inability to answer the new questions of the day, sociologists turned to alternative perspectives. The more radical among them blamed these upheavals and inequalities on the dynamics of the capitalist system, and so turned to Marxism, while others, still working within a Western democratic framework, effectively turned functionalism on its head, accepting some of its premises but not its most fundamental one, drawing inspiration not from Durkheim so much as from Weber, and thus developing the tradition of conflict theory.

Possibly the chief theoretician of this group was **Ralf Dahrendorf**. Although Dahrendorf claimed to have been heavily influenced by Marx, his writings on conflict were not in any obvious way Marxist. In many respects, Dahrendorf can be described as providing a middle ground between the functionalists who we discussed in Chapter 2 and the Marxists who we turn to in the next chapter. The functionalist project, he suggested, was still worthwhile and had much to contribute, but it had fallen short because it only looked at one side of society – consensus. Conflict and consensus co-exist, Dahrendorf claimed, like the two sides of a coin. So while the functionalist perspective helps us understand societies based primarily on consensus, conflict theory can add to it by helping us make sense of societies based on conflict. While the consensus model applies to most modern industrial societies, the conflict model applies in most other situations. However, for Dahrendorf, the Marxist theory of conflict was too narrow, in that it focused purely on class relations in economic terms (again, more on this in Chapter 4). For Dahrendorf, this ignores the basic point of class relations, namely, that they are defined by an uneven distribution of *power*. In modern

Source: Getty Images/AFP

Ralf Dahrendorf

societies, said Dahrendorf, class relations are better defined in terms of access to power and authority – those with, and those without. This is important to remember when we come to discuss the role of interest groups according to conflict theory.

It is worth mentioning that, unlike functionalism, conflict theory was never presented as a coherent 'grand theory' with an all-encompassing systematic explanation of human action. Instead it used existing models, and turned them upside down. As we've already suggested, Dahrendorf never intended to entirely discard the insights of functionalism, he merely highlighted its shortcomings and developed his conflict theory as a complement to it. Another writer, Lewis Coser, introduced a version of conflict theory that stayed much closer to functionalism. In his most famous book, Coser (1956) looked for *The Functions of Social Conflict*, clearly then trying to present a *functionalist theory of (the functions of) conflict* in society rather than an actual *conflict theory*.

Other writers associated with conflict theory used Marxism (which we discuss in the next chapter) rather than functionalism as their starting point. For example, various British-based sociologists, such as

C. Wright Mills

**John Rex,** David Lockwood and John Goldthorpe, who were much more explicitly influenced by Weber than Dahrendorf or Coser ever were, placed the conflicts between social status groups at the centre of their analysis, in much the same way as Marxists had drawn attention to the conflict between class groups in capitalist societies, while a young British sociologist, **Anthony Giddens**, provided an analysis of the British class structure which was decidedly non-Marxist. Meanwhile, in America, **C. Wright Mills,** who had been, during the 1950s, one of the few heavyweight American sociologists to actually *challenge* the functionalist dominance, had provided a fresh perspective on the hierarchies of power in American society – the **power elite** – that showed how high-ranking interest groups in business, government and the military, conspired to protect each other's interests and sustain power.

Still others developed versions of conflict theory from other existing perspectives. For example, the American sociologist Randall Collins (whose work we won't be discussing in any detail in this chapter, and who has been more influential in the United States than elsewhere) used the so-called 'micro-sociological' approaches (those which start with the experiences of people rather than with abstract social systems) of interactionism and ethnomethodology (see Chapters 7 and 8) as his starting

51

ʋoint, and proceeded to examine the dynamics of conflict between individuals with different views. Finally, also influenced by Weber, a new historical sociology was developing which sought to critique evolutionist approaches to social change (such as functionalism and Marxism). This rich tradition, associated with such names as Barrington Moore, Jnr, Norbert Elias, Theda Skocpol, Charles Tilly and Michael Mann, is not usually included under the banner of conflict theory, but I do think a case can be made for doing so here, and I will return to it towards the end of the chapter.

In any case, this is what I mean when I say that conflict theory does not really exist as an all-encompassing school of thought, like functionalism. Rather, it is a loose coalition of contributions derived from all over the world of sociological theory. But what unites these contributions, sociologically at least, is that they *begin* with the view that societies are sites of difference, and such differences often, naturally, come into conflict with one another. Now, after reading Chapter 2, you may have decided that the functionalist analogy, of society as a system, was a useful one. However, if you follow this chapter, you may understandably be tempted to think otherwise. It's probably fair to say that, at one level, the basic premise of conflict theory – which forms its major criticism of functionalism – is perhaps entirely *obvious*, and if that is the case, then the functionalist metaphor of society as a system is clearly flawed. Naturally, the reality is a little more complex than this but if we were to present the case for conflict theory simply, it would follow rather like this:

1 People and groups in societies do not necessarily share the same values or desire the same ends.
2 Sometimes, the ends desired by one group are incompatible with those desired by another.
3 In such instances it may be possible for a compromise to be reached, but if no such compromise is possible, conflict may be inevitable.
4 Whoever achieves dominance is likely to present its values as *the* values – history, as they say, is written by the winners.

What we are left with, then, is a vision of society as a kind of marketplace, in which each trader is trying to do a bit better than the others, to gain a greater share of power and influence. If functionalists tell us that society is naturally a rather harmonious place thanks to those good old shared norms and values, conflict theory presents us with a far more aggressive picture. But remember that conflict theory is not a political ideology, it does not necessarily provide us with a programme for what *ought* to happen in the world, it presents a sociological model of what society *is*, namely, riddled with conflict. In actual fact, among those we can list as conflict theorists, some, such as C. Wright Mills, are clearly quite radical as they want to expose the stark inequalities and abuses of power in society. Some, such as Rex and many of those British Weberians, are a bit more centre-left: they highlight inequalities but don't necessarily endorse a radical overhaul of the system. A number of them, including Ralf Dahrendorf, are more identifiably liberal in their politics: they believe that while conflicts are an inevitable part of society, these can be effectively contained within the Western liberal democratic model of government (in the related discipline of political science, such an approach is known as 'pluralism'). But there are also some quite conservative contributions to conflict theory that have appeared in recent years: Samuel Huntington's 'clash of civilisations' thesis, which has inspired American neo-conservative academics and politicians to worry that cultural diversity might stifle 'Western values', can be read in this vein.

So, to summarise, in this chapter we are looking at a sociological viewpoint which defines its subject matter – society – as an arena of contestation, akin to professional wrestling's 'King of the Ring' competitions, in which the participants are actively trying to promote their own interests *vis-à-vis* those of their rivals. The interests being promoted can be political, economic or cultural in character – the point is that there is no 'consensus' which defines any one society, but a plurality of opinions and values. How one should react to this world of difference is a question of ideology, not sociology. In order to grasp what conflict theory tells us about society, particularly through its single most important concept, that of the *interest group*, we need to look more closely at the anti-functionalist philosophy which underpins it. Central to this philosophy is the idea of cultural relativism, which we need to turn to now.

## Cultural relativism

The theory that all cultures and communities contain their own particular value systems is known as **cultural relativism**. This position has been influentially advanced in social anthropology through the writings of such luminaries as Franz Boas (1940), Ruth Benedict (1934) and Margaret Mead (1928). These writers submitted a powerful challenge to the universalist and evolutionist approaches dominant in their discipline, which reflected the dominance of functionalism in sociology. Instead of seeking to locate general laws about how all societies 'operate', the relativists advocated the need to understand particular practices in their contexts. These derive from the *Geist* or 'spirit of the people'. Cultural relativists thus emphasise the diversity of human cultural, linguistic and genetic characteristics, and are deeply critical of attempts to impose external values upon local cultures.

Cultural relativism in social anthropology largely emerged as an attempt to overcome the perceived ethnocentrism of the discipline at the time. That is to say, it was commonplace for an American (say) researcher to extrapolate from his or her observations of American society a set of generalised rules. When Mead studied the 'coming of age' of young women in Samoa, she explicitly drew comparisons with the American experience that challenged any such presumptions of universality.

In sociological circles – where it is often referred to as 'subcultural theory' – the theory of cultural relativism has had limited appeal but has nonetheless made important contributions to a handful of fields, especially the sociology of language, thanks to the writings of William Labov, the sociology of poverty, via the interventions of Oscar Lewis, and the sociology of crime and deviance, through the work of Walter Miller and various others. Labov, for example, stressed that the language patterns of African-Americans did not constitute an 'inferior' form of communication, but rather were, in their own way, every bit as complex, as elaborate, as meaningful, and as linguistically consistent, as those of the 'mainstream' (white) society against which they were being measured. Similarly, for Lewis (1959, 1961, 1967) poorer families do not subscribe to the presumed values of wider society, which they see as providing only false hope for work and financial security, and families in poorer countries are not interested in having the values of wealthier countries imposed upon them, because they do not address the actual needs and daily lives of members of those communities. Instead, in rejecting these false promises, they develop and subscribe to an alternative set of values that allows them to make the most of their lives (Lewis lists, for example, the celebration of masculinity to the point of machismo, immediate rather than deferred gratification, sexual promiscuity and fatalism). However, as these values are internally derived, they cannot be easily divorced from the condition of poverty and underdevelopment upon which they are based, and so result in a 'culture of poverty'. Thus, traditional models of welfare provision or development misunderstand the socio-cultural dynamics at work within these communities.

In each of these examples, the lesson that is being presented is that one should not 'measure' ways of life – the complexities of different ways of speaking, the values of different socioeconomic groups – as if they exist on some shared universal continuum. Rather, each needs to be understood *in its own context*. Perhaps the clearest example of how a cultural relativist position differs from functionalism is found in Walter Miller's work on delinquent gangs. In a direct assault on the functionalist tradition, Miller rejects the idea that subcultures emerge when groups of people are unable to realise the values of the dominant culture. The norms and values of these subcultures in fact constitute a dominant culture in their own right. Delinquency is not, therefore, deviance from or resistance to the norms of wider society, but a natural expression of certain 'focal concerns' that constitute the way of life in particular cultural groups, particularly 'lower-class culture', taken to their extremes (Miller, 1958). It is, in its own way, a wholly conformist, and positive, manifestation of core values, the product of *normal* working-class socialisation rather than 'abnormal' middle-class socialisation (Downes, 1966).

It is important to note that cultural relativism in the social sciences requires us to appreciate and respect the existence of different value systems, and to understand them in context. When applied to questions of morality, i.e. questions of what one *ought* to do in any situation, it commands us not to measure the appropriateness of a particular action against some imaginary universal scale. What it most certainly does *not* do is open up the floodgates to a kind of nihilistic moral relativism where one action is 'as good as' any other. Make sure you are absolutely clear on this distinction – just because a cultural practice makes sense in one context does not mean it is easily transportable to another. As an example of this, Weber himself championed the relativist cause in his analysis of different sources of legal authority. Weber – and his disciple Radbruch – claimed that each local form of law should be measured according to its respective form of rationality and its relationship to justice. The emphasis for Weber was on historical and cultural difference. He suggested four ideal-type models of law, as outlined in Table 3.1, but the point of his argument was not that any one system was superior to the others, nor that they were all equally acceptable anywhere, but that each form of law made sense in its own context.

**Table 3.1** Weber's types of legal system

| System of law | Justification |
| --- | --- |
| Substantively irrational | Judgements based on *ad hoc*, emotive or interest-driven considerations |
| Formally irrational | Judgements based not on an offence but on appeal to some additional criteria (e.g. trial by combat, or advice from the gods) |
| Substantively rational | Judgements based on a legal system derived from non-legal sources, such as religion |
| Formally rational | Judgements based on a complete system of law derived from legal principles |

Cultural relativism is a central concept in sociological conflict theory, although it is by no means particular to it: interactionism and structuralism, just to take two examples of sociological perspectives which we discuss in later chapters, owe a great debt to it as well. (When you get to Chapter 9, and come across Dumont's anthropological work on the Hindu caste system, you should recall this discussion: in a sense, structuralism provides a *via media* between the generalising tendencies of functionalism and the contextually specific focus of conflict theory.) Conflict theory, though, is inherently relativist, in that it recognises the centrality of *difference*. However, while anthropological relativists and subcultural theorists in sociology tended to concern themselves with highlighting *cultural* differences, often across societies, conflict theorists in sociology have tended to take this a step further, and look at how, *within* societies, there is a seemingly infinite array of different persuasions, preferences, values and priorities, which in practice manifest themselves as competing voices trying to be heard. This is not just about recognising the existence of different voices and values but about seeing how they coexist. This is an inherently *political* issue – the promotion of particular *interests*.

## Interest groups and the pursuit of power

So, let's recap – following Weber, conflict theorists tend to subscribe to the cultural relativist position, which highlights the diversity of cultures, lifestyles and values that exists between and within societies. Its sociological direction has largely gone the way of analysing how societies are defined by the conflicts that arise when the positions of different groups are incompatible. In effect, as I've already suggested, societies are akin to marketplaces, in which rival interest groups compete with one another for scarce resources. The interest group is the key unit of analysis for much conflict theory. Broadly speaking, an interest group is any collective of people united by shared interests, and each of us belongs, in one capacity or another, to a multitude of interest groups. Women, students, Catholics and vegetarians are all examples of quite general interest groups. Students – despite their numerous other differences – are united in seeking to promote their interest *as students*. Supporters of a particular football team constitute an interest group, when they are united in defending their team against another, or advocating a better deal for themselves. Each of these interest groups effectively reflects a part of an individual's identity. The clearest articulation of this identity is when claims are made in respect of it, and in this respect, appropriate representative bodies are formed to speak 'on behalf of' those interests. A university lecturer may seek support from her trade union if she wishes to raise an issue relevant to her in that capacity, but she will not, of course, do so in order to promote her interests as a supporter of a particular football club. Society is, then, a mesh of interwoven interest groups making demands appropriate to their constituents, and is thus a heavily political machine.

> **EXERCISE 3.1  What interest groups do you belong to?**
>
> Make a list of ten interest groups that you belong to. Next to each one, try to think of one or two examples of the specific goals or values which unite members of that particular group.

In most cases, interest groups are not naturally in competition with one another. One's identity as a woman, a university lecturer and a supporter of a particular football club is perfectly reasonable because these interests do not result in conflicting demands. But in almost every case, an interest group has its nemesis, that which it is not, the group whose interests are entirely in opposition to its own. In such cases, power, which is defined as the securing of influence so as to protect one's own interests, is a zero-sum game: it is not infinitely expandable, so for one to achieve it, it means another must go without. Those who support fox-hunting and other field sports are in direct competition with anti-hunt protestors, because their respective interests are so specifically defined that for one to secure influence it is necessary for the other to fail to do so.

> **EXERCISE 3.2  Competing interests?**
>
> Take five of the ten interest groups you defined yourself as belonging to in Exercise 3.1. In each case, try to identify another interest group whose goals are in direct competition to yours. In respect of each pair, try to think of how this competition is actually played out. For instance, what goals conflict? Is compromise possible? What kind of conflict ensues between the competing groups?

This is where the 'marketplace' metaphor is best applied. If a trader makes a living selling fish then she or he is not threatened by the presence of a fruit seller setting up stall nearby. However, the arrival of another fish seller presents a direct challenge to the trader's self-interest. Both want a monopoly. It may not be possible to achieve that, so they may decide to reach a compromise, or they may engage in all-out competition to wipe the other out of business. You have already listed some of the interest groups you belong to, and in some cases listed direct competitors. This is why, at the level of experience at least, the central claim of conflict theory seems obvious. *Of course* we all belong to different interest groups, I hear you shout! And *of course*, sometimes my interest clashes with someone else's. And *of course* I want to get my way even if it means someone else doesn't, and that means I have to gain *power* at their expense. But sociological conflict theory isn't *just* about stating this rather obvious point (although it *is* important). What many of them actually want to do is investigate what happens when interest groups compete with one another for *real* power, *structural* power, which is located in the machinery of the state.

This is the question which was posed by the founders of what we now call 'political sociology': *if* conflict between interest groups is an inevitable feature of society, then how can we best *manage* this conflict? There is no single answer to this question – it depends on your analysis of the political machinery itself. James Madison, Alexander Hamilton and John Jay were the authors of *The Federalist Papers*, which are central to the American political system but also crucial to the field of political sociology. Their account (specifically attributed to Madison) begins explicitly with this problem, the problem of multiple conflicting interests or voices wanting to be heard, and the authors proceed to list the checks and balances necessary in a democratic society to ensure that all reasonable voices are wherever possible heard and that a fair verdict is reached in cases of competing interests. Within political sociology many writers, who as I mentioned above we refer to as 'pluralists', have taken their lead from Madison *et al.*, to show that Western-style democracies are best equipped to deal with such potential conflicts of interest. However, not all conflict theorists have been so inclined to accept this benign view of Western politics. Many have concentrated instead on the processes through which structural inequalities are sustained, and the voices of rival groups silenced by those who have achieved, and who wish to maintain, a position of power and dominance. Such a tradition harks back primarily to Max Weber, and by returning to his famous concept of 'status' we can follow the process a little more carefully.

Weber emphasised the importance of status as a measure of the influence of interest groups. Status groups, which Weber lists alongside class groups and parties as sources of conflicting interests, are not easy to define, and the distinction between the three categories identified by

Weber is not always obvious. Certainly, in some societies, inequalities based on status distinctions form the basis for all other inequalities. The Hindu caste system, in so far as it is a form of social distinction, can be interpreted in this respect. W. Lloyd Warner (1936) famously described the system of segregation in the United States as akin to a caste system, which was always interwoven with a class-based system. Warner makes the point that, as in the case of caste, in systems of segregation, privileges and opportunities are unevenly divided between groups, and social sanctions serve to maintain these distinctions, such as the absence of intergroup relationships or of social mobility. Caste, therefore, is necessarily a closed system, as opposed to social class, which must involve some degree of social mobility and interclass relationships. Warner's thesis was supported by Gerald Berreman (1967), who listed three characteristics of a caste system. First, it is hierarchical and closed. Second, the society is culturally plural but one group has achieved a monopoly of power. Third, interaction between groups is restricted through these power relations.

The conflict tradition thus draws considerable attention to both cultural pluralism and political violence. Taken together, these clearly signify the conditions for ethnic conflict. Leo Kuper's account of the structural conditions which allow for genocide to take place, and John Rex's work on the conditions which breed racial conflict, both clearly belong in this tradition (see for example Kuper, 1981; Rex, 1970; Rex and Moore, 1967). According to Kuper and Rex, as for Berreman, the primary condition for either racial violence or, in extreme cases, genocide is that the society in question is a plural society. This is not the same as a *pluralist* one. A pluralist society might be based on multicultural tolerance, but a plural society, while similarly diverse in its ethnic, religious and racial constitution, may be characterised – in its extreme form at least – by stark inequalities between these groups, and by the subordination by one group of another. In a plural society, diverse social and ethnic groups compete with one another for resources of money and power, and as a result, inequalities and patterns of discrimination exist within the economic, political, cultural and social spheres. These, then, are the conditions which make such acts of ethnic violence possible – one group seeking to stamp its superiority in the most extreme fashion over another. Rex suggests that racial violence emerges out of the interlinking of the three conditions already presumed by conflict theory: the unequal plural society; clear distinctions or boundaries between the groups within that society; and a cultural system, upheld by the dominant group, which justifies discrimination.

In addition to these conditions, Kuper stresses, in true Weberian fashion, that the site for these struggles is the state, and that the state plays a key role in administering this violence. The state is, after all, the location and machinery of power, the centralised means of violence. In the competitive marketplace of interest groups, the group which successfully gains control of the state gains control over the administration of society as a whole. Indeed, the conditions described by Kuper are the conditions which Weber himself used to describe, with due pessimism, the modern nation state: a society characterised by competition between different social groups, administered by a highly bureaucratic, technologically rational, centralised power structure. If these are the conditions which make genocide possible, then the rather disturbing conclusion is that such an atrocity could happen anywhere, at any time. While it certainly isn't *normal*, it *is* a logical extension of the *normal* state of affairs.

So, for conflict theorists, complex societies are characterised by a diverse plurality of different social, cultural and political groups, each with its own set of norms and values, and its own interests, and conflict between these groups as they seek to further their own specific interests is inevitable. Power is not so much an end in itself, but rather a means to another end, that is, the protection of self-interest. Law and politics are not independent of these interest groups, rather, they are constructed *by* them *in their interests*. Those with the power *make the laws*, they *drive the politics*, and they *define the crimes* in society (Chambliss and Seidman, 1971; Quinney, 1970; Vold, 1958).

In analysing how interest groups sustain power once in a dominant position, many conflict theorists reject the liberal view of power presented by political pluralists, who maintain faith in the potential for Western democracy to minimise conflict. They argue, in direct opposition to the pluralists, that power is always held by a handful of important decision-makers, or elites. These elites represent a variety of constituencies, including business, military, religion and community, and at various times each elite may succeed in gaining *some* power, but conflicts between them make it impossible for any one of them to secure *absolute* power (Rose, 1967; Hewitt, 1974). What tends to happen is that these elites come together in somewhat clandestine fashion. This is precisely what C. Wright Mills (1956) argued in his classic work from the 1950s: that rather than serving the interests of the people, the political machinery at work in America was dictated by an unelected power elite of business, military and political leaders 'scratching each other's backs', as it were.

---

### EXERCISE 3.3  Who rules?

In 'democratic' societies, elections take place which give members of the public a chance to decide who they want to govern the country. But who actually 'rules'? Does the elected government have total power for its time in office, or is it accountable to other interests? Taking Mills's classic *The Power Elite* as your lead, think about the different interest groups that might have a say in how a country is run – and about any possible conflicts of interest that you might be able to identify among them.

---

## Historical sociology

We have spent a lot of time in this chapter on the core concept within the conflict theory tradition, which is the concept of the interest group. Although relatively simple in its meaning, this is a surprisingly important and complex idea. It is important because, if we accept that interest groups are the building blocks of societies, then we must immediately dismiss the functionalist perspective with its emphasis on the social system and shared values (not to mention the Marxist perspective, which we cover in the next chapter, which takes social conflict down an altogether different route). It is complex because it then presents us with a logical process of how conflicts are played out, as part of the competition for the scarce resource of real, structural power. Those who achieve power want to keep it. To this end they may strike deals or negotiate compromises with other powerful interest groups (the power elite model), they may introduce laws which serve to criminalise, or impose economic sanctions which serve to marginalise, their rival voices, or in extreme cases they may undertake nothing less than the annihilation of that rival voice.

If we follow the logic of conflict theory as we have so far discussed it through to its next step, though, we might see that it also provides us with a theory of social change that is very different indeed from the quasi-evolutionist model presented in the preceding chapter and attributed to the functionalists. If you recall, for functionalists (and also for the Marxists we encounter in the next chapter), history appears to be pre-written; it follows a set pattern. Such approaches are criticised for being 'ahistorical' because they approach history and social change from the point of view of general laws that are applied objectively, be they (for functionalists) evolution and natural selection, differentiation and modernisation, or (for Marxists) historical materialism, without any attention to *history* itself. But if the story of society is really a story of interest groups for ever competing with one another for power and influence, then it begs the question, *whose* story is being told? Surely, according to such a perspective, history does not proceed along a predetermined path, but rather is dependent for its direction upon whichever interest group happens to gain power at any historical moment. Given the vast range of possible alternative interest groups who could seize power and thus 'write' history, the 'story' of social change would have to be seen as wholly unpredictable and subject to an endless variety of possible directions.

This is precisely the challenge laid at the feet of other theorists of social change by conflict theorists. Advocates of such a 'historical sociology' want to rewrite the rules for understanding social change by bringing in the perspectives and motives of actors involved in those situations. Conflict theory, applying the methods of historical sociology, thus suggests that human agents are the active creators of history to specific social and historical fields. They pay attention to the roles of collective actors, such as social movements and revolutions, political, military and economic factors, and 'figurations' of people and social relationships, which are viewed as key agents in social transformation (Elias, 1978; Giddens, 1985; Skocpol, 1979). What unites historical sociologists in this tradition is their refusal to apply generic schemes or frameworks to processes of social change, preferring instead to focus on the specific historical conditions that influence change, as well as the interplay of different influences upon it (Skocpol, 1979). For example, Barrington Moore, Jnr (1966), whose work was crucial to the development of this new historical approach, presented a direct challenge to the functionalist modernisation literature by uncovering the *multiple* routes towards democracy taken by different states, and the way that twentieth-century political systems such as democracy, fascism and communism result from specific historically contextualised interactions between the aristocracy, the emerging bourgeoisie, the proletariat and the agrarian peasantry.

In fairness, few if any of the above listed authors or others like them would explicitly identify as conflict theorists in the way described in this chapter. Even so, it seems perfectly reasonable to identify the *project* of this new historical sociology as being within the spirit of conflict theory (at least at this introductory level – the reader may wish to locate them elsewhere in the labyrinth of sociological theory at some later stage of her or his course). After all, it reminds us, in the last instance, that those *in* power use it to *maintain* that power and to exclude others from it.

## Summary and final thoughts

While recognising that there isn't exactly a single, unified body of thought that we can call conflict theory, I have tried in this chapter to pull together a variety of important contributions to sociological theory which *start* from the assumption that the world is first and foremost defined by *difference*, and that these differences are articulated in the form of competing interest groups vying for power. Max Weber was one of the first sociologists to recognise this and to place it at the centre of his view of society. Since then, a number of sociologists have defined society in terms of the strategies employed by any one group to secure power and then to sustain it. For them, society is similar to a marketplace, where each trader tries to shout louder than the next to secure your custom. I've also asked you to consider some of the interest groups *you* belong to, and to recognise that, in each case, someone, somewhere in the world belongs to a rival group that is entirely *incompatible* with it.

As most commentators point out, though, in so far as conflict theory might exist as an identifiable school of thought, it does so primarily as a direct alternative to functionalism, rather than as an explicit perspective *in its own right*. Perhaps, then, to conclude, we should look again at how conflict theory differs from its functionalist predecessor, usefully in tabular form (Table 3.2).

**Table 3.2** Comparing conflict theory to functionalism

|  | Functionalism | Conflict theory |
| --- | --- | --- |
| *Core assumption of the constitution of society* | In its 'natural' state, consensus: a 'healthy' system comprised of functionally necessary component parts | In its 'natural' state, conflict: a marketplace of competing actors pursuing their own interests and values |
| *Fundamental units within wider society* | Shared norms and values | Interest groups, with distinctive norms and values |
| *Theory of stratification* | Division of labour resulting from specialisation and functional differentiation | Class, status and party as coexisting forms of difference |
| *Engine of social change* | Social evolution, progression, 'modernisation' | Historical power relations |
| *Cause of social problems* | System malfunction, breakdown in social integration | Competing values, dominance of one interest group over another |

There is little doubt that conflict theory presents us with a different way of looking at society to functionalism. Indeed, we should bear in mind that it is not only in the discipline of sociology where the idea of conflict as the natural state of affairs has been influential. In the study of international relations, for example, it presents a powerful alternative to some older theories of how nation states engage with one another. In such a perspective, conflict – for example, as manifested in extreme cases as war and violence – is an inherent property of the international political system, just as it is of the social structure (Waltz, 1979). The state itself thus becomes a kind of collective actor, an interest group, pursuing its interests within the wider international system, competing with other such actors, other states.

How are we to judge the contribution of conflict theory to our understanding of society? For a start, it seems right to criticise functionalism for its ignorance of inequality and power hierarchy in society, its 'rose-tinted' view of the world. And in identifying the significance of interest groups – which are, after all, crucial components of social structure and its dynamics – it adds an important dimension to our sociological understanding. But if we were to find fault in it, we could say that it either goes too far, or doesn't go far enough, such that ultimately it fails to deliver on its promise of providing a radical theorisation of society. It goes too far because it gives too much autonomy to specific group interests and cultures, ultimately at the expense of casting any moral judgement on particular actions, always a problem with cultural relativism. It does not go far enough because in many cases it maintains an implicit reliance upon a relatively benign view of the world, the idea of a 'natural state', just as functionalism does, and shies away from engaging with more pressing questions about how inequalities and conflicts are not only inherent in *but also reproduced through* the dominant system. Its suggestions for reform are superficial and piecemeal, rather than radical. More radical voices such as Marxism, which we cover in the following chapter, would say it fails to condemn the inherently unjust capitalist system – indeed, it maintains that with proper management the system is in itself unproblematic. In its largely social democratic policy suggestions, it remains functionalist, albeit with a recognition of the natural state of conflict *contra* one of consensus. While it is true that conflict theory does not suppose this conflict to be inevitable, it does fail to engage in enough depth with the causes of this conflict, instead taking as read the great philosopher Jean-Jacques Rousseau's observation that society 'breeds' inequality and conflict. Sociologists who found conflict theory to be an inadequate critique of functionalist dominance turned instead to Marxism, in one or another of its forms. Others welcomed the Weberian concern with interests and motivations, but argued that such things need to be understood in the context of individual, rather than general, desires, and turned to various forms of social constructionism, including interactionism or ethnomethodology, which we deal with in Chapters 7 and 8.

## Key terms

*Definitions for the key terms listed below can be found in the Glossary on page 227.*

- Class, status and party
- Cultural relativism
- Interest groups
- Plural society
- Power elite
- Social class

# Biographies

*Short biographical descriptions for the names listed below can be found on page 240.*

- Ralf Dahrendorf
- Anthony Giddens
- C. Wright Mills

- John Rex
- Max Weber

# 4 | Marxism

In this chapter we will be:

- introducing the key ideas that underpin the theoretical approach known as Marxism;
- identifying the significance of Karl Marx in the development of these ideas;
- contrasting different types of Marxist-influenced sociological theory which have emerged in the last hundred years or so;
- looking at Marx's theory of historical change, called historical materialism, and considering some criticisms of this idea;
- looking at the suggestion that Marxism is a form of economic determinism, and how those sympathetic to it have sought to overcome this problem;
- discussing the core Marxist idea, that capitalist societies are defined by unequal class relations, and asking what these terms mean;
- considering some contemporary developments in Marxist theory in the light of more recent changes in society.

## Marx and Marxism

Marxism is the broad sociological and political tradition named in honour of its 'founder', the nineteenth-century German theorist and activist, **Karl Marx**. If you are already reasonably familiar with sociology, you are probably already aware that Marxism has made a pretty significant contribution to the history of the discipline. If you are not, though, you may be associating it and its founder more with a certain kind of political theory, 'communism', which, for a large chunk of the twentieth century, was the way of life in what was then the Soviet Union and eastern Europe, and stood in stark contrast to the **capitalism** of the West. When

I was throwing out some old notes from my sociology classes at school, I found it amusing that the first sentence on Marxism stated that 'two thirds of the world is run under this system'. Looking back on it, I realised how unhelpful it must have been to have seen Marxism first and foremost in relation to a form of political organisation, which was duly demonised as the 'enemy' of the West during the Cold War – talk about prejudicing a choice on the merits of a Marxist theory! And that is the point – Marxism is a general *theory* of society, not a 'system' of state administration. Far better to start with an evaluation of Marxism as such a theory, which draws particular attention to what is *wrong* in modern, Western, capitalist societies, and which seeks solutions to those problems, and leave it to politicians to derive from that theory a 'better' system of organising society, which may or may not be true to the spirit and the intentions of the man whose ideas it claims to represent.

So, it is Marxism as a *sociological* theory we are discussing here. And there is much to discuss, because the theory has much to offer. More so than possibly any of the other perspectives included in this volume, it is a theory which develops around its own set of very clearly defined key concepts – capitalism and **social class** are the two big ones, and attached to them are 'historical materialism', **'alienation'**, **'ideology'**, **'base and superstructure'**, 'exploitation', and dozens more besides. The beauty of a Marxist approach is that while *at the next level* it is incredibly complex (we won't be dwelling on the very detailed contributions Marxists have made to economic theory!), and there are certainly many different and often competing interpretations of Marxist theory (which we will be discussing), at its most *basic* level, Marxism can be quite easy to grasp. Once you understand what these core concepts mean, you will find, I think, that they actually hold together in a coherent way, presenting Marxism as a total, joined-up way of seeing the world, and making it relatively straightforward for you to understand how you would go out and *do* a Marxist sociology. Of course, whether you agree with the Marxist *description* of society in the first place is an altogether different thing, but that's a challenge you should find yourself facing when you come to evaluate *each* of the perspectives in this book.

To be honest, as a marking tutor, I am rather bored with essays on Marxism which always state that Marx himself was born in Trier (in the German Rhineland) in 1818, and that he died in 1883, although these are undeniable facts. Far more important is that, having studied philosophy and law at Bonn and Berlin, he became not an academic but a freelance scholar, journalist and ultimately an activist, that he moved to London in 1849, and that he formed a close relationship with a fellow German, Friedrich Engels, who was wealthy enough to serve as his sponsor. Marx is actually buried in Highgate cemetery in north London (in close proximity to Herbert Spencer, one of the other great founders of sociology, but please don't let the amusing fact of this detract you from your continued attention), and his residence in England is of absolute significance to his status as one of the most important intellectuals – and I don't mean just sociological theorists, or even social theorists broadly defined, I mean *intellectuals*, of the calibre of Plato, Aristotle, Charles Darwin, Albert Einstein and John Maynard Keynes – ever to walk the planet. What Marx did in establishing the relationship between the economic conditions of the society around us and the way we live our lives is actually quite breathtaking. And it was largely due to his analysis of his adopted country. England was where the Industrial Revolution started. It was the site of so much radical social change, as factories were being built and entire new ways of life established around them. Marx was fascinated by all of this, and from it sprang his observations that capitalism, the new model of society, was inherently flawed and undeniably unfair, and that it would ultimately be replaced by a new, fairer system, communism.

So, Marx himself developed what would become known as the Marxist theory (obviously!), but there have been a number of significant variations on it since then, such that it is not entirely accurate to treat Marxism as a single theory (plus, of course, there is Marx's own famous quotation on the subject – 'All I know is that I am not a Marxist'). It *is*, however, fair to pull these together under the broader umbrella of a Marxist *tradition*, because they address familiar Marxist *themes* (primarily, the social inequalities resulting from capitalism), and use Marxist *tools of analysis* (a materialist approach, a focus on *class* relations, a commitment to radical social transformation). The best way I think to incorporate these different variants of Marxian-inspired theory within this chapter is to locate them within a conversation with what we might call an 'orthodox' Marxist approach. For me, such an approach would be focused around three key propositions, and these form the structure of this chapter:

Source: Corbis/Swim Ink.

Karl Marx

1 the theory of **historical materialism** – Marx's theory of how social change can be understood as the transformation from one economic system to another;

2 the theory of **economic determinism** – the claim that the economy operates as the engine of society, its 'base', and that other factors, such as cultural and political ones, are subordinate to it and form the 'superstructure';

3 the theory of class analysis – that in a *capitalist* society, an inevitable schism and thus conflict exists between two *classes*, the owners (the 'bourgeoisie') and the workers (the 'proletariat').

So, an 'orthodox' position (if one truly exists) would hold each of these propositions to be true, but, as we shall see, each has its own problems, and the subsequent history of Marxist social theory has been to overcome these problems while maintaining the integrity of the Marxist project. The Russian revolutionary leader V.I. Lenin was among the first to 'adapt' Marxism, when he provided a reassessment of historical materialism to justify the revolutionary transformation to communism in Russia without going through a capitalist stage. Lenin also drew attention to the *expansive* nature of capitalism, spreading ever-outwards like a hungry beast seeking new markets to consume, in his theory of *imperialism*. Another important development came from the Italian revolutionary Antonio Gramsci, who studied political and cultural processes not solely as empty reflections of the economic base but as strategic forces in capitalist reproduction, through his theory of *hegemony* (in a nutshell, how capitalism thrives on the manufacture of *consent* from those it exploits, akin to turkeys voting for Christmas!).

In the mid-twentieth century, two very important movements emerged which sought to rescue the promise of Marxism from its limitations, although they had very different ideas about what that promise, and those limitations, actually were. The first was associated with the 'Frankfurt School', a group of intellectuals based at the Frankfurt Institute for Social Research, who wanted to repackage Marxism as a critique of *domination* rather than just of capitalism, and thus extend its critical reach beyond obviously capitalist societies to the fascist regimes of Europe and the Soviet-dominated dictatorships to the east. Also, like Gramsci, these Frankfurt scholars, who came to be associated with 'critical theory', wanted to show that the processes Marx was writing about in the nineteenth century had, by the middle of the twentieth, extended to incorporate the *cultural* as well as the economic realm. In doing so, scholars such as **Theodor Adorno** and **Herbert Marcuse** were not necessarily *abandoning* Marxism so much as *updating* it to take into consideration recent changes in the nature of capitalism (more on which below).

The second movement emerged in France and its inspiration was a philosopher named **Louis Althusser**. Unlike the Frankfurt School, Althusser did not think that the real promise of Marxism was in its emancipatory potential. Schooled as he was in the tradition of *structuralism* (which we discuss at length in Chapter 9), he had no time for the *humanist* pretensions of Marx's earlier writings (the idea that the central concept in society must be people and their experiences of the world), but found in Marx's later contributions, and especially in his three-volume tome *Capital*, the definitive scientific analyses of the workings of the capitalist *system*. What Althusser and his followers went on to do – quite brilliantly, some would argue – is effectively abandon all three of these core propositions, and, in a sense, redefine capitalism itself. Again, more on this later.

Other variants of Marxism have come onto the scene, with different degrees of longevity and influence. In Britain, for example, a very distinct branch emerged which detached the non-economic aspects of society from the capitalist economy altogether. For example, Ralph Miliband refuted the claim that the state (the locus of political activity) in a capitalist society must inherently be a capitalist state; rather he claimed it should be seen as an empty boardroom which has to be *occupied* by the agents of capitalism, thus making it possible for a socialist state to be established through parliamentary rather than revolutionary means. Also, the end of the twentieth century saw a plethora of Marxist-inspired writers trying to engage with some very specific and contemporary debates (including **post-modernity, globalisation** and the perceived crisis of the nation state, which we discuss at length in the concluding chapter of this book) within a Marxist framework, effectively doing what the Frankfurt School had tried to do – updating Marxism to take account of changing conditions. Elsewhere still, a collection of scholars began to make use of a range of heavily *analytical* philosophical tools (including rational choice theory, which we discuss in Chapter 6) to address the *problems* posed by Marxist theory, but without all the additional questions of ideology and politics. And in the United States, **Immanuel Wallerstein** and his collaborators at the Fernand Braudel Center at the State University of New York, Binghampton, were busy recasting the entire Marxist project from being one about power relations between *classes* to one about power relations between *states* within the *world* capitalist system – not so much updating Marxism, then, as dismantling it and rethinking the entire history of capitalism.

We will return to some, but not all, of these different forms of Marxist theory later in the chapter. Suffice to say that, in so far as this book is designed to present eight very broad traditions in sociological theory, they can all be suitably located within the Marxist camp, but they are quite distinct and at times they are in total contradiction with each other and with what I have called 'orthodox' Marxism. Once you have grasped Marxist theory in its simplistic form, you should investigate each of these in more depth to see how they differ from one another. To help you, I have put them into tabular form (Table 4.1).

**Table 4.1** Types of Marxist theory

| Type of Marxist theory | Disagreement with 'orthodox' Marxism | Key propositions | Key names |
|---|---|---|---|
| *Critical theory* | Its economic determinism and its emphasis on class analysis | Culture has been collapsed into the economy; class is no longer the only form of oppression | Theodor Adorno Max Horkheimer Herbert Marcuse |
| *Structural-Marxism* | Its historical materialism, economic determinism and class analysis, plus its humanism | Capitalism is not just an economic system but an entire 'social formation' that manifests and reproduces itself in cultural and political as well as economic forms | Louis Althusser Nicos Poulantzas |
| *Liberal-Marxism* | Its economic determinism and implicit revolutionism | Capitalism is purely an economic system which takes over cultural and political practices but these are autonomous from it | E.P. Thompson Ralph Miliband |
| *World-systems theory* | Its historical materialism and class analysis, and its nation-state bias | Capitalism has always been a world system in which powerful 'core' states exploit weaker 'peripheral' ones | Immanuel Wallerstein |
| *Analytical Marxism* | Its heavily outdated normative bias | The problems identified by Marx remain largely the same but more rigorous analytical tools are required to better understand them | G.A. Cohen |
| *Neo-Marxism* | Its inappropriateness for dealing with contemporary problems unless it is duly updated | The current phase of 'late capitalism' is distinct from the earlier phase so Marxist theory must accommodate this | Jürgen Habermas David Harvey Frederic Jameson Leslie Sklair |

However, for the purpose of introducing Marxist theory in its broadest possible terms, I will turn to each of these three core propositions, to explain what they mean, and present examples of how they have been criticised or developed. In the conclusion I will try to bring these together into a summary of Marxist theory in sociology.

## The materialist theory of history

The central idea in most traditional forms of Marxist sociological theory is that the social world has to be understood in *materialist* terms. This is probably the hardest thing to grasp about Marxist theory and, once you are clear about it, much of what follows should slot into place neatly. It means that what actually drives societies forward, what serves as their *engine* if you like, is comprised of *real, substantial* things ('products') as opposed to *ideas*. The world is not something *imagined* by philosophers, but something that is *lived* by people – people who need to eat, to have shelter and clothing, to work. We should study society, says Marx, in terms of its capacity to provide us with these material things. The great ideas of the world, like religion and culture, are not somehow superior to the mundane reality of it (such an assumption would be considered heavily elitist and conservative). This is beautifully summed up in a quote from the playwright George Bernard Shaw, in his play *Major Barbara*: 'I can't talk religion to a man with bodily hunger in his eyes'.

But Marx did not merely prioritise the real material struggles over the great ideas in his social theory, he also devised from that a theory of how we should study the world itself and its various transformations. He developed a theory of social change which has come to be called historical materialism. Here, he was consciously reacting against the *idealist* theory of history proposed by the great German philosopher Georg Hegel. Hegel had suggested that change comes about in what he called a *dialectical* fashion – meaning, a dominant *idea* of the world (in Hegelian terms, a *thesis*) is confronted by its opposite, its *antithesis*, and from these comes a new *synthesis* which itself becomes the dominant idea for a new world, and which of course goes on to clash with its antithesis to produce a new synthesis, and so on. Marx was very fond of this dialectical approach, this emphasis on how change comes about through the clash of opposing forces producing a new way forward, but he was less enamoured of Hegel's insistence that these forces were *ideas*. So, Marx set about taking Hegel's dialectical method but applying it to *material conditions of existence* rather than to ideas.

But first, how does one measure material conditions of existence in a meaningful way? Marx answered this by focusing on *production*. Each

75

society, he argued, can be understood in terms of how it produces the material goods needed for survival. You have to bear in mind that Marx was writing in nineteenth-century England, and the Industrial Revolution was still ongoing. Marx was acutely conscious of how the new technologies, the factory system and so on, were fundamentally changing not only how goods were being produced but, by extension, how people were living their lives and society itself was being organised. Agricultural production methods of the pre-industrial era required forms of organisation (politics) and ways of life (society) that seemed a world removed from the realities of people living in the new industrial towns such as Manchester. So what Marx did, and what makes him a brilliant theorist, was to build from this specific interest in changing methods of production a much broader social theory about nothing less than the constitution of society itself. First of all, we have what Marx called the *means of production*, a bit of jargon for sure but not at all complicated, because it means precisely what it looks like it should mean: the strategies and technologies available for producing goods. Then, we have what he referred to as the *relations of production*, which simply means the relationships different people have to the means of production: this is a source of division in societies because some people relate to the means of production as *owners* and thus exercise more power over it than those who relate to it merely as *workers*. So, we have here a direct link in any society between *how goods are produced*, and what kind of *hierarchy* is present in that society. Finally, Marx suggested that we could study each society as a form of economic organisation defined by its means and relations of production: as a specific *mode of production*. A mode of production is just a way of categorising different societies. It's no different from saying that Italy is a Catholic society while Saudi Arabia is an Islamic society, or that the United States is a democracy while Pinochet's Chile was a military dictatorship. However, whereas in these cases we are using religion or political system as the central means of defining and comparing societies, Marx was using the type of economy as his fundamental factor.

So, what exactly did he do with Hegel's dialectical method? Remember, Hegel was talking about how change comes about, and that is precisely what Marx did as well. He took his idea that different societies could be understood as distinct 'modes of production' and tried to present them in a teleological order, one following another, to show how societies change across the course of history from one such mode of production to another in dialectical fashion. That is to say, each mode of production (replacing Hegel's dominant idea as the *thesis*) intrinsically creates the seeds of its own destruction by producing its own opposition (its *antithesis*), which results in a *synthesis* and thus a new mode of production.

Marx theorised history in terms of a five-stage sequence, showing how one mode of production was replaced by another. In some respects there are similarities between what Marx was suggesting and the ideas of the nineteenth-century evolutionists like Spencer and, later, Durkheim, who we discussed back in Chapter 2, and it is true to say that Marx's theory of historical materialism has been criticised for being overly evolutionist just as those others have. Indeed, many subsequent Marxists have maintained that while focusing on societies as *modes of production* is vital, because it enables us to understand the *real* forces of domination at work in any given society, it is not necessary to buy into this whole chronological sequence that Marx gives us. There is truth to this, and Marx himself recognised the flaws in his system later on, but at the same time, appreciating how one mode of production is superseded by another in the necessary course of history is crucial to understanding the other important part of a Marxist theory, which is its commitment to not only identifying the inherent *problems* of the current system, but also to showing how they can be overcome when the system is replaced with a 'fairer' one. We'll return to this later. For now let us try to grasp the basic five-stage sequence Marx suggested was occurring in (Western) societies. First of all, he suggested, there was a very early stage of *primitive communism*, which was effectively classless and defined by an early example of mutual exchange, the sharing of goods and resources for the benefit of the group. However, from this emerged the earliest form of hierarchical society, which Marx called the *ancient mode of production*, which operated as a largely military-controlled economy and in which power relations were defined by the institution of slavery. In such a society, the distinction between the 'haves' and the 'have-nots' was one of *master and slave*. Naturally, the slave-based society created its own tensions and inequalities, and as a result a new *synthesis* emerged from it, the *feudal mode of production*. In the feudal mode of production, the slaves are 'free' but at the same time *not* free because they remain dependent on the elites. The feudal mode of production was characterised by an agricultural economy and by a hierarchy between the aristocracy which owned the land and the *serfs* who worked it.

The feudal mode of production was thus based on a heavily ascribed form of stratification. There was no social mobility as such. Medieval romances notwithstanding, the serf was largely predestined to live out his or her life as a serf, there was no system in place which allowed them to show initiative and get promoted to the role of lord or lady of the manor. Herein lay its inherent contradiction, and it was a contradiction Marx argues that became more and more apparent as the new industrial technologies emerged. The more enterprising among the serfs were able to exploit these new technologies and establish themselves as a new *middle* class. As feudalism gave way to the new *capitalist* mode of production characterised by industrial technology, an entirely new way of life emerged, a new hierarchy, in which those with control over the new technologies were now in possession of real power. The old aristocracy was thus supplanted by this new middle class, the *bourgeoisie* which had emerged from the ranks of the serfs, as the dominant player. Make no mistake, then, capitalism was a *revolutionary* force because it overthrew the old status distinctions based on birthright, but, inevitably, and in true dialectical fashion, it quickly constructed its own hierarchies and its own contradictions. In addition to the bourgeoisie who own the means of production, there are those who have to do the work, the *proletariat*. Marx argued that capitalism is inherently exploitative, because it necessarily requires that some people reap the benefits of other people's work. The distinction between bourgeoisie and proletariat, the social classes of the capitalist mode of production, is crucial to Marxist social theory generally and we will have much more to say about it, and why Marx thought capitalism was inherently exploitative, later in the chapter. Suffice to say at this point that the exploited workers would, according to Marx, eventually realise their position and overthrow the system, ushering in the fifth stage, a new classless communist society in which those who do the work receive the appropriate reward for it.

As I have already suggested, the theory of historical materialism has been somewhat Janus-faced in Marxist theory more generally. On the one hand, it has provided Marxists with the ammunition to refute any suggestion that the Russian revolution of 1917, which was carried out in the name of Marxist theory, could have ever led to a true communist society as Marx himself envisaged. After all, historical materialism tells us that these stages of history, these modes of production, are *sequential*, and so to reach that ultimate stage, a society first has to progress through the others. Russia was a feudal society at the time, so could not properly transform into a communist one without going through the capitalist phase. Commentators such as Bill Warren, a Marxist economist and sociologist of development, have made this point in respect of the progression of 'underdeveloped' societies – that, for all its faults, capitalism remains an essential stage in the evolution of any society. But on the other hand, it locks Marxist theory into a rather stagnant and one-dimensional view of the world, not to mention a very insular one, in that these modes of production seem to be entirely based within nation states. This last point has been taken up by the American academic Immanuel Wallerstein, who, as I stated earlier, has an interesting relationship with Marxist theory: he uses its tools, he talks about divisions between rich and poor, and he targets capitalism as the cause of the problem, so to all intents and purposes he is part of the Marxist tradition, yet he explicitly refutes the core theoretical basis of Marxism, which resides in Marx's account of the emergence of capitalism. For Wallerstein, capitalism is not just a mode of production, a stage in a country's history, but an entire world *system* of production *and exchange*, which has been in operation for hundreds of years. It hardly matters whether a particular country goes through the capitalist 'stage' or not, as it is already intrinsically locked in to this broader, *world* capitalist system. A very different rejection of historical materialism comes from Louis Althusser, who looks at capitalism as not just a mode of production but as an entire social formation which manifests itself in different ways, thus consigning Marx's overly teleological and rather predictable and simplistic view of history to the rubbish bin in favour of a more dynamic view, capitalism constantly adapting and evolving in often unpredictable ways.

## Base and superstructure

The second core proposition we need to explore is the claim made by Marx that the driving force in society is its system of production and the resultant distribution of its goods, i.e. its *economy*. Whether or not the theory of historical materialism is appealing to you, it is important that you treat this claim on its own merits, because it is the single underlying claim of Marxist sociology.

For many critics, Marx's claim that the economy takes priority over other forces in our lives, such as politics and the realm of ideas we call culture, renders Marxist theory open to accusations of economic determinism. Marx does not just say, they point out, that it is more important for us to *study* the material conditions of existence, but goes further to say that the economy *drives* these other areas of life and that they are subordinate to it. Politics and culture, law and religion are not only less important than economics, they are reflective of it and determined by it.

This is the 'classical' Marxist position, although it is not one that is embraced by all subsequent Marxist sociologists, and in fairness it was never one that was actually embraced fully by Marx himself. Nonetheless, one can see how the confusion has arisen. If Marx famously said that 'religion is the opium of the people' it was to suggest that religion serves a particular function to support and uphold the dominant economic system by placating the exploited workers and offering them a better deal in Heaven rather than on Earth. Note the use of the word *function* here. There are similarities between this kind of (crude or vulgar) Marxist analysis and the functionalist perspective we covered in Chapter 2. The difference, of course, is the emphasis on artificial power relations in Marxist theory contrasted with some 'healthy' state of equilibrium in functionalist theory. The institutions of society – the political system, the legal system, the religions, the education system, the media and so on – do not provide functions to service and sustain the 'natural' state of society, but to protect and reproduce the interests of the dominant capitalist system, to which they are entirely subordinate and thus from which they have no autonomy. Marxists refer to the economy as the *base* of society, upon which sits the *superstructure* comprised of all these other things. The superstructure cannot exist without the base, and has no substance independent of it. This relationship between base and superstructure is usually presented in the form of a simple triangle (Figure 4.1).

However, there is a clear contradiction here between Marx's apparent economic determinism and his dialectical advocacy of revolution

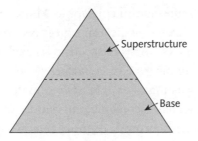

**Figure 4.1** The base–superstructure triangle

(which surely comes from ideas, not least that of class consciousness). It may very well be that if we take 'orthodox' Marxism to its logical conclusion, then it is highly *illogical*. But that is not to deny its relevance. For a long time, for example, in the field of 'cultural studies' (a term we use now, but did not then), the Marxist approach to culture corresponded very much to these rules. For such writers, literature and other cultural forms reflect not the autonomy and creativity of any specific artist, but rather the material conditions within which the art form is constructed (see Caudwell, 1946; Hauser, 1951, 1958). A similar argument is presented within the sociology of education, in the 'correspondence theory' of Samuel Bowles and Herbert Gintis (1976), for whom education serves to prepare the pupil for work in a capitalist society, and indeed the education system within a capitalist society represents something akin to a training ground for the actual workplace.

---

### EXERCISE 4.1 What the superstructure does . . .

Taking hints from what has been suggested above, think of some of the ways the following 'superstructural' institutions might serve the interests of capitalism:

1 Education

2 Religion

3 Law

4 The media

5 Politics and the state

---

One Marxist who seeks to overcome the apparent simplicity of this approach is Theodor Adorno, one of the members of the 'Frankfurt

School'. For Adorno, the central concept in Marx's work was **commodification,** the process through which an object becomes part of a marketplace, and its use value becomes reduced to its exchange value (the table that you build, for example, receives a *market* value). Adorno accepted that in Marx's day, this was mainly applicable to material goods, but in *late* capitalism, culture itself has become a commodity. We buy and sell symbols, ideas, brands and sounds as much or more than we do tables. They have their own market value; this is what he called the 'culture industry'.

If Adorno adapted Marxist theory by showing how culture had been collapsed *into* the economic base, the French Marxist theorist Louis Althusser championed an even more radical break with economic determinism. Althusser rejected this proposition by rethinking the definition of capitalism itself. In his view, it is not merely a mode of production, an economic system, but rather an entire *social formation*, a social system which comprises economic, cultural and political aspects, each of which exercises 'relative autonomy'. In certain societies, said Althusser, the economic form is sufficiently advanced to present itself as the dominant face. But even then it is sustained through the machinations of the 'ideological state apparatuses' (such as the media, religion and the education system), and, if necessary, the 'repressive state apparatuses' (such as the police and the army). And, where the economic face is insufficiently stable, the capitalist social formation takes on a different form of control – perhaps through its cultural face, as with certain tribal or heavily religious societies, or through it political one, as with military dictatorships. In effect, Althusser takes the good old triangle and suggests that rather than being rigid, it is flexible enough to turn on its side and allow a different form of domination to take the lead (Figure 4.2).

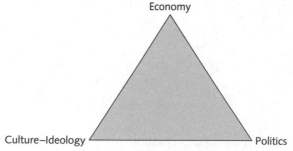

**Figure 4.2** The social formation of capitalism

It was precisely Althusser's suggestion that capitalism should be treated as an entire social formation that inspired one of the most famous discussions about Marxist economic determinism in the field of political sociology – the 'Miliband–Poulantzas' debate in the 1970s. Both writers wanted to address the role of the state within a Marxian framework but did not want to treat it merely as something entirely determined by the economic base. Inspired by Althusser, the Greek sociologist Nicos Poulantzas claimed that the state, the political machinery of society, acts in such a way that it is attached to but not entirely dependent on the economy – it has *relative autonomy*; however, in the last instance, it remains part of the capitalist system and so in a capitalist society will necessarily be a capitalist state. Ralph Miliband suggested, by contrast, that the state is an empty vessel, an *instrument* which is not directly attached to or at all dependent on the economy, and that for capitalism to be dominant it has to *appropriate* the machinery of the state. Miliband's aim was to show that the state is not inherently capitalist so that, if occupied by an elected socialist government, it could serve to introduce a socialist society in place of the capitalist one. However, many Marxists felt that in granting the state full autonomy he had strayed too far from the spirit of Marxism.

## Class in a capitalist society

So, let's take stock for a second. Are you clear what Marxists mean when they refer to capitalism? Remember, it is a *mode of production*, a way of organising the economy. Very often we hear the word used in a much more general sense, but for Marx it has a much more specific definition, while for Althusser it is a *social formation* which is more than just an economic system, although it predominantly presents itself as such.

What about the idea of social class? Again, Marx has a very clear definition of what this means. It is a method of classifying people according to how they relate to the means of production. Even more so than capitalism, we hear class used to refer to all sorts of things. Sometimes it is used as a complex system of categorising people according to the type of job they do (in the UK we have the so-called 'Registrar-General's Scale', which 'ranks' types of work into different class categories).

Sometimes, though, we think of class as part of our identities, and associate it with certain lifestyles and values. For example, football is a 'working-class' sport (unless you count the so-called 'prawn sandwich' brigade in their corporate boxes!), while rugby union is a 'middle-class' sport. 'Being' working class, in this sense, has nothing to do with whether or not you hold down a manual job or rather work in an office, or as a teacher (which are more 'middle-class' jobs), but it has to do with your attitude towards the world – pub culture, tabloid newspapers, simple food are all 'working class', but art galleries are not.

Marx's use of the term conveniently gets rid of all those subjective aspects of class and defines it in clearly objective terms. It is purely about whether you *own* or *control* the means of production, and thus benefit from the labour of others, or whether you are one of those forced to sell your labour for a wage so that others can enjoy the profits. It is thus a *power relationship* defined by your economic position within a capitalist society, and it is a source of inevitable conflict.

Why is this? This is perhaps one aspect of Marxist social theory that is most misunderstood. We *know* that Marx was heavily critical of capitalism and that he advocated a 'fairer' kind of system, communism, in its place, but we rarely bother to find out *why*. It is all too easy for us to just dismiss Marxism at this stage as revolutionary nonsense, which is perhaps an understandable knee-jerk reaction from people brought up in a capitalist society, and superficially at least quite fond of it, especially when compared with an abstract alternative mistakenly associated with the dictatorial politics, relative poverty, rigid bureaucracy and thoroughly unglamorous lifestyle of the old Soviet Union. But remember, dear reader, that we are not going to make that mistake here – we are going to focus on Marxism as a sociological theory, and at the heart of that is the claim that for all its apparent freedoms, capitalism is an inherently unjust and exploitative system.

The problem comes from what Marx calls *species-being*. By that, he means a variation of the old philosophical chestnut, 'human nature'. Humans are, of course, *homo sapiens*, thinking beasts, but for Marx, we are also *homo faber*, creative ones. It is human nature to create, and to enjoy the product of our creativity. But capitalism denies us this. It forces us to turn the very essence of our humanity, our creativity and labour power, into *commodities* that are bought and sold.

Commodification, if you recall, is a Marxian term which refers to the process of attaching a price tag to something so it can be situated in the marketplace. When we sell our labour power for a price (a wage), we commodify ourselves. We have no control over the process of creation, nor any ownership of the product we are creating. We are distanced from it, detached from the very thing that defines us. Marx calls this alienation. Capitalism as an economic system – a mode of production – is all about this: we work while others enjoy the profits from the product of our efforts. This is, by any definition, exploitation. And – assuming we agree on the meaning of that word, 'exploitation' – this is not something that Marx's critics would dispute. Capitalism *is* a system which requires some to struggle and work so that others can live in the lap of luxury. Not everyone can own – who would do the work? Contra the closed system of earlier feudalism, capitalism offers you the *possibility* of social mobility, of doing well for yourself, but not everyone can actually succeed. This is a fundamentally *moral* problem, not a sociological one *per se*. Many will say that there is nothing at all immoral about this situation, because the fairness of a situation resides in ensuring that everyone has the *chance* to succeed. Marx and his followers would disagree. It is as simple as that.

So, a Marxist sociological analysis of capitalist society would focus on the dynamics of this system of exploitation. It would draw attention to the way the working classes are required to 'sell themselves' so that the already-rich get richer, focusing on the *distribution of wealth* in society and how it is decidedly polarised, and on how the uneven distribution of life chances and of quality of life in general is a direct consequence of this polarised distribution of wealth.

Marx himself had a solution – of sorts. Although he is most famously associated with the idea of a communist society, he said very little about it. He suggested that it would come about when the workers, who are forced to compete against each other to survive and thus exhibit 'false class consciousness' (fail to recognise each other as a single exploited group and thus to address the real cause of their misery), finally come to realise their shared position and achieve 'true class consciousness'. From this will come the revolution that will see the unjust capitalist order overthrown and replaced by the new system where power reflects actual work.

Clearly, there is an issue with the theory of class analysis. Is it really so easy to divide power up in such polarised terms? Consider the following exercise:

## EXERCISE 4.2  Class and power in the university

Consider the university as an example of a micro-capitalist society, where the product is knowledge itself. Who represents the 'bourgeoisie', the owners of the means of production? Who represents the 'proletariat', who work to produce it? How do the different agents exercise power in respect of each other? Where do students fit into the power structure?

I wouldn't be surprised if you thought, at first, that students represent the proletariat, and are powerless, while the university represents the hierarchy of power almost as some kind of monolith, with academics in collusion with executives. But I hope you can see, on further insight, how wrong this is. In most universities these days, academics are *employed* for their skills as workers, but exercise precious little power over the institution and receive scarce reward from it save their salaries. If the *function* of the university is to pass on knowledge through teaching and research, then academics carry out that function, just as the chap on the assembly line does when putting together a car. OK, they have more *creativity*, more involvement in the design of their courses and articles and thus more say in *how* their product is created, but a standard Marxist analysis of their role would be to say that they represent a position *within* the proletariat, rather than one of management. In a crucial contribution to Marxist theory, Harry Braverman (1974) drew attention to the extent to which workers are increasingly subdivided and specialised. Despite this, the 'white-collar worker' remains a *worker*. And what of the student? Spokespersons of various political persuasions are keen to describe the twenty-first century student as a *consumer*, suggesting that she has power *over* the institution, in some contractual way. This is actually just rhetoric – the student is *not* a consumer, at best she is a *client* of the university. In any case, this is surely an excellent case study of Marxist theory – it shows quite clearly how something which exists *outside* the system and thus challenges it is quickly dragged into it: higher education used to be about knowledge for its own sake, now it is about producing healthy capitalists; it used to be an arena of debate and critique, now it concerns itself with conformity. Her very existence as a student has become *commodified*, or, to use the language of the neo-Marxist, **Jürgen Habermas**, her 'lifeworld' (that part of her which is *not* part of the economy, which defines her cultural and social affiliations), has become infiltrated by the commodifying logic of the marketplace.

But, having said that, what is her relationship to the lecturer? How does she exercise her voice within the university community? To what extent does she hold power over, say, the security guard who cheerfully patrols her block at night? To what extent does she really exercise *any power at all* in the university 'community', outside perhaps of the influence she might wield over the new colour schemes for her college bar or common room? After all, if we were to follow the logic of Bowles and Gintis and their 'correspondence theory', then the university, like the school, merely prepares students for their outside work, in which case students *are* the exploited lab-rats of a capitalist institution. It may very well be that these are complex questions, not easily answered within a standard Marxist framework, and this may well be why critical theory, as inspired by the Frankfurt School, has somewhat supplanted Marxism as the theory of choice among radicals, because it restates the problem as one between *powerful* and *powerless*, rather than just *bourgeoisie* and *proletariat*. But perhaps also, to go down that route is to miss entirely the point of a Marxist theory of class in a capitalist society, which is a theory of *exploitation*.

There is, of course, *another* problem with class analysis, and that is that it presumes that the working class is *capable* of being this great revolutionary agent. In his 1964 book *One-Dimensional Man*, the Frankfurt School theorist Herbert Marcuse presented a very serious challenge to this idea. He suggested that in late capitalism, the working class had become so integrated into capitalist society that it had lost its potential to 'see outside the box' and thus *challenge* it. The system had, in effect, successfully colonised the working-class lifeworld (to use Habermas's term) – hegemony and commodification rolled up into one. Marcuse put his faith in those *other* exploited groups who remained outside the system, whose exploitation was not necessarily *material* (based on the distribution of wealth) but *cultural* (based on their rejection of the dominant ideology or belief system). He turned to hippies and environmentalists, women and ethnic minorities, intellectuals and, above all, students, to participate in the new 'great refusal', the refusal to participate in the dominant capitalist game. Perhaps, if he were writing now, he would have much the same to say about students as he did about the working class back in the 1960s – that they have themselves been subjected to the kind of commodification we discussed above. But that other great Marxist theorist of an altogether different ilk, Althusser, would have something quite different to say: no such 'agent of change' is possible because none can exist outside the 'text' of society itself, all are necessarily constructed by it, and thus ultimately bound within it. But that is Althusser the *structuralist* speaking, and I will return to him in Chapter 9.

## Summary and final thoughts

In this chapter I have only touched the surface of the rich body of knowledge that is Marxism, but I have tried to select those aspects of it which best help you understand the contributions Marxism makes as a sociological theory. I have suggested that from Marx's own writings, a tradition of 'classical' or 'orthodox' Marxism emerged which was heavily reliant on three core propositions: historical materialism, economic determinism and class analysis. The first provides us with a distinctive account of social change, in contrast to those we have already covered in previous chapters. The second provides us with a description of how society works, so that if we use the analogy of a car, the economy serves as the engine which makes the whole thing work, the rest plays its collective part but is still dependent on the engine. The third provides us with an account of the dynamics of capitalist society – that it is inherently divided into two opposing forces, the owners who cream off the profits and the workers who do the work but receive no immediate benefit from it. However, these three propositions have been challenged by those writing within the Marxist framework, so as to rescue the broader Marxist perspective from the perceived problems and contradictions that arise from them.

Orthodox Marxism is fraught with such problems, as its own disciples have pointed out. Its economism – its belief that all historical and social relations are reducible to economic factors, with cultural and political forces rendered dependent on the economy – is hardly attractive. Ditto its historicism, which presents an overly teleological and perhaps naive view of society, never mind its humanism – the faith it puts in the achievement of true class consciousness and thus the possibility of revolution.

Perhaps, as some would suggest, Marxism was just a creature of its times. When Marx himself was writing, capitalism was a relatively new thing, and a pretty unsophisticated one at that. It may have made perfect sense to think about the new society in terms of the simplistic division between owner and worker. But the world has moved on since then! We have a far more complex class system, if we even have a class system at all (according to some). Capitalism has provided opportunities for all (well, all who live within its central radius, maybe) and the subsequent consumer society we take advantage of and the freedoms we enjoy are a direct result of that. I don't doubt that is what many of you think. And I don't doubt also that it is very, very hard for you to imagine *not* living in a capitalist society. But for a second, be a good sociological theorist about this. Do you *really* think that the *sociological* point Marx was trying to make about society in his lifetime is any less relevant today? Not only have we all experienced the knock-on effects of the recent economic collapse, but our lifestyles remain contingent upon our economic position, even if in a way different from how Marx described.

There are those who speak of the contemporary world as being so wildly different from the one Marx lived in that it seems acceptable to call it not 'modern' but '*post*-modern'. In such a world, we are no longer bound by the old hierarchies, and the old rules, of which people like Marx spoke. But there are also those who look at this rather anarchic new world and suggest that it is nothing more than the manifestation of a *new* form of capitalism, a 'late' capitalism, which operates quite differently from the old form – it is no longer bound up in nation states and is rather spread out across the world in a transnational way (Sklair, 2002), it is disorganised and unstructured and requires new unstructured forms of culture to sustain it (Harvey, 1989), or it is subject to periodic crises of legitimacy and thus requires adaptation (Habermas, 1976). But it is still capitalism. And as long as it is still capitalism, it is still exploitative. And as long as it is still exploitative, it can still be subjected to Marxist critique.

## Key terms

*Definitions for the key terms listed below can be found in the Glossary on page 227.*

- Alienation
- Base and superstructure
- Capitalism
- Commodification
- Economic determinism
- Globalisation
- Historical materialism
- Ideology
- Post-modernity
- Social class

## Biographies

*Short biographical descriptions for the names listed below can be found on page 240.*

- Theodor Adorno
- Louis Althusser
- Jürgen Habermas
- Herbert Marcuse
- Karl Marx
- Immanuel Wallerstein

# 5 | Feminism

In this chapter we will be:

- introducing the key ideas underpinning feminist sociological theory, i.e. a sociological theory that highlights inequalities, and power relations, between men and power;
- comparing different types of feminist theory;
- distinguishing between 'sex' and 'gender';
- discussing the core term in feminist sociology, which is patriarchy, and looking at how the perceived dominance of men over women is reproduced through social institutions such as the family, education and religion;
- looking at how some feminists have drawn attention to women's experiences and values which have been ignored by male-dominated disciplines such as sociology.

## Types of feminist theory

Feminism is one of those perspectives in social theory that is broadly generic across a range of disciplines – feminist contributions to international relations, criminology, political science, socio-legal studies, development studies, social anthropology, social policy, social psychology as well as sociology, have made similar criticisms of their own disciplines as well as of society itself. Across the fields and disciplines, feminists draw attention to the exclusion of women – women's voices, women's experiences – from the academic and political debates. They seek to show that, in so far as these debates are dominated by male voices, they necessarily promote male interests and marginalise or subordinate the interests of women.

However, while this provides a shared platform for feminist theory, feminists are often divided on the necessary direction that theory should take to overcome these problems. As we shall see, feminism, like Marxism in the previous chapter, is an incredibly diverse collection of approaches united under a loose umbrella, a general condemnation of the gender imbalance in society. To understand feminism as a theory in sociology, we first have to appreciate that it is indeed an umbrella, covering a diversity of ideas and a fair amount of internal disagreement. The various 'types' of feminism are well covered in text books, and while their respective approaches to the concept of male power are also well documented, perhaps what isn't clear is precisely how these different variants are distinct from one another. A straightforward way of approaching this problem is to compare how the different versions of feminist theory view the relationship *between* men and women.

Early feminism in the late nineteenth and early twentieth centuries was concerned with the extent to which women were excluded from the otherwise progressive politics of modern society. Basic equalities and freedoms in society, including political rights such as the right to vote, were being extended to men, but not to women. Feminists from early pioneers such as Mary Wollstonecraft and Harriet Taylor Mill through to more recent contributors such as **Betty Friedan** and **Jessie Bernard** have thus demanded equal treatment. This form of feminism is called *liberal feminism*, because it effectively accepts the premises and promises of modern, liberal society – the contract between citizens and state in which the citizens are allocated certain rights – but highlights the exclusion of women from it. In other words, the problem of women's ostensibly inferior position in society is due to the fact that the liberal ideal has not been fully realised so as to incorporate women, rather than to any problem inherent in the system itself. Some liberal feminists have extended this concern with inequality into the private sphere of the family, pointing out that marriage is often an unequal contract which empowers men but disempowers women (Bernard, 1976).

For subsequent feminists, the idea of simply incorporating women into the existing system was not enough. The unequal position of women in the system was seen as a result of a problem in the system itself. So, for example, a tradition of *socialist or Marxist feminism* emerged, in which the subordination of women was blamed on the class system in

Source: Corbis/Bettman Archive

Suffragettes lobbying for votes for women

capitalist societies. We have already discussed Marxism in Chapter 4, so readers will already be familiar with its accusations that capitalism is inevitably divisible into two distinct groups, those who own the means of production and benefit from exploiting the labour of others, and those whose labour is exploited. In capitalist societies, women form a reserve labour force that is cheap and easily exploitable. They are also often restricted to specific areas of what is deemed to be 'women's work' (such as unpaid household labour, or low-paid jobs in the caring sector) and thus become financially dependent upon men. Thus women, because of this basic lack of recognition and reward for their efforts, are part of the exploited proletariat. Accordingly, overcoming capitalism will inevitably result in a restructuring of the gender imbalance. A major influence on this strand of feminist theory is Marx's collaborator, Friedrich Engels, who identified how capitalism, which emphasises ownership and *private* property, is quietly dependent on maintaining this family structure. Subsequent writers have been concerned with the material conditions of women's existences, extending in many cases beyond simplistic Marxian economism, and with what **Dorothy E. Smith** has called the **relations of ruling** (not just the *fact* of it but the *way* power operates between men and women). Juliet Mitchell and Jacqueline Rose, Michèle Barrett and **Ann Oakley** are among those who have made significant contributions to the development of socialist and Marxist feminism.

However, the relationship between feminism and Marxism or socialism has for many feminists been an uneasy one. In orthodox Marxism, all other forms of social stratification are subordinate to class inequalities. Thus, even Simone de Beauvoir, whose work *The Second Sex* is hailed as one of the greatest contributions to feminist theory in the twentieth century and who, together with her equally famous partner Jean-Paul Sartre, was otherwise quite sympathetic to the Marxian project, largely rejected Engels's analysis of gender inequalities. Some Marxist feminists – notably Mitchell and Rose – sought to overcome this problem by turning to Althusserian structural Marxism (again, see Chapter 4, and how Louis Althusser redefined capitalism as a total 'social formation' and not just an economic system), and through that lens viewing **patriarchy** (the name given to a social system that privileges men at the expense of women) and capitalism as separate but mutually interdependent 'dual systems' operating within the broader social formation. Barrett (1980) undertook a similar project, while Eisenstein (1979) coined the term 'capitalist patriarchy' to look at the specific role played by the private sphere in reproducing structural inequalities. Christine Delphy (1984) went further in seeing capitalism and patriarchy as distinct modes of production operating respectively in the public (industrial) and private (family) spheres.

But even if the subordination of women is not solely reducible to the dynamics of capitalism, must it be nonetheless allied to it in such a dual systemic form? Many feminists were understandably uncomfortable with the idea that such a distinct and fundamentally important issue could be reduced to factors unrelated to gender itself, such as class. Such commentators wanted to shift the emphasis on how women are structurally oppressed away from capitalism and firmly towards patriarchy and how it impacts on **gender identity**. One such project involved incorporating elements of psychoanalysis into feminist thinking. Such a *psychoanalytical feminism*, associated with Nancy Chodorow, Laura

Mulvey and others, views the oppression of women as the result of patterns of socialisation and the construction of patriarchal personalities. However, from a sociological point of view, a more significant attempt to understand the dynamics of patriarchy is that undertaken by proponents of an alternative tradition, *radical feminism*, which has made a number of significant and distinctive contributions to feminist sociology, as well as being instrumental in the further development of the political 'women's movement' during the 1970s. Like Marxist feminists, radical feminists – whose number includes such well-known scholars as Andrea Dworkin, Catherine MacKinnon, **Shulamith Firestone** and Adrienne Rich – have argued against the perceived naivety of liberal feminists in believing that the position of women could be improved simply by extending existing measures to incorporate women. They wanted to show how the subordination of women is directly related to the very structure of such a society, and that the only way to promote the interests of women is to radically overhaul that society. But the structural problem at fault is not capitalism, in which women are reduced merely to invisible members of the working class, but patriarchy, which is not only wholly independent of capitalism but pre-dates it significantly. After all, capitalism represents a relatively recent phase in world history, yet the subordination of women can be traced back to the earliest records of history, so how can this particular form of oppression be accurately viewed as a consequence of capitalism? Radical feminists thus make a significant sociological point, that the original and dominant inequality in society is between men and women, and that women are effectively assigned inferior status because men are enjoying positions of power. Furthermore, social institutions exist to reproduce that power imbalance, such that religion, the family, the media and so on serve the interests of patriarchy in much the same way as Marxists believe they serve the interest of capitalism. Put simply, radical feminists want to locate the origin of women's subordination in the social relations of gender itself, and thus in doing so present a kind of 'pure' feminism that is not dependent for its ideological ammunition upon some other form of social theory, such as liberalism, Marxism or psychoanalysis. As Terry Lovell usefully points out, radical feminism is unique because it 'does not point to some other area of theory or politics but, rather, enhances solitary pride in independence' (Lovell, 2000: 305).

A related branch of feminism that actually predates the radical feminist movement is *cultural feminism*. Like radical feminists, cultural feminists, from **Charlotte Perkins-Gilman** and Jane Addams through Virginia Woolf to Dorothy E. Smith and Carol Gilligan, are concerned with the distinctiveness of women, rather than with efforts to stress the potential sameness of all people, but they celebrate this distinctiveness by concentrating more on the lived experiences of women, and on highlighting the distinctive contributions women might make to the public realm, simply because they are women and have outlooks, practices, virtues and ethics different from men (for example, Gilligan speaks of an 'ethics of care' which is distinctive to women). Cultural feminists thus bridge the divide between liberal and radical feminists – like radical feminists, they focus on difference, but they then seek to utilise this difference to strengthen the liberal feminist concern with ensuring equality in the public sphere. Also, cultural feminists are more inclined than other variants to make use of philosophical approaches, such as existentialism and phenomenology, which tend to inform micro-sociological analysis (which we discuss in more depth in Chapter 8) in order to understand women's experiences.

The most recent broad school of feminist theory is *post-modern feminism*. Here, the emphasis is more on gender identity, 'difference' and forms of knowledge. In general, post-modernist theory (which we discuss in greater detail in the concluding chapter to the book) challenges traditional forms of knowledge, which, it claims, are bound up in binary opposites – such as 'man' and 'woman' – that ignore differences at a very local level. Post-modern feminists have criticised earlier feminist scholars for focusing largely on white, middle-class, Western women, as if such experiences are applicable to women in general (hooks, 1984). Post-modernism is thus a celebration of difference and an ostensibly radical critique of the constraints imposed upon us by dominant 'discourses'. Post-modern feminists are, therefore, necessarily concerned not only with how appeals to such 'grand narratives' – attempts to 'explain' the world in monolithic terms – such as liberalism and Marxism are politically problematic, but also how cultural and radical feminists overemphasise the uniformity of women at the expense of differences *between* women. Post-modern thinking has appealed to scholars – one of the most celebrated being Patricia Hill Collins – wanting to 'tell the story' not of women as a universal category, but of black women (Collins, 1990), lesbian women, women in the developing world (Afshar, 1985; Mohanty, 1988; Momsen, 1991), and so on, and how these different forms of oppression – oppression based on gender, 'race', sexuality, economic position, and so on – comprise a complex 'matrix of domination' (Collins, 1990).

Let us compare and contrast these positions. Liberal feminists are ultimately concerned with the inherent sameness between men and women. We are all humans, they argue, and so we deserve to be treated with the same respect, and allocated the same rights, as each other. That modern society has yet to extend its commitment to equality in this vein to women is reason enough for feminism to maintain a strong political voice in its opposition. Marxist feminists are also concerned with sameness, but not between women and men as a whole, rather between women and their fellow members of the working class, and stress the differences between women as members of the working class and the bourgeoisie. Radical and cultural feminists shift the argument entirely, to a focus on the differences between men and women. We should, they argue, concentrate on, and duly celebrate, the distinctiveness of women from men. Radical feminists thus call for 'sisterhood' in opposition to male power (see Morgan, 1970), while cultural feminists make more modest demands for women's contributions, skills and values to be recognised. Post-modern feminists take an even more radical view of difference, by focusing on the differences between women, and thus call to mind the distinctiveness of the experiences of different lifestyles, ages, ethnicities, sexual orientations and so on. If we begin, with the liberal feminists, with a view of society as a block in which all parts are potentially equal and the same, and then see that splintered by the cultural and radical feminists, we finish up, thanks to post-modern feminism, with the idea that society is indeed a block but each component part is so distinct that sameness is a myth and an impossible pursuit, in a way that transcends simple gender (or class) distinctions.

To further summarise, we can locate these traditions in tabular form (Table 5.1).

In the sections that follow, these distinct traditions within the broader feminist perspective will re-emerge, but the intention of this chapter is not to focus narrowly on such distinct contributions, but rather to

**Table 5.1** Types of feminist theory

| Type of feminist theory | Nature of women's subordination | Proposed solution | Key names |
|---|---|---|---|
| *Liberal feminism* | Absence of basic rights and freedoms | Extension of liberal project to accommodate women | Mary Wollstonecraft<br>Harriet Taylor Mill<br>Bettie Friedan<br>Jessie Bernard |
| *Socialist feminism* | Exploitation of women's labour | Economic reform to recognise women's contributions | Ann Oakley<br>Heidi Hartmann |
| *Marxist feminism* | Exploitation of women's labour | Overthrow of capitalist system | Juliet Mitchell<br>Michèle Barrett |
| *Psychoanalytical feminism* | Distorted socialisation | In the last instance, radical reform of the institutions of socialisation | Nancy Chodorow<br>Laura Mulvey |
| *Cultural feminism* | Contributions and virtues of women left out of public realm | Reform of system to blend male with female virtues | Charlotte Perkins-Gilman<br>Jane Addams<br>Virginia Woolf<br>Dorothy E. Smith<br>Carol Gilligan |
| *Radical feminism* | Patriarchy as a system of oppression | Sisterhood as a rejection of patriarchal system | Andrea Dworkin<br>Catherine MacKinnon<br>Shulamith Firestone<br>Kate Millett<br>Adrienne Rich |
| *Post-modern feminism* | Matrix of domination subordinating local identities | No single 'solution', but recognition of complex interplay of factors and 'small acts' of resistance | Patricia Hill Collins<br>Judith Butler<br>bell hooks |

introduce you to the core themes which unite them under the banner of feminism, and which serve as the key feminist contributions to sociological theory, and then to highlight some of the different interpretations of these themes between feminist scholars. Three such key contributions will be discussed: first, the distinction between sex and gender; second, and easily the largest of the three themes, the analysis of the various institutions and practices which serve to reproduce the patriarchal system; and third, the attempt to bring to the fore the contributions, experiences, forms of knowledge and virtues of women hitherto neglected by both sociology and society itself. However, you should bear in mind throughout that this is a chapter about changes and debates in feminist *theory*, and not about actual changes in society itself. As with all theories, feminism offers an *interpretation* of the world.

---

### EXERCISE 5.1 Women at the top?

This exercise involves a little research on your part. Try to get a feel for how many women are in senior positions in industry or politics compared with men. Select an established list of high-ranking companies and find out how many of them have women in executive positions. If you prefer you can focus on one type of industry, for example the media. Why do you think the ratio of men to women is as it is?

---

## Sex and gender

Early sociological perspectives – including early functionalist approaches, which we have already covered in Chapter 2 – concentrated largely on the extent to which sex is a fixed category. Because of this, the **sexual division of labour** was seen as legitimate because of its universality. Some commentators looked for the basis of this universality in biology. Coming at it from a slightly different angle, some functionalists such as George Peter Murdock viewed it as the outcome of basic processes of social evolution, that have apparently resulted in the most 'efficient' methods of organising society. In either case, whether it is biologically or culturally prescribed, the sexual division of labour was treated as natural.

This claim has been criticised for conflating sex with gender. Most feminist theory begins with the assumption that there is a fundamental difference between sex, which is a biological classification, and gender, which is a social construct. Feminists, especially cultural and radical feminists, are largely concerned with the social construction of femininity. Simone de Beauvoir made this claim in her definitive feminist text, *The Second Sex* (1973) – that one has to *become* a woman, to 'learn the roles' that wider society expects of a woman. This is echoed in the works of subsequent feminists, such as Judith Butler, who treats gender as a performance, which we are engaged in 'doing'. Similarly, Dorothy E. Smith has argued that feminists need to see femininity as a matrix of different accounts and perceptions, defined by participants, rather than just as some objectively defined 'category' which is reproduced through socialisation (1990a).

More recent feminists have, in fact, sought to take the argument for social construction even further, by showing how sex as well as gender is a negotiated social construct. The body itself is not, they claim, as fixed and rigid as some previous theorists may have presumed – rather, it is very much a contested thing, as fluid as is identity, subject to change. For example, drawing on post-structuralist thought (see Chapter 9), Judith Butler has challenged the assumption that the sex–gender distinction is equivalent and reducible to that of nature–culture, arguing instead that sex is itself a product of discourse that creates and regulates bodies, while gender is the cultural process through which the category of sex is validated as 'natural' and pre-social (Butler, 1993). However, for much of the history of feminist thought, the focus has very much been on the way in which social institutions have served to reinforce the reduction of gender to sex, by shaping women's cultures and identities, and thus uphold a male-dominated social system.

## The dynamics of patriarchy

The name given to a social system in which the position of women is inherently subordinate to that of men is patriarchy. Patriarchy is to most feminist sociologists equivalent to what capitalism is to Marxists – the very definition of existing social structure, the dominant ideology that is the cause of inequality and oppression and thus has to be opposed. For most feminists, patriarchy is not reducible to other such forms of oppression, such as capitalism or colonialism and racial oppression; rather, it is the foremost and the original such system which pre-dates all others. It is through patriarchy that men learn to dehumanise and oppress women as 'the Other', and indeed men have a vested interest in reproducing patriarchy and keeping women in subordinate positions, as it satisfies their sexual desires and provides them with a domestic slave labour force. Most feminists would not be so crude as to suggest that this is an active, conscious position taken by men. Rather, it is a subconscious desire to sustain the unequal power dialectic. Rather like Marx's bourgeoisie, the role of men in this dialectic is not at all dependent upon how they feel or what they believe, as the inequality between men and women is the product of a system of social relations rather than individual motivations. Patriarchy is reproduced through all social institutions and practices, whether in the direct form of physical violence – think of such historical and contemporary practices as rape, sexual abuse, forced surgery, female genital mutilation, *sati*, honour killings, the burning of witches, domestic violence, forced prostitution and female infanticide, and how each of them serves to reproduce and in some cases legitimise male dominance over women – or in the more covert form of symbolic violence, examples of which might include media representations of women, pornography, unpaid household work, religion, expectations associated with fashion and beauty, or male-dominated medical practices and professions.

---

### EXERCISE 5.2  Patriarchy in practice

Find one or two examples of how the following social institutions might serve to discriminate against women, or present them in a subordinate position to men:

1  The family
2  Education
3  Religion
4  The media

---

Now that you have tried this exercise, let us see how experienced feminist academics have answered the same question. **Kate Millett**, in her important book *Sexual Politics* (1970), provides a list of the different ways in which – and the different means through which – patriarchy is successfully reproduced. The first is *ideological* – women are usually assigned an inferior status to men through socialisation. Some feminists, such as Nancy Chodorow and Juliet Mitchell, have drawn on Freudian psychoanalysis to show, for example, how a distinctive, subordinate, personality type is imposed upon girls in the early phases of socialisation.

The second is *biological* – the female body itself is an agent of patriarchy (a point taken much further by Shulamith Firestone whose work we will discuss below), and the myth is commonly promoted that gender is dependent upon the biological category of sex. The third is *sociological* – male dominance originates in the family structure. Indeed, according to one of the great pioneering feminist sociologists, Charlotte Perkins-Gilman, ever since the dawn of society, men have used force to relegate women into domestic roles in the family structure, perpetuating the myth that women's roles as mothers and carers means they are unsuitable for paid employment. Jessie Bernard's classic text *The Future of Marriage* (1976) similarly suggested that the origins of male dominance lie in inequalities in the family structure. This is further reproduced in the *educational* sphere, where women are often encouraged to specialise in particular areas, the result of which is that women are prevented from gaining entry into traditionally 'male' preserves where political power is exercised. *Religious* practices and institutions are also active in sustaining the subordinate position of women. Many religions present negative images of women, as seductresses or 'whores', in some cases directly

*Source*: Topfoto/The Granger Collection, New York

Charlotte Perkins-Gilman

responsible for the 'fall of man' (think of Adam and Eve in the Bible), and most religious institutions are very open in how their hierarchies prevent women from having too much influence. This point was also made by Perkins-Gilman (1923).

Millett suggests that social *class* also serves to reproduce patriarchy, because it divides women from each other, thus preventing what we might call a 'true gender consciousness'. Women are similarly oppressed in the *economic* sphere, an example of which is how the domestic work often carried out by women is unpaid and unrecognised. This is a key argument made by socialist or Marxist feminists, that the capitalist system itself is quietly dependent upon the exploitation of women in the domestic sphere. The feminist sociologist Ann Oakley famously listed the various jobs expected to be carried out by the housewife, from childminder and carer to cleaner and cook, and suggested that, if women were actually paid for such work at its market value, the effects would be disastrous for the economy. Similar claims have been made by feminist contributors to the study of social policy. Patriarchy positions women in the role of carers, as if this position is 'natural', and in doing so allows welfare providers to ignore the importance of the informal caring sector, including the family, in which much welfare work is done. Recognising the crucial role played by the economy in suppressing women, Perkins-Gilman had famously argued for the professionalisation of domestic and care services.

*Force* is also a key factor in women's subordination, whether it is legal force or unofficial sanctions, such as rape and domestic violence. Feminist studies have shown how violence against women in the family is still often treated as if it is different from any other form of violence, perpetuating the myth that the contract of marriage implies the 'ownership' of the wife by the husband, and thus implying the 'right' of the husband to treat his 'property' in a violent way. Susan Brownmiller (1975) has suggested that the practice of rape, for example, has been historically and anthropologically defined and reproduced. Men are, for the most part, structurally and physiologically capable of inflicting violence against women, so while the 'first' rape (she is referring here not to an actual historical instance but to a convenient fiction) may have been accidental, once men realised they could do it, they proceeded to do so purposefully, transforming the practice from one designed solely for the benefit of sexual desire to one used to sustain male dominance over women. Catherine MacKinnon (1993) has also shown how agents of the state often engage in systematic and purposeful violence against women, including rape, as strategies during war – such as for the purpose of torture or even genocide – and that such atrocities have been conveniently overlooked throughout history.

With all this working against them, Millett suggests, it is hardly surprising that the last process through which patriarchy is reproduced is *psychological* – in order to survive in a male-dominated world, women might feel the need to buy into these stereotypes, to humiliate themselves, to accept their 'inferior' status. This aspect of patriarchy was the subject of Betty Friedan's earlier text, *The Feminine Mystique* (Friedan, 1963). Women's acceptance of a subordinate position is the product of an on-going socialisation process – they are 'taught' from an early age that women *should* look and act feminine, carry out 'women's jobs', and accept the dominance of men. Technology and social progress may have liberated women from overt drudgery, but only so that they could dedicate themselves to perfecting their roles as wife and mother. The greatest goal for women to achieve, accordingly, is the perfection of their femininity. While the ideology of progress appears superficially to support women, in so far as it seems to value this femininity, in reality it undermines women by locating them firmly in subordinate positions.

To Millett's list, we can add various other spheres through which women's subordination is sustained. The first is in the sphere of media culture, through the process of representation. Many feminists, including Friedan herself, have focused on the portrayal of women in the media, in advertising and in women's magazines. As Gaye Tuchman (1981) has pointed out, the representation of women in the media often amounts to a process of 'symbolic annihilation'. Media images often portray women in stereotypical positions – if they bother to portray them at all. They are in trivial roles, supplementary to men, submissive to male power, either as housewives or as little more than objects of male sexual desire or conquest, or they are manipulative, devious and treacherous, the 'Lady Macbeth' model. While some liberal feminists suggest that this situation can be overcome through media reform and the extension of basic principles of social justice, others claim that such representations reflect a patriarchal system which is intrinsically embedded in the very language of the media and popular culture (Modleski, 1986), and in the sexual dynamics of the male gaze and the objectification of the woman (Mulvey, 1975). From a radical feminist perspective, Andrea Dworkin has looked in particular at the role of pornography in reproducing patriarchy. Dworkin (1979) reminds us that the term pornography actually means 'writing about whores', and so is inherently oppressive. She suggests that it is not enough to say that pornography provides the foundations for violence against women – rather, it actually *is* a form of violence against women. However, the demand made by radical feminists such as Dworkin and MacKinnon, that pornography be banned, is not universally accepted by feminists. Opponents have claimed that such censorship would go against the interests of women, because the feminist movement itself was born out of a fight against censorship, and that its struggle lies in allowing women's voices to be heard and women to be in control of their own bodies.

## EXERCISE 5.3 Media representations of women

Select one day to undertake a thorough trawl through the media. Look at a few newspapers and magazines, and watch as much television as you can, including news programmes, popular entertainment, films and so on. In each case, how are women represented? What stereotypes are being presented? What language is being used to describe women? Keep a scrapbook of your findings and then ask, what common themes might exist across the different media which might serve to 'place' women in society?

A second addition to the list of patriarchal institutions is the political sphere. Catherine MacKinnon (1989) has referred to the realm of formal politics as the 'masculine state'. Patriarchy reduces women to the private or domestic realm, identified with roles such as mothers and carers. This private realm is outside the domain of the state, which is the public realm of formal politics. Thus, the state, as the site of formal politics in which political decision-making occurs, is necessarily masculine, driven by masculine practices and values, and protecting masculine interests. The practices of the state, such as war and security, are on the one hand gender-driven, and on the other serve to reinforce gender divisions (Tickner, 1992).

For most feminists, patriarchy as a 'reality' is socially constructed and reproduced through these various social institutions and practices. It is not a 'natural' state at all, and therefore strategies can be found to overcome it. Thus, many cultural and radical feminists have argued for women's solidarity, sisterhood, as expressed through the Women's Movement (Morgan, 1970), and for some degree of separation from and less reliance upon men. Feminists – Brownmiller's observations on male physiology notwithstanding – have rarely accepted material or biological explanations for patriarchy, because such essentialist views can easily be inverted to give legitimacy to the unequal and oppressive system. Two important contributions that trace the sources of patriarchy in part to the female body, and thus engage more with biological arguments, have come from Ernestine Friedl and Sherry B. Ortner. As an anthropologist, Friedl (1975) studied hunter-gatherer societies, and concluded that patriarchy emerges from the suitability of the male body towards hunting, which has culturally been constructed as a primary source of power within the social group. Note that Friedl's argument on how patriarchy is still effectively a sociocultural one – there is no natural reason why the role of hunter should carry with it greater power. Ortner (1974) takes this argument a step further by suggesting that patriarchy is largely sustained not by the biological body itself but by sociocultural perceptions of women's biology and psychology, which surface in well-trodden claims that women, because they are after all biologically capable of giving birth, are 'closer to nature', and this is reflected in women's behaviour, attitudes, virtues and so on. Ortner suggests that as most societies tend to value culture – which gives us knowledge, the arts, religion, progress – above nature, such false presumptions about female biology and psychology have contributed towards the continued subordination of women.

Both Friedl and Ortner acknowledge the role of the female body in sustaining patriarchy, but for both of them, its contribution is distorted through a cultural lens. The body itself is not the actual problem, but the sociocultural prejudices that emerge as a result of it. A very different account of the role of the body is found in the work of the radical feminist, Shulamith Firestone, in her book *The Dialectic of Sex* (1972). Firestone suggests that one of the fundamental agents of patriarchy is the female body itself, and in particular its capacity for biological reproduction. Because of this capacity, women do not have the same control over their bodies as men have, and this reproduces the dialectic of power between men and women. Firestone's solution to this involves a transformation in the social relations of production, the utilisation of new technologies to create artificial wombs so that women were no longer required to act as birth-givers, these wombs to be controlled by the community as a whole and not by men or the male-dominated medical profession.

Other feminists have provided additional media through which patriarchy is reproduced, including the way language is constructed, the act of sexual intercourse itself, and the promotion of a heterosexual sexual identity as 'normal'. For example, Monique Wittig (1982) has claimed that in linguistic terms, the concept of 'woman' is itself dependent upon that of 'man'. Because the concept of 'woman' is socially constructed in terms of its femininity, it is defined by its relationship to that of 'man', and the institution of heterosexuality is thus promoted as 'normal' – a situation referred to as 'compulsory heterosexuality' (Rich, 1980). This is an artificial power relation, claim writers such as Anna Koedt (see Koedt, Levine and Rappone, 1973), because female sexual pleasure is not at all necessarily reliant upon the penis. Similarly, Wittig posits the view that, just as 'woman' is an identity dependent upon that of 'man', lesbian identity is free of this, and thus empowers women. Adrienne Rich (1976, 1980) has made a similar argument using Freudian psychoanalytical theories. Freud famously claimed that the sexual desire of men for women is wholly natural because it originates in the act of birth itself, in the bond formed between the boy-child and the mother, the maternal desire or 'Oedipus complex'. If this is true for the boy-child, Rich asks quite reasonably, is it not also the case that it is true for the girl-child? Rich suggests that, if we follow Freud's line of thinking, female heterosexuality is actually unnatural, and is, in fact, socially constructed and reproduced through social institutions and through the various sanctions that are in place to actively promote it. Rich's account is, of course, problematic, because it renders male homosexuality as 'unnatural' as female heterosexuality, and acceptance of it is entirely dependent upon one's acceptance of its Freudian premise, but it is an interesting observation nonetheless.

The concept of patriarchy is central to radical and much psycho-analytical feminism, but has been subjected to criticism by some contemporary, post-modern feminists, who view it as too rigid a description of the structure within which gender identities are shaped and controlled. Sylvia Walby (1990) has responded to these criticisms in a useful defence of patriarchy as an analytical tool, with a theorisation of patriarchy that is more sensitive to historical change and sociocultural differences than previous versions. According to Walby, patriarchy is not a single system of oppression but a mesh of six independent but interrelated structures. While these do for the most part echo concerns already raised by Millett, Oakley, MacKinnon and others, Walby repackages them in a useful way:

1 the exploitation of women in the household;
2 the exploitation of women in the labour market;
3 the state as a masculine institution;
4 male violence against women;
5 the sanctions that are imposed upon sexuality, including the presumed normality of heterosexuality as well as the double standards that exist in respect of male and female sexual behaviour;
6 the patriarchal gaze of major social institutions, including religion and the media.

Walby suggests that over the last hundred years or so in the West, we have seen a shift from a 'private' patriarchy, occurring largely in the domestic sphere as the purposeful action of individual men, to a 'public' patriarchy, in which the patriarchal processes are embedded in the structures and institutions of society itself. It is worth bringing some of the contributions of Walby, Millett and others together in tabular form, to more clearly understand the arguments presented about how patriarchy is reproduced (see Table 5.2).

Walby insists that an analysis of patriarchy must appreciate the complex way in which it is intertwined with other systems of oppression. Juliet Mitchell and others had already usefully developed a 'dual systems' approach to understand better the relationship between patriarchy and capitalism, but as we have seen, many feminists have insisted nonetheless on the prioritisation of patriarchy as the original system of oppression. An important further development within feminist theory

**Table 5.2** The sources of patriarchy

| Patriarchal institution | Method of reproducing patriarchy | Key sources |
|---|---|---|
| *The body* | Capacity for childbearing constrains women, and renders them seen as closer to nature | Shulamith Firestone<br>Sherry B. Ortner<br>Ernestine Friedl |
| *Class* | Women are divided against themselves | Kate Millett |
| *Economy* | Women's labour is exploited, and housework is unrecognised | Charlotte Perkins-Gilman<br>Christine Delphy<br>Kate Millett<br>Ann Oakley<br>Sylvia Walby |
| *Education* | Women are streamed into particular disciplines | Kate Millett |
| *The family* | Marriage contract amounts to ownership; domestic violence becomes normalised | Charlotte Perkins-Gilman<br>Kate Millett<br>Jessie Bernard<br>Sylvia Walby |
| *The media* | Representations of women portray them in subordinate roles, either sexual or inferior | Betty Friedan<br>Andrea Dworkin<br>Gaye Tuchman<br>Angela McRobbie<br>Sylvia Walby |
| *Psychology* | Women are forced to accept and internalise the roles assigned to them to succeed | Betty Friedan<br>Kate Millett |
| *Religion* | Women are presented in a negative way, and denied access to influential positions | Charlotte Perkins-Gilman<br>Kate Millett<br>Sylvia Walby |
| *Sexuality* | Heterosexuality is treated as the norm, such that women's identity becomes reliant upon sex with men; double standards exist between how men and women behave sexually | Adrienne Rich<br>Monique Wittig<br>Anna Koedt<br>Sylvia Walby |
| *Socialisation* | Socialisation produces distinct and subordinate female personality | Nancy Chodorow<br>Juliet Mitchell<br>Kate Millett |
| *The state* | The state, and indeed the public sphere as a whole, is driven by, and in the interests of, masculine values | Catherine MacKinnon<br>Sylvia Walby |
| *Violence* | Men routinely exploit their physical capacity to inflict violence against women | Susan Brownmiller<br>Sylvia Walby |

has sought once again to understand multiple forms of subordination within the context of a sociology of knowledge, in which 'formal' and 'official' systems of knowledge are counterposed with the everyday experiences and voices of women and other marginalised groups. It is to this development that we now turn.

## The experiences and contributions of women

Across the humanities and social sciences, feminists have launched powerful internal critiques of their own disciplines, which are charged with historically ignoring or downplaying the contributions of women, and seeing their subject matter from an exclusively male gaze. For example, in the study of culture, media and the arts, feminist theory has, since Virginia Woolf (1929), been concerned with the exclusion of women from the cultural realm, and the material constraints imposed upon women's participation in literature and the arts, closing down the possibility of a distinctive 'female tradition'. Woolf posed the question of women's literary contributions by introducing the fictional character of 'Shakespeare's sister' and asking whether she might have received the same degree of success as her brother, had she written his plays.

Similarly, sociological studies of crime, deviance and law have been subjected to feminist interrogation (Smart, 1976, 1989). Traditionally, the sociology of crime and deviance had focused on men (such as the classic delinquency studies which were almost exclusively concerned with working-class boys) and had very little to say about women. The law, it is claimed, is largely written by men and thus reflects male values and interests, and upholds male dominance. As an approach which locates gender at the centre of its analysis, feminism effectively extends the definition of crime, and in particular draws attention to crimes such as rape, sexual abuse and domestic violence, which are often committed by men against women – sometimes in the private sphere, which, we have already seen, is considered to be marginal to the 'male' public sphere – and serve to reinforce a violent patriarchal system. Clearly, such crimes cannot be understood without first recognising the gender politics underpinning them. Feminists have also sought to expose discrimination and gender insensitivity within the criminal justice system.

Feminist analyses of social policy and formal institutions of justice and politics have also made the claim that the dominant knowledge within the sector is masculine – as we have seen from MacKinnon's concept of the 'masculine state'. Against this, Carol Gilligan (1982) has stressed the distinctive contribution that women can make to the development of 'ethical society', which she suggests would be a blend of the male 'ethic of justice', which focuses on the achievement of equality for all, with the female 'ethic of care', which is better able to respond to individual needs.

The core problem, then, is not so much that women have been excluded from involvement in the development of these disciplines and professions (although they have), but that the knowledge upon which each of these disciplines and professions is based is itself gendered. Subsequently, theoretical contributors – even those coming from more critical perspectives – have uncritically presumed the gender blindness of the knowledge systems of which they are a part (Fraser, 1989). To counteract these distorted perceptions, feminist scholars have sought to draw attention within their disciplines to both the experiences of women in general, and to the particular forms of knowledge contributed by women to those disciplines. In respect of the former, no feminist theorist has done as much to highlight the lived experience of patriarchy as Dorothy E. Smith. Smith points out that the struggle faced by women is that they exist in a world so dominated by male assumptions, emotions and definitions, that they have effectively been denied a language within which to articulate their criticisms of that world (Smith, 1990a). As an example of how in the public realm there is an underlying 'taken-for-granted' assumption that women's knowledge is inferior to men's, she famously describes how during a medical inquiry members of the court treated (male) doctors with reverence equivalent even to their own respective stations, but in their treatment of the (female) nurses, they were dismissive and rude. Now, one might say that surely doctors – who have undergone more intense training – have a greater grasp of medical knowledge than nurses, and so should be treated as a more significant authority, but the inquiry in question concerned mysterious deaths in a children's ward, so given this, the knowledge possessed by the nurses should have been equally if not more significant than that of the doctors (Smith, 1990b).

Smith's fundamental point here is that knowledge itself is gendered, or rather, the knowledge we uncritically give value to is located within a gendered system of relations. In other words, patriarchy is so pervasive that even a critical and political feminist analysis appears condemned to operate within its boundaries. Given her views on this, it would be understandable for the reader at first to locate Smith within the radical feminist tradition which calls for separatism and sisterhood, but instead Smith takes a different route, drawing heavily on ethno-methodology and phenomenology (see Chapter 8), as well as elements of Marxism (see Chapter 4), to uncover the experiences of women and then locate these experiences within the structural, patriarchal relations of ruling. These relations of ruling exist and operate at all levels of formal society, and serve to silence the voices of women and other mar-ginalised groups. For Smith, and other leading feminists such as Patricia Hill Collins (1990), the relations of ruling are far more complex than some analyses of patriarchy might suggest, involving as they do the 'intersectionality' of gender, 'race', sexuality, class and so on as sources of oppression.

Smith's solution to this is to develop a 'standpoint theory' in which the actual voices of the marginalised groups can be heard, and then be understood in the context of these broader power dynamics. Smith's is a distinctly dialectical feminism, because it looks at the dynamics between the formal, patriarchal norms and values existent within the relations of ruling, and the 'taken-for-granted' experiences and voices of women at the level of everyday life (Smith, 1987). It is also significant because it contributes not only to feminist sociological *theory* but also to the development of feminist research methods, not directly the topic of this book but worth exploring further nonetheless.

## Summary and final thoughts

In this chapter, I have discussed some of the key contributions of femin-ism as a sociological theory. Recognising, of course, that feminism is far *more* than just a sociological theory, I have tried to contextualise these contributions within the broader feminist engagement with society itself. Feminism makes political demands which transcend any one academic discipline, but there simply isn't space to do justice to those here in this chapter. You need to be clear, though, about the extent to which feminism doesn't just provide you with a lens through which to theorise about society, it also makes demands about how you and all of us see and act in the world, about how our very lives are *gendered*. My concern here has been with introducing you to feminist *theory*, and to this end I have suggested that while there are numerous types of such a theory which are actually very different from one another, the core underlying *sociological* observation they share is that societies *are* gendered, and that, certainly in Western society and in many others besides, this takes the form of unequal power relations between men and women. This power imbalance is termed *patriarchy*, and you should be aware of how patriarchy operates all around us in multiple, sometimes very subtle, ways. Recognising such subtleties is the mark of a good theorist. Finally, it is worth pointing out that I have concentrated my efforts on discussing feminist *theory* but that feminists have also pioneered distinctive research *methodologies* which are in practice inseparable from those theories (because such feminists have emphasised the indivisibility of theory from practice).

As a man writing this book, I am drawn to two questions in evaluating the feminist contribution to sociology. The first is, am I in a position to even write this chapter? Am I in a position to present feminism at all to a wider audience? I have taught radical feminism as a perspective in social theory to my students for many years, and I have always asked them to contemplate the same question, while justifying my position – with due irreverence – in terms of staff workloads. But this is no joking matter. Seriously, can a man understand the perspective of a woman? Can a man – who is, after all, part of the problem – understand and explain patriarchy? Or should the question be reframed – Is it not imperative that I, as a man, *can* teach feminism? Your response to this depends upon how you perceive the structural conditions that make the subordination of women possible.

This leads me into the second question. Should we not all be feminists? In other words, aren't the feminist arguments so convincing as to be incontrovertible? That Britain has in the past elected a female prime minister does not negate the fact that women still remain under-represented in positions of power. That female icons, from Marilyn Monroe to Madonna and beyond, have become major celebrities and, in some cases, have taken control of their own destinies does not negate the fact that men have an easier chance of success in their chosen field than women. Current generations of young women no doubt do enjoy greater freedoms and more rights than their antecedents, but does that make feminism as a body of knowledge redundant? Clearly not. The task of feminist theory today may very well be to re-engage contemporary audiences with the politics of gender inequality and oppression in ways applicable to their conditions. Another quite interesting engagement I have with my students is over the issue of positive discrimination. While discrimination is never truly desirable, there is an argument that it is sometimes necessary to promote people from particular demographic groups, such as women or ethnic minorities, if such groups are under-represented at the higher echelons of their particular hierarchies. It is sometimes surprising to me that female students occasionally reject such a programme in favour of the open market approach – may the best candidate win! Ideally, they are surely correct, but pragmatically, the foundations upon which such decisions are made are clearly done so within conditions that favour men. You may wish to set up a debate in class about this issue. You may also wish to think about the advances made by women in society in recent years and speculate on what you think the position of women will be in, say, twenty years' time – and whether there will be any real need of a dedicated feminist tradition in sociology.

In my personal view, feminism still has a huge part to play in sociological theory, whether or not it is amalgamated with other traditions such as Marxism, interactionism, structuralism or ethnomethodology, all of which are discussed in other chapters. The question does remain, though, as to whether the subordinate position of women is overcome by piecemeal changes to the existing social structure, or by radical overhauls of a system that is inherently patriarchal. Can the position of women in society be protected through existing systems? Is the male lecturer complicit in reproducing patriarchy? These and other questions clearly sustain the role of feminist theory in the broader realm of sociological, indeed social, theory, for some time to come.

# Key terms

*Definitions for the key terms listed below can be found in the Glossary on page 227.*

- Gender identity
- Patriarchy
- Relations of ruling
- Sexual division of labour

# Biographies

*Short biographical descriptions for the names listed below can be found on page 240.*

- Jessie Bernard
- Shulamith Firestone
- Betty Friedan
- Kate Millett
- Ann Oakley
- Charlotte Perkins-Gilman
- Dorothy E. Smith

# 6 | Exchange theory

In this chapter we will be:

- discussing the theoretical movement in sociology that could be called 'exchange theory', but which currently exists under the more limited name of 'rational choice theory';

- exploring the origins of this theory in psychology, and in particular in a certain approach to the study of child development;

- showing how a sociologist named George Homans developed this psychological perspective to accommodate the kinds of things sociologists are interested in;

- interrogating the concept of 'rational choice', and how exchange theorists use certain models to predict the kinds of choices people make in social situations.

## The origins of exchange theory

Okay, here's a quick backtrack: way back in Chapter 3 I briefly mentioned Weber's analysis of different systems of law. I did so in order to describe the idea of cultural relativism to you, but in this chapter I am going to take it in a different direction. Remember, Weber listed four different kinds of 'rationality' upon which different legal systems were based. Now, in the context of Chapter 3, the point was to show that different societies do things differently. In the context of *this* chapter, I want you to think about what we (and Weber) mean by *rationality*. When we say something is 'rational', we imply it makes sense, according to some kind of accepted logic. Weber told us that, in some societies, that 'logic' against which the rationality of something is measured might be grounded in religion, or tradition, or the whims of the monarch, or a trial by strength. But he also said that in 'modern' capitalist societies, it is based on an objective system of *rules*. Weber called this kind of system 'formally rational'. Bear that in mind as we make our way through this chapter.

What we are going to do here is discuss a very different kind of theoretical perspective in sociology to the ones we have already covered. It has had its highs and lows, its die-hard champions and its vitriolic opponents. It has gone by different names both within sociology, and across the social sciences in general. It is also possibly – at a superficial level at least – the most non-sociological of all the major sociological theories, because its explanations are for the most part derived from other social science disciplines, especially from psychology and economics. For the purpose of this chapter, I am going to refer to this broad perspective as 'exchange theory'. It could just as easily be referred to as the 'utilitarian' perspective, the 'behaviourist' perspective, or 'rational choice theory'. All of these names are adequate but to some extent incomplete when referring to the movement as a whole. Exchange theory was the name preferred by **George Homans**, a Harvard University professor (who was thus a colleague of Talcott Parsons, the eminent functionalist), who made the most important case for such a perspective back in the 1950s. These days, the term 'exchange theory' is largely associated with Homans's approach. Most who fit into this camp today would not identify with it so much as they would with the term 'rational choice theory' (the difference is in the extent to which the latter has largely abandoned the former's reliance upon psychology, but I will explain what I mean by this later in the chapter). However, for the purpose of discussing the perspective in a broader sense, I will treat rational choice theory as an aspect of it rather than its entirety, and much the same can be said for utilitarianism and behaviourism.

I have said that this is a very different kind of sociological perspective. Back in the first chapter, I suggested that functionalism, which for a time during the 1950s was so dominant as to be synonymous with sociology itself, came under fire from two different angles. Some critics argued that it was too conservative, and could not accommodate conflict and inequality in society. As a result, there was a fresh interest in conflict theory and in Marxist and feminist sociologies, which we have already discussed in the previous three chapters. But the other set of criticisms focused around the charge that functionalism was too structural in its approach. By that I mean that functionalism, and by extension much of sociology, was biased towards looking for explanations for human behaviour *outside* of the individual, in that strange big thing called 'society' itself. The focus was very much on the workings of the social system, and individuals like you and me were rather marginal to that, at least within the context of the functionalist theoretical perspective. Individuals were seen as acting in ways largely determined by external factors, like norms and values, and the processes of social integration. So what about *choice*? Curiously, Parsons himself had begun his massive journey through grand theory with a genuine interest in the problem of voluntary human action, but had quickly moved from there to the level of the apparently over-deterministic social system. Conflict theorists tried to bring choice (in the form of *interests*) back into the equation, but still largely focused their efforts on the structural dynamics of interest groups. Most (but not all) Marxists were similarly engaged with this kind of *macro*-sociology (the kind of sociology that looks at large-scale concepts like society itself), concentrating as they were on such structures as capitalism and sweeping historical processes. Even those feminists concerned primarily with the dynamics of patriarchy as a social system seemed to fall into the same trap. Across the board, then, academic sociology had seemingly neglected the role of the poor old individual. Leading the charge for a shift in focus was Homans, who famously used the occasion of his inaugural address as President of the American Sociological Association to make a plea to 'bring men (*sic*) back in'. Homans's use of the word 'men' here had nothing to do with any backlash against sociological feminism! Rather, he was talking about 'men' as individual people in contrast to 'man', that generic category which sociologists are prone to take for granted. Against the apparent structural bias in functionalism and much of the rest of mainstream sociology, Homans called for **methodological individualism**.

Part of the reason for sociology's concern with structural factors comes from its academic mission statement, especially as developed from Durkheim through Parsons. Durkheim made it quite clear that the discipline of sociology should be firmly distinguished from that of psychology. While these two approaches may cover much of the same ground – they may both seek to explain why individuals commit crimes, or why some people do better in education than others – the explanations

George Homans

they provide for these fields of inquiry are quite distinct. Durkheim spelled this out in his study of why people commit suicide. A psychological explanation would look for causes within the personality of the individual. A sociological explanation would seek these causes in factors external to the individual, within the wider context of norms and values, institutions and other people, which form the society into which she or he is born. From a sociological point of view, psychology cannot provide adequate explanations for social action because it focuses on the individual in total isolation from these external influences.

What Homans did was precisely to advocate a programme for sociology derived from psychology. To be fair, he did not say that sociology should be entirely subsumed within this other discipline, but he did suggest that sociologists should start with psychological understandings of people and work outwards from there, and utilise the tools and methods developed by psychology for this purpose. He was advocating nothing less than a radical break with the normative tradition (emphasising things like 'culture') that had dominated sociology since Durkheim. Let

119

us start our sociological journey, Homans said, by understanding what it is to be human, and by examining the choices that we make as we go about our lives. This is where psychology has the edge on sociology, he suggested.

The project initiated by Homans did not come out of some intellectual vacuum. Rather, it was his attempt to introduce into sociology a way of thinking about people – about who people are and what they do and why they do what they do – that had been around in other disciplines for centuries. For example, one of the most important and influential movements in moral philosophy – the study of ethics, of what constitutes the 'right' thing to do – has been **utilitarianism**. Advocated and developed in different ways (which we don't need to go into detail on here but which the reader is encouraged to research independently) by a range of key historical writers, including the philosopher and reformer Jeremy Bentham, the educationalist James Mill, the liberal political theorist John Stuart Mill, the sociologist **Herbert Spencer** and the economist Alfred Marshall, utilitarianism is effectively a theory of ethics which locates the moral justification for an act in its consequences – crudely, an act can be justified if it results in the greatest amount of happiness for the greatest number of people. At the heart of this theory of utilitarianism is an implicit psychological proposition, that through their actions individual human actors seek to achieve and enjoy the maximum level of satisfaction, or happiness, and avoid unhappiness.

Precisely the same proposition had been developed in psychology, in the form of **behaviourism**. A theoretical subfield of behavioural psychology (the psychology of how people *act*, rather than how and what they *perceive*, which would be cognitive psychology), behaviourism took shape due to the pioneering works of scientists such as John B. Watson, Ivan Pavlov and, later, B.F. Skinner. I want to spend a bit more time on behaviourism in the next section, but for the purpose of introducing it here, suffice to say that it is a way of exploring the construction of the human personality through a process of *learning*, of 'trial and error', of identifying certain actions with rewards (and thus with happiness) and others with punishments (and thus with unhappiness). For behaviourists, our knowledge of such outcomes is not due to some innate, biological characteristic, nor is it directly the result of factors external to us such as norms and values, but emerges through this process of learning, usually in the infancy phase. While behaviourism was primarily presented as a theory of child development, Homans was greatly influenced by it and, as we shall see, wanted to use it as the basis for a general theory of social action.

A third sibling project derived from the same general assumptions had taken hold in the discipline of economics, particularly classical economics and econometrics. This has come to be known as 'rational choice theory' and has, as I indicated above, become a significant approach within sociology in its own right. Economists influenced by rational choice theory had been actively studying human economic behaviour in terms of a process of 'weighing up' the relative pros and cons of one course of action against another. Again, as with utilitarianism and behaviourism, the assumption here is that the individual will seek to pursue that course of action which is deemed *rational* for her or his self-interest; specifically, that which will yield her or him the maximum exposure to happiness. To ascertain what that might be, researchers have often turned to a novel methodology called *game theory*. I want to come back to this and say more about it later because it is crucial to the sociological tradition we are discussing in this chapter.

So, from these three sources, conveniently brought together by Homans and his supporters, emerged a new perspective in sociology which was and remains easily the most self-consciously individualistic perspective in the discipline. It is a perspective which begins with a simple and fundamental psychological premise – that all humans are motivated by self-interest, by the desire to maximise their personal happiness and minimise their unhappiness, and that this motivation directs the choices that we all make. Thus, the basic unit for sociological analysis must, according to Homans and his followers, be the individual. This is why exchange theory is a definitive example of methodological individualism. Homans tried to construct a general sociology that begins with the individual. Another significant American writer, **Peter Blau,** tried to apply these principles to questions of power in more structural settings. Others made equally significant contributions to the development of exchange theory, often trying to overcome the perceived limitations of Homans's own approach, including Richard Emerson and Karen Cook. More recently, firmly within this tradition, the American sociologist **James Coleman** presented his *magnum opus*, called *Foundations of*

*Social Theory* (1990), which sought to 'rescue' exchange theory from its psychological foundations in behaviourism by focusing instead on the pure econometric basis of social action. After the work of Homans and other early exchange theorists fell out of favour with sociologists, Coleman's work was instrumental in reviving interest in the approach, under the stripped-down banner of sociological 'rational choice theory'. As a result, the major focus of this chapter will be on this idea of rational choice, because it is central to the entire tradition. However, before addressing that, we need to locate the tradition with a broader history of ideas, and in particular address the psychological theory of behaviourism which provided it with its fundamental premise.

## The debt to behavioural psychology

Reader be warned: the story about to be told is all about dogs, rats and pigeons, and infant children finding their way in life. In itself, it is not in any way a sociological story. But as you read through this and get to grips with the basics of the theory of behaviourism in psychology, remember throughout that the point is not so much to question it as a theory of *child development* (let us leave that to the psychologists themselves – and trust me, there have been a fair few criticisms made of it), but to consider whether or not it might have any use as the basis for a sociological theory of social action.

The first thing we need to appreciate is the difference that is made between two types of behaviour: *respondent* (or reflex) behaviour and *operant* behaviour. As we will see, understanding these is crucial to understanding what Homans goes on to do in his sociological exchange theory, and he provides a useful summary of the two. Respondent behaviour is, primarily, biological. It consists of those 'knee-jerk' responses over which we have no direct control. The Russian physiologist Ivan Pavlov famously observed how dogs salivate when they are near to food. In an early statement on social engineering, Pavlov suggested that it would be possible to modify the natural behavioural responses, and to condition in animals such as these dogs engineered responses to different sets of stimuli. Operant behaviour, as defined by the American psychologist B.F. Skinner through his famous experiments involving rats and pigeons, is also primarily biological in origin, because it is behaviour driven by our natural hungers and desires, but it takes on a psychological dimension. It comprises those strategies which we construct in order to *satisfy* our needs. Let us take an obvious example. If I experience a hunger for food, my body will express this in certain ways, such as the unfortunate sensation of my stomach rumbling (rather like the salivating dogs). This is respondent behaviour. But in order to satisfy my hunger, I need to find something to eat – and for that, I need to know that my rumbling and my pain will go away if I put food in my mouth. This requires a process of association that has to be *learned*. This is an example of operant behaviour. After all, I don't necessarily know that the rumbling stomach won't be cured if I do something else, like pray. And if we return to Weber, we will recall that in some cultures, this response might be considered perfectly valid.

## EXERCISE 6.1 Operant and respondent behaviour

List five examples each of operant and respondent behaviour in humans.

Psychological behaviourism is keen to discover how we learn to perform operant behaviour of this kind, and in doing so is an unapologetically *empirical* theory. Empiricism is the doctrine that holds that we can only truly 'know' that which we can experience through our senses – we have no innate knowledge of anything. According to the empiricist philosopher John Locke, and many others, we are all born *tabula rasa*, our minds are like clean slates, empty. As we go through life, we collect various 'sensations' and 'impressions', which we store in our minds. Thus, to 'remember' something is to locate one of these stored experiences and retrieve it, to 'forget' is to be unable to do so, and to 'imagine' is to play with different experiences and produce a new idea. Of course, as we find our way in life, we come to 'associate' certain experiences with certain presences in the real world – for example, fire is hot. This is called 'associationism'. The level of association becomes more complicated as we begin to ascribe to these associations courses of action. Such courses of action are influenced by whether we associate the experiences with pleasure or pain – it is a fundamental feature of behaviourism (and thus of exchange theory, following utilitarianism), that people are inherently self-serving, interested only in experiencing pleasure and avoiding pain. Fire is not just hot, it burns, so we do not want to get too close to it. Water is not just wet, it is refreshing, so we might want to drink it when we are thirsty.

At this point in what is otherwise a necessary detour through a psychological theory (this is after all supposed to be a book on sociological theory, but hopefully the relevance of all of this will become clear), let us consider whether there are any parallels in the social world. What about the associations we make in respect of criminal activity? Through a similar kind of 'social engineering', we come to recognise that crime is 'bad' and subject to punishment, so we avoid it, and that 'good behaviour' is subject to reward. Clearly, we do not merely make associations based on scientific and natural qualities, we also make them based on moral ones – but more on the example of criminal behaviour later.

The interesting question asked by the behavioural psychologist is: *How* do I know that a particular action will result in the satisfaction of a particular desire? It was John B. Watson who famously took Pavlov's observations about the behaviour of dogs and used it to form the basis of a 'hard' science of psychology, making the important distinction between *conditioned* and *unconditioned* reflexes in human behaviour. Some reflexes, he said, are innate and biological, but others are conditioned through learning. Rather than possessing some pre-social, biological knowledge (given that we are born *tabula rasa*), Watson argued that we, like any other animal, have to *learn* it. We achieve this through trial and error. Ultimately, this rests on basic psychological premises. One such premise is that an action which results in a reward is likely to be repeated, while an action which results in a sanction is likely to be avoided in future. But this premise alone is not sufficient. There may, of course, be no necessary link between the action which is rewarded and the drive itself. Animals are, in any case, more likely to repeat any action which produces a reward. The second premise, then, is that an action is dependent upon particular circumstances, *stimuli*. So, to briefly summarise, if, in a certain set of conditions, a particular behavioural act results in a reward for the actor, the likelihood is that under those same conditions, the animal will reproduce the act in order to receive the same expected reward. The more often the relationship between stimuli, action and reward is reinforced, the more likely it is to be reproduced.

This third condition is called *reinforcement*. Again, the premise is simple, and largely familiar. Imagine that last week I ordered a pizza, which I enjoyed. The next morning, I found myself suffering from a nasty stomach upset (you know the kind!). I may not have associated the latter with the former at the time, as any number of things could have caused it. But if I ordered the same pizza a week later and, once again, the next day fell ill, I would be inclined to give that pizza a miss in the future. This theory was developed by B.F. Skinner, whose contributions to the theory of behaviourism had an even more direct influence on the development of exchange theory in sociology than those of his predecessors, due in no small part, no doubt, to the fact that he was professor of psychology at Harvard where Homans was based. It was Skinner who devised the theory of operant behaviour. His experiments involving pigeons led to his conclusion that animals associate the arrival of a treat (food for the hungry birds) with whatever actions they were performing at the time (even if these were actually irrelevant), and that this association would be reinforced through repetition.

Source: Getty Images/Time & Life Pictures

B.F. Skinner at work in his laboratory

These, then, are the factors which influence operant behaviour, and this is the belief which underpins the work of behavioural psychologists such as Watson and Skinner. Watson believed that using behavioural psychology as a tool, we would be able to familiarise ourselves with likely responses to all manner of stimuli, such that we could predict behaviour. Necessarily, if behaviour can be predicted, it can also be modified – hence the controversial relationship which exists between behavioural psychology and social engineering. Skinner devoted much of his subsequent career to showing how operant behaviour could be influenced by **conditioning**, and inventing a variety of gadgets, from controversial baby cribs and teaching aids to missiles, based on this principle. In a sense, though, behaviourism had always had an implicit association with conditioning. Over a century before, the great utilitarian philosopher James Mill had stated that the purpose of education is to make it possible for the child to associate her or his experiences with external realities in a way best suited to the smooth and moral organisation of society. Mill suggested that the child should be persuaded, through frequent positive engagements with them, that certain sensations associated with the process of learning are pleasurable, and that through conditioning the child to aspire to these noble qualities, society as a whole benefits in terms of the greatest happiness to the greatest number.

So, behaviourists have extrapolated from experiments on various creatures that organisms respond in ways that can be predicted and actually conditioned. They have gone on to tell us a lot about how children, born with no innate knowledge, learn to cope in the world and become fully socialised adults. But is this where its influence should stop? Or can the insights of behaviourism illuminate our understanding of the social world more generally? Certainly, prior to or independent of Homans, scholars in related social science disciplines have presented accounts of sociological processes and institutions based on behaviourist principles. Gabriel Tarde, one of the pioneering names in criminology, had suggested that criminality results from imitation, often of those in positions of authority, which is why crime is more prevalent in heavily populated urban areas (see also the work of Bandura, e.g. 1973). Developing the behaviourist-influenced approach to criminality, some (such as Eysenck, 1970) have discussed conditioning as a means of reducing crime. But it was Homans who first sought to develop these behaviourist principles into a full general theory of social action. Homans does that by going beyond respondent and operant behaviour and introducing a third level – *social* behaviour – which is primarily associated with rational choice. This is what we need to turn to now.

## Social exchange and rational choice

So, behavioural psychologists such as Skinner carried out their research using non-human animals, such as pigeons. Clearly, it would not be a straightforward step to go from those experiments towards any theory of human behaviour. George Homans makes it clear that behavioural psychology provides the basic tools for a sociological theory, but not necessarily all the answers.

This is where Homans carves out a role for the sociologist distinct from the psychologist. He makes an important distinction between *individual behaviour*, which is one-directional, and *social behaviour*, which is reciprocal. The psychologist is best equipped to deal with the former, but the role of the sociologist is to understand the latter. Sociology is the study of social relationships, says Homans, and these always involve some form of reciprocal interaction. Inspired by the ideas of the classical economist Adam Smith, **social order** – rather than being something largely static and external to the individual – is instead seen as the dynamic product of trade and barter between self-interested actors. This is something social anthropologists had understood for some time, through a rich tradition of work best exemplified by Durkheim's protégé, Marcel Mauss, and his writings on the gift relationship. Such a tradition views societies as comprised of multiple 'modes of exchange', including *market exchanges*, in which social relationships are grounded in economic transactions, so that an object costs a certain amount of currency at which it has been valued in the market (such as when you handed over a certain amount of cash for that last CD you bought, because the market ascribed a price to it) and *gift exchanges*, which are grounded in reciprocity, the understanding that when something is given to someone, the recipient does something in return (Mauss, 1965). In sociology, the issue of exchange and its centrality in social interaction was highlighted by **Georg Simmel**, a German sociologist of the 'classical'

127

era. Simmel was interested in the way in which the *concept* of exchange is embedded in social relationships – a 'deal' between two people becomes more complicated when another person gets involved, and so on. Homans extends this tradition by presenting a conscious development of psychological behaviourism into the realm of human social interaction in the form of his seven propositions. These are basic statements of all social behaviour, according to Homans, and the first six are taken straight out of the manual of behavioural psychology, while the seventh gives the list a sociological flavour. The propositions are:

1 *The success proposition.* The likelihood of an actor repeating an action corresponds to the number of times that action has been rewarded in the past.
2 *The stimulus proposition.* An actor is more likely to repeat a previous action if the stimuli at the time are similar to those which occurred when that action was rewarded.
3 *The value proposition.* An actor is more likely to perform an action if the outcome of that action is of importance to the actor.
4 *The deprivation–satiation proposition.* The value of any reward depends largely on its scarcity. Rewards become less valuable the more frequently they are granted. This could also be understood as a *cost–profit proposition.* Action involves weighing up costs against profits. An action is more likely to be performed if the actor believes the profit to be sufficiently worthwhile.
5 *The aggression proposition.* An actor is more likely to be angry and aggressive if she or he is denied any reward which might have been expected, or indeed punished rather than rewarded, and the value invested in this action increases.
6 *The approval proposition.* An actor who receives no punishment when punishment may have been expected, or who receives an expected reward, is more likely to be happy and approving, and the value invested in this action increases.
7 *The rationality proposition.* When deciding upon a course of action, an actor is most likely to choose that the result of which would yield the greatest profit, relative to the probability of achieving such a result.

At the heart of exchange theory, then, is the concept of rational choice, which is presented in the seventh of Homans's propositions.

This proposition is taken directly from rational choice theory in economics, and is most directly reliant upon utilitarian premises. As was suggested earlier, rational choice theories have grown prominent across the social sciences and have been applied to a wide variety of social situations, including criminal behaviour (Becker, 1968; Cornish and Clarke, 1986), family dynamics (Becker, 1981), political decision-making (Buchanan and Tullock, 1962), and legal decision-making (Becker, 1976; Posner, 1972, 1981). In all these cases, the emphasis is on understanding human behaviour according to the principles of mathematics and economics, namely, 'rational' decision-making and cost–benefit calculations. Rational choice theory is primarily a methodology for explaining and predicting social action, based on the idea, familiar now to readers, that humans are calculating actors whose actions are the outcome of strategic decision-making. The situations people find themselves in are considered to be perfectly *normal*, not at all extraordinary. Take crime. Some scholars treat criminals as different from other people, either because of their biological make-up or because of their social upbringing. But, *rationally speaking*, if one has ready access to criminal involvement (remember Tarde, who I mentioned briefly earlier in the chapter?), then criminality is in fact nothing more than a 'routine activity' (Clarke and Felson, 1993), and the decision whether or not to participate in it rests upon weighing up the relative advantages and disadvantages of doing so.

This premise may be utilitarian, but is not necessarily behaviourist. In his mammoth book *Foundations of Social Theory*, James Coleman (1990), already known as a leading exponent of the use of mathematical models in sociology, suggests that the principles of rational choice theory are capable of providing a greater understanding of the dynamics of social interaction without recourse to behavioural psychology. Implicit in all rational choice theory is the assumption that outcomes are quantifiable commodities to which can be ascribed values dependent on their relative benefits. In this respect, rational choice theorists often make use of various forms of 'game theory', which amounts to the application of mathematical modelling to the study of human behaviour initially developed by Von Neumann and Morgenstern (1944), of which the most famous variant is the 'prisoner's dilemma'. We will come to that shortly.

What precisely do we *mean* by 'rational choice'? If a friend asked you whether or not something you did last night was the 'rational' thing to do, how would you respond? Rationality as a concept has a mixed history in sociology – since Max Weber, as we should know by now, we have been aware of the multiple forms of rationality that can be identified. The German Marxist critical theorists of the Frankfurt School (introduced back in Chapter 4), notably Max Horkheimer and Theodor Adorno, and more recently Jürgen Habermas, have juxtaposed the *narrow* concept of rationality, those means–end calculations they associate with economic activity, with a 'true' rationality concerned with human freedom. The rationality of rational choice theory is very much of the narrow, economic variety, substituting for a basic equation about how people are likely to behave in social situations. Homans's rationality proposition is clear on this: it is about the likelihood of Person A carrying out a particular action given the amount of benefit Person A would achieve by successfully performing that action, multiplied by the likelihood of Person A actually achieving this beneficial outcome. In a sense, our choices are equivalent to those made by the contestants on the game show, *Deal or No Deal?* For those of you unfamiliar with the concept, a player is surrounded by boxes which contain undeclared sums of money, from small to large. She is asked to eliminate the boxes one by one, in the hope that she discards those which contain small sums and is left with those that contain bigger pots, as the amount contained in the last box is what she goes home with. At regular intervals, weighing up which amounts have gone and which remain, she is given the choice of either accepting a token lump sum, or else playing on. If she chooses the latter, she might get lucky, but she also runs the risk of ending up with only a small payout. Whether to play on or to take the money and run thus becomes a calculated choice she has to make.

Long before this game show appeared on our television sets, Anthony Heath (1976) conveniently broke the idea of rational choice down into three distinct types of choice:

1 Riskless choice. Here, an actor knows the rank order of her or his preferences, knows how to achieve those preferences, and knows the consequences of the action.

2 Risky choice. Here, an actor knows the rank order of preferences, and knows how to achieve those preferences, but is uncertain about the consequences of the action.

3 Choice under uncertainty. Here, an actor is uncertain about the order of preferences, the ability to achieve them, and their consequences.

The game show contestant thus seems to be engaged in *risky* choice. Give some thought to these three types and then have a go at the next exercise.

---

**EXERCISE 6.2  The rational choices of a student**

To what extent can you apply the principles of rational choice theory to your everyday experiences as a student? Think about attending lectures (or missing them), submitting coursework on time (or not!), and other such activities.

---

## The prisoner's dilemma

Earlier, I mentioned that rational choice theorists often make use of a methodology known as 'game theory'. This was first proposed by Von Neumann and Morgenstern (1944), and involves a particular form of mathematical modelling. When people engage in 'games', they tend to weigh up the pros and cons of their situations, evaluate the strengths and weaknesses of their opponents, and try to ensure the best possible outcome for themselves, namely, victory. There is little place in such a scheme for altruism! In game theory, all social interactions can be read as games (Caplow, 1959; Coleman, 1960). This model provides a framework for predicting the behaviour of two or more 'players' whose interests may to varying degrees be in conflict with one another. It is based on the assumption that each 'player' has an identifiable number of possible actions which she or he can perform, and that the likely outcome of each action can be ranked numerically according to how it correlates to the preferred outcome of each player. In Scenario A, the ideal outcome for me is Outcome B, but failing that, it would be Outcome C, and then maybe D, but at all costs I want to avoid Outcome A, and so on.

Probably the most famous (and simplistic) illustration of the theory of games is the 'prisoner's dilemma'. This is based on an imaginary

|  | Actor 2 | |
|---|---|---|
|  | Remains silent | Confesses |
| **Actor 1** Remains silent | 2, 2 | 0, 1 |
| Confesses | 1, 0 | 1, 1 |

**Figure 6.1** The prisoner's dilemma

scenario in which two prisoners, charged with a crime they allegedly committed together but held for questioning in separate rooms, are placed in a conundrum by their captors. Each is told that if she or he confesses, then she or he will receive a light sentence. However, each is also told that if she or he does not confess, but the other does, then the one who has not owned up would receive a heavy sentence. If they both confess, then, they are sure of receiving only a moderate sentence, but (in more complex versions of the game at least) not as light as they would have received had the other one not confessed, because the value (to the captors) of each individual confession is diminished by the confession of the other. However, if neither confesses they both go free, as their captors don't have enough evidence to charge them with anything. Naturally, they are not allowed to discuss their options. We can see this dilemma in diagrammatic form (Figure 6.1), in which each outcome is given a numerical indicator proportionate to the extent to which it matches the interests of the actors. In this diagram, the figure 2 represents the best possible outcome, 0 the worst. Clearly, the *best* outcome for both actors is to remain silent, because then they both go free. However, silence is dangerous in the event of the other person confessing. At least if the actor confesses he or she knows her sentence will be relatively light whatever decision the other actor makes.

### EXERCISE 6.3 The prisoner's dilemma

Play the prisoner's dilemma. What would you do?

The idea of the prisoner's dilemma is that we all find ourselves in situations where our choice of action is determined by the relative value we give to its outcome. Here's an example for the British reader (because it is easier to provide, thanks to the way the country's political system works), but you can take the point and adapt it to where you are. The general election is upon us and you are a voter in a marginal constituency. Your natural tendency is to vote Labour, but in this part of the country, the Conservatives are in power, and the Liberal Democrats are close behind. Your ideal scenario is for Labour to win the seat (2 points in the above diagram). But if you vote Labour with this goal in mind (bearing in mind you do not know what the other voters are doing), you may simply help to split the anti-Conservative vote and therefore keep the Conservatives in power (0 points). You are advised by experts to exercise such a thing as 'tactical voting' (i.e. vote for the Liberal Democrats, despite the fact that you are a Labour supporter), and if all Labour supporters did that, then the Conservatives would be beaten, and the Liberal Democrats would win the seat (1 point).

The classical prisoner's dilemma is based on rational and strategic thinking involving two players (in the example above, you and the rest of the local electorate, but in the original example, the two prisoners). Clearly, most social situations are not so straightforward. For example, where four persons are involved in a game, and two contrive to defeat a third, what is the best option for the fourth player? She or he is likely to see it in their best interests to side with the majority, because of the balance of power, even if this conflicts with her or his individual and strategic interests. Here we see two major flaws with the rational choice model proffered by sociological exchange theorists in its traditional form: first, its explicit methodological individualism, according to which it focuses largely on the factors that influence *individual* decision-making; and second, its apparent inability to cope with the problem of *power dynamics* in social relationships. A third problem is the problem of *unequal exchange* – so far, we have looked at social exchange from the point of view of a participant as if it is largely a benevolent process. Unsurprisingly, writers in the exchange theory tradition have responded to all three criticisms.

First, according to some of its chief exponents, including Coleman (1990; see also Caplow, 1959; Friedman and Hechter, 1988), rational choice theorising is sufficiently flexible to accommodate collective as well as individual interests. For Coleman, society itself emerges from a state of individuals working together to secure their rational individual and also collective interests. Caplow (1959) illustrates this using a modified version of game theory, in which a weaker player in a multi-person game is likely to form a coalition with two stronger players, or to unite with other weaker players so as to outnumber a stronger player. In either case, the weaker player is able, through a strategic playing of the game, to achieve a stronger position. Caplow's argument relies heavily on the inclusion of factors outside the traditional mandate of rational choice theory, such as 'irrational' presumptions of prestige. Coleman agrees that the orthodox definition of rationality has to be expanded in order to accommodate collective decision-making – factors such as trust and norms. He points out, for example, that in some cases it is beneficial for individuals to surrender their interests to the wider community. The major problem that needs to be overcome, according to Coleman, is the power exerted over individuals by institutions.

According to exchange theory, power is essentially the capacity for one actor to obtain compliance from another actor. Power, then, is a resource exercised by one at the expense of another. This is known as an *instrumentalist* theory of power – that power is akin to an instrument, a possession, that one *uses*. We have already come across such an approach to power in Chapter 3. Necessarily, a power relationship is an exchange relationship in which both actors seek to maximise their personal interests. In such a situation, where you and I are the respective actors, I am involved in a process of bargaining with you, and to maximise my chance of winning the game, I need to obtain your compliance at as little cost to myself as possible. I hold the upper hand (power) in any scenario whereby I can offer something that you want, and you and I both know that other people want it as well (I can raise my price owing to the demand for my services), and not many other people can offer what I am offering. But if I show you that I want to give you what I can offer, or suggest that I desperately want something in return, then I actually lose some of my bargaining power. At such a point, *you* have something over *me*. So, while all relationships have an unequal balance of power, based on this principle, the 'game' to achieve final power in any exchange remains open, and contested.

So, exchange theorists have sought to accommodate problems of inequality within their broad theory, but doubts remain as to its legitimacy as an explanatory mechanism. We should conclude by weighing up (in true exchange theory fashion) the relative pros and cons of the perspective.

## Summary and final thoughts

So, in this chapter we have come across the sociological version of a familiar approach in the social sciences. It is the theory that the social world – society itself – is merely the sum of the calculations we make as individuals when we go about our business. Exchange theorists tell us that we (as sociologists) can best understand 'society' if we begin with the way we as individuals go about *negotiating* with one another.

As ever, the strengths of exchange theory are synonymous with its weaknesses, namely its reliance upon psychological behaviourism and rational choice theory. Indeed, its relationship with sociological theory has always been tenuous. Homans certainly argued that its ultra-individualism was actually one of its biggest strengths, although its critics are quick to point out that if we reduce everything to the motivations of individuals, we necessarily ignore those structural factors which certainly impose upon us, even if they don't actually determine us. This is where the functionalists, Marxists and others are strong – they highlight the extent to which such external things as our class or status position have a big influence on the choices we make and the actions we perform.

Which leaves us with the other perceived weakness of exchange theory: if we put aside its individualism, which may or may not be a good thing, we are left with its description of human nature. Are we really so strategic, so instrumental, so self-serving, and so ultimately predictable? Exchange theory tells us we are. In so far as rational choice theory presumes that humans are constantly engaged in a process of rational decision-making, say some critics, it duly ignores those factors, such as emotion or tradition (which Weber listed as *other* forms of rationality), which also influence our choices and actions. In short, such critics may say, humans are not calculating machines but fiery and passionate animals. In response, exchange theorists have either defended the validity of their position and downplayed the significance of these 'non-rational' factors, or extended the definition of rationality so as to incorporate them. In any case, as an explanatory mechanism, exchange theory, with its rational choice foundation, becomes redundant. Take the following example. The other week, in a competitive game of whichever sport you like, when in a winning position, I called a foul on myself (owned up to an accidental breach of the rules) that the referee and my opponent had not spotted. Where is the rationality in this? It gave me no strategic advantage – I went on to lose the match. Was I being driven by a broader set of norms and values not reducible to instrumental rationality – the 'spirit of the game'? If so, rational choice explanations for behaviour are inadequate. Or was I operating under the influence of some much greater sense of strategic rationality, such as the belief that in admitting the foul I would earn the respect of my peers which would serve me better in the long term? Perhaps I was just unwilling to risk *not* calling the foul, because I did not know that the referee had not seen it and to have it called against me without having owned up to it first would have yielded greater disadvantage than to have tried to get away with it (now this is a classic prisoner's dilemma!). If so, let's be honest – what use is a theory if I can simply bend its parameters to incorporate anything I like?

Its usefulness as a sociological theory aside, another controversy surrounding exchange theory with its rational choice foundations is its association with a particular type of political theory. This may seem a bit odd to the casual reader at this point. After all, Marxism is a good example of a perspective which has an explicit relationship to a particular political ideology, but exchange theory is supposed to be neutral, scientific, value free. It is an empirical theory, concerned with how things *are*, not how they should be. It is associated with **positivism** in sociology. But the pretence to scientific objectivity is itself ideological, as Habermas has told us, because it protects the status quo, and silences the voices of the alternatives. But even more than this, exchange theory is implicitly ideological in its strict individualism. The very idea that the individual is the centre of the social world is closely associated with the Western liberal tradition in political theory. Individualistic liberalism champions the absolute sovereignty of the individual against authority from above, the weak state against the strong one, freedom against equality, and the free market against economic planning.

Early exponents of the rational choice model – adherents to utilitarianism – tended to be political liberals. That is, they tended to champion the values listed above and adopted a rather benign view of government as a 'servant of the people'. However, the founder of sociological exchange theory, George Homans would probably not have thought of himself as a conventional liberal – he was a keen follower of, and indeed wrote a definitive book on, the Italian sociologist and economist Vilfredo Pareto (a political elitist who grew to prominence under the fascist regime). In fairness, Homans was more impressed by Pareto's methodology than by his political persuasions. More recently, though, many people who adhere to modern rational choice theory have been unapologetic advocates of the right-wing political ideology known as 'neo-liberalism', or the 'New Right'. If you think about it carefully, it might seem perfectly logical to connect the theory of rational choice to this kind of political ideology. Neo-liberals are committed (if I may summarise quite crudely a complex set of ideas) to the old liberal belief in the primacy of the individual over the state, and thus to the belief that government should not intrude upon the affairs of private persons, but whereas old liberals couched this in a benign view of human nature, neo-liberals are far more cynical. These private persons, these individual rational actors, are far more driven by self-interest and prone to exploit situations to that end, often operating for example as 'free riders' (Olson, 1965). So, distrustful as they are of the pure idea of democracy, it is hardly surprising that many modern rational choice theorists champion a particular role for the state to prevent such abuses without unduly interfering in private activities. Let's think again about the problem of crime – if crime is just a 'routine activity' that people engage in because it makes 'rational' sense for them to do so, then the solution to this *problem* is not found in any 'cure' or any practice of rehabilitation, but in the more direct state project of crime *prevention*, and thus of *deterrence* (Clarke, 1992; Clarke and Felson, 1993). Exchange theory, with its basis in behaviourism and rational choice theory, naturally lends itself to such ideas of social engineering and conditioning.

Much of this, of course, depends on whether you accept the idea that humans are naturally cynical, self-serving actors. If you don't buy into this, then there's no reason why you would make the leap from the sociological perspective of exchange theory to the political ideology of neo-liberalism. It certainly has to be said that this approach is not solely popular among those on the political right – many sociologists who are committed to the project of Marxism, such as Jon Elster and John Roemer, have been drawn to the use of rational choice methods to help them understand the dynamics of power and inequality in capitalist societies. But the implicit problem with exchange theory is not just that many of its exponents treat us in such a cynical way – it is that they treat us as largely *predictable*. Few if any of us would consciously subscribe to such a self-description. We would see ourselves as unpredictable, driven by impulses that cannot be explained through objective scientific method. The school of thought that takes up this particular challenge is known as interactionism, and is the subject of our next chapter.

## Key terms

*Definitions for the key terms listed below can be found in the Glossary on page 227.*

- Behaviourism
- Conditioning
- Methodological individualism

- Positivism
- Social order
- Utilitarianism

## Biographies

*Short biographical descriptions for the names listed below can be found on page 240.*

- Peter Blau
- James Coleman
- George Homans

- Georg Simmel
- Herbert Spencer

# 7 | Interactionism

In this chapter we will be:

- introducing the sociological perspective called interactionism (or 'symbolic interactionism');
- tracing the roots of this perspective to a particular philosophy of knowledge called pragmatism;
- focusing on the idea of the 'self', with particular emphasis on how Mead and Cooley suggest what the self *is* and how Goffman describes how it is *presented*;
- relating the interactionist perspective to a particular kind of methodology called ethnography;
- showing how, through a theory of 'labelling', this approach allows us to understand how power operates in social interactions.

## Sociology at the University of Chicago

In the previous chapter, we discussed the perspective, which in sociology came to be known as exchange theory, which grew out of the behaviourist tradition in psychology. In sociology, it emerged as a critique of the functionalist dominance, which allegedly overplayed the significance of structural factors at the expense of understanding the behaviour and actions of individuals.

On the one hand, readers might have been rather sympathetic to this critique. Nobody is keen to see themselves as merely the product of external, structural forces. But on the other, an astute reader might have felt more than a little aggrieved at the way exchange theory seems to portray the individual in question, as a rather predictable, calculating, self-interested actor whose choices are dictated either by conditioning or by some inherent capacity for 'rational' thought. On the surface of it, this perspective seems to present a no more sympathetic view of the person than does functionalism. Most of us would rather see ourselves as rather unpredictable, passionate, and above all, *free* to do things which may not be reducible to 'rationality'.

This is perhaps why, in my experience, the interactionist tradition – or to give it its proper name in sociology, *symbolic* interactionism – often seems to be quite popular with students (although you may disagree!). While it focuses on individuals, rather than abstract structures, it avoids treating them as the object of scientific study, whose actions and intentions can be defined objectively by the social scientist, and seeks instead to find out what they mean to the individuals themselves. Rather than trying to provide a *science* of how people behave, interactionism is concerned with presenting what we might call a *documentary* of how particular people in particular settings make sense of the world around them. Two other possible reasons for its apparent popularity among my students spring to mind: first, that the perspective seems to be less concerned with abstract theorising than it is with the 'real world' (a horrible phrase!), although as we will see, it most certainly does have a theory; and second, that researchers in this tradition have produced fascinating studies of some of the more unusual, exciting, perhaps 'seedy' walks of life, such as jazz musicians, street-corner gangs and marijuana users.

The term 'symbolic interactionism' was coined by **Herbert Blumer**, but the real 'founder' of the movement is **George Herbert Mead**. Mead was not a sociologist as such, but rather identified more as a philosopher and a social psychologist. He taught at the University of Chicago and, as we will see, that place is especially associated with this particular tradition. Blumer was a graduate student there and attended Mead's lectures, astutely assembling his lecture notes which he and his peers produced in Mead's name, posthumously, as *Mind, Self and Society*. And with that, interactionism was born.

Mead's lectures summarised his particular philosophy. He was evidently influenced by **behaviourism**, but he wanted to take that psychological theory a step further, and identified himself as a 'social behaviourist'. Rather than treat **socialisation** as a process which occurs during the childhood phase, he suggested that it was on-going throughout life, and that our 'self' was never complete as such, but rather constantly adapting as we interact with other people. Interactionists ever since have spoken of life as a process of 'becoming', or learning one's way around, rather like a 'career' which is never fully accomplished. In developing this perspective, Blumer set it against two alternative viewpoints, which he called 'realism' and 'psychologism'. 'Realism', he said, claims that the meaning of any event is inherent in it and objective to individual perception, while 'psychologism' suggests that actors discern meaning through psychological processes. 'Interactionism', by contrast, holds that an actor *attributes* meaning to an event, and that the meaning she or he gives is dependent on social context and subject to interpretation by those involved.

A number of themes characterise the interactionist tradition in its various forms (Plummer, 2000: 194). First, society is by its very nature *symbolic*, and symbols are understood through the interpretation of meaning. Blumer stressed that we cannot actually 'know' the meaning of any event – all we can do is take into consideration the different *interpretations* made of that particular event by those who witnessed it. Second, societies are constantly changing. Third, attention is paid not to individual actions or consciousness, nor to some abstract notion of society as a 'thing in itself', but to the shared experiences of individuals, their *interactions*. Fourth, the tradition has an empirical rather than theoretical focus. Indeed, there are only a few general theoretical contributions that have been made by interactionists. On the whole, these sociologists respect *grounded theory* – theory that emerges from, and is useful in, a particular situation (Glaser and Strauss, 1967).

The relationship between interactionism and a particular kind of research methodology is crucial to our understanding of the tradition. Because of its roots in **pragmatism**, which we shall discuss below, interactionism has never cared for abstract 'grand theories'. Some of its most important contributions have been more methodological than theoretical – its exponents have championed qualitative methods. This is particularly true of the many studies carried out by interactionists on criminal or delinquent groups, school children, or professionals at work. Sociologists such as Becker, Strauss, Davis and others have employed **ethnographic methods** such as participant observation as a research technique. For the most part, such researchers prefer to 'hang out' with the people they are researching, asking questions and taking notes so as to document their activities, rather than speculating about them from a distance. Perhaps this is inherited from some advice given by two of the 'founders' of the tradition. At Chicago, **Robert Ezra Park** – who had been a journalist and social activist (he worked with the civil rights campaigner, Booker T. Washington) before becoming a practising sociologist and who had himself become fascinated by the flux and flow of everyday life after spending some time studying in Europe under **Georg Simmel** – had famously encouraged his graduate students to go out into the field and 'get their hands dirty'. Meanwhile, at Michigan, Charles Horton Cooley recommended a method called 'sympathetic introspection', which called for sociologists to put themselves in the place of the person they are studying in order to better understand the reasons for particular behaviour.

Interactionism resulted, then, from a series of developments in philosophy, psychology and sociology, mostly at Chicago. From Park (courtesy of Simmel) came this fascination with the dynamics of small-scale social interactions, and the call to arms for sociologists to 'get stuck in' to the world around them, particularly the underside of life, those spaces on the margins of the city, in the shadows of the increasingly complex modern world. From Cooley came this interest in understanding the world *from the point of view of the participants*, an interest that was shared by William Isaac Thomas at Chicago (about whom more below), by the great American jurist Oliver Wendell Holmes, who said we should try to see the law the way a criminal sees it, and by those who adhered to a philosophical tradition called pragmatism. One cannot truly understand interactionism without first understanding pragmatism – the former is perhaps best described as the sociological variant of the latter (in much the same was as exchange theory is the sociological variant of behaviourism). Mead identified himself as a pragmatist, alongside such contemporaries as John Dewey, William James and Charles Sanders Pierce. I want to discuss pragmatism in more detail in the next section. Then, in the remainder of the chapter, we will be looking at some of the practical contributions interactionism has made to sociological theory and research, first by providing a theory of the self, and then by showing how the self is being constantly renegotiated through the process of **labelling**. The reader should pay careful attention to how these contributions all fit together to form a rather rich sociological theory of *who we are*, *what we can know*, and *how we relate to one another*.

---

**EXERCISE 7.1  Who am I?**

Although interactionism is most closely associated with the University of Chicago, there was a rival tradition that emerged at the University of Iowa, and was spearheaded by Manford Kuhn. While the Chicago group championed ethnographic research, participant observation, Kuhn thought it was possible to provide a more 'scientific' form of interactionism by studying the responses people would give to the question, 'Who am I?', his famous 'twenty statements test'. Try this for yourself. List twenty of your own responses to that basic question.

---

## The pragmatist theory of knowledge

So, what do I mean by 'pragmatism', this philosophical movement that provides the backbone for interactionism in sociological theory? In short, it is a way of looking at the world in terms of how it appears to us at the time. To carry out work within the interactionist tradition is to adopt a pragmatist view of knowledge and understanding, even if only implicitly. The very fact that interactionists make no pretence to scientific neutrality or generalisable 'truths' when they conduct their research, preferring instead to see themselves as storytellers, documentary makers, is down to their origins in this movement. For pragmatists such as James, Dewey and Pierce, those scientists who claim to have revealed the 'truth' are somewhat misguided. It is not so much that there is no such thing as an objective truth, just that we cannot actually *know it*. What we come to call 'truth' emerges instead out of an appreciation for *meaning*, and the meaning of something, and therefore its 'truth', relates to the *practical* qualities of some statement, or some concept or object, such as its effects. 'Truth', said William James, is a kind of convenient fiction which we construct in order to make sense of our lives. It has to be understood in context. Knowledge is not, therefore, a library of 'stock information', to which we can seek access, but an incomplete project which is driven forward by new human experiences; it is not advanced through the reflections of isolated individuals, but through collective associations and experiences; it should not be measured against some abstract scale of importance, but by its usefulness and its effectiveness, in the service of human needs and interests. Influenced by these ideas, the Chicago sociologist William Isaac Thomas suggested that the reality of any situation is dependent upon the extent to which the actors involved in that situation *define* it as being 'real'.

An example of pragmatism 'in action' is Dewey's approach to education (and it is worth contrasting this with James Mill's views on the subject, which were mentioned in the previous chapter as illustrative of a behaviourist or utilitarian approach). He felt that the task of education was to produce people capable of reaching their potential in modern, complex societies. Education should not, then, be 'subject-centred', but should be 'child-centred'; its role should be to allow children to learn co-operation, teamwork and problem solving. In the child's real world, the strict theoretical problems of mathematics and language mean very little. Dewey proposed instead an education based around the setting of various tasks through which the child, either alone or in a group, could come face to face with problems and develop skills in overcoming them, and understanding their nature. Above all, Dewey was opposed to the separation of school from wider society – such a schism is meaningless in the real world. Just as learning is not an activity which occurs only in schools, so should schools not be seen as factories reproducing some specific, sacred form of 'academic' knowledge. The tasks undertaken by the children should not be purely academic in the formal sense, nor should they be set by teachers. Instead they should emerge from the real problems experienced by the child. This view is echoed in how later pragmatists came to view the role of politics or the law – as strategies for problem solving, for 'dealing with' real issues, rather than as absolute commands in their own right. The same view underpins Richard Rorty's famous treatment of the idea of 'human rights' (Rorty, 1993): Rorty controversially agrees that such rights cannot be 'universal truths' and are indeed best seen as reflections of dominant Western ideals, but they must still be championed, because their power lies in their usefulness as the 'best' or most appropriate 'story' available to us at this particular point in history.

Pragmatism, then, is core to the interactionist tradition, thanks to its focus on the perspective of the actors involved, and its insistence that the 'best' we can do is understand the meaning of something in its particular context. But if this gives us the interactionist *epistemology* (its theory of what we can *know*), then from Mead and Cooley, with their respective theories of the ever-changing self, we get its *ontology* (its theory of what we *are*).

## The self in social interaction

Mead's biggest contribution to sociological theory was in his development of a theory of the self as being in a state of permanent transition. Heavily influenced by the pragmatists, especially Dewey and James, Mead divided the self up into two distinct components: **'I' and 'me'**. The 'I' is the *subjective* self, the self that is locked up inside a person. The 'me' is the *objective* self, the self that engages in interaction with others and presents itself to them. When an individual interacts with others, she or he comes to reflect upon their sense of self by internalising the symbols and expressions of the group, effectively coming to see themselves as they believe others see them.

George Herbert Mead

Mead claimed that various aspects of the self are formed according to three stages of child development. In the earliest stage, the stage of 'pre-play', a child's action is largely imitation. There is no consciousness or understanding of meaning, no ability to recognise the position of any other person. It is in this stage that the 'I' is formed. However, in a second phase, the 'play' stage, the child develops the ability to take on the role of the 'significant other' (meaning a direct co-participant in any interaction), and thus begins to recognise himself or herself as being a participant in interaction. During this stage, then, the 'me' – the social face of the self – is developed. Only in the third phase, the 'game' stage, though, is the child able to see himself or herself, and others, as part of a broader, more complex network or community, to recognise the 'rules of the game', and to appreciate the role of the 'generalised other' (meaning others in general, beyond immediate interaction). It is at this stage that the 'self' is developed. Socialisation for Mead is thus a learning process in which an individual grows to recognise the role of the other – both the direct or significant other, and latterly the indirect or generalised other. This engagement occurs not through reflex responses, as a behaviourist might suggest, but through making sense of action through various symbols including gestures, hence *symbolic* interaction.

This idea that the self is constructed through social interaction – the idea of the **looking-glass self** – originally comes from **Charles Horton Cooley**. Although associated with the Chicago tradition, Cooley was actually a member of faculty at the University of Michigan, where Mead, significantly, had taught before moving to Chicago. Perhaps because of this connection, his theory of the self influenced the later generation of Chicago scholars. Cooley insisted that the 'self' is not an absolute or permanent thing. It is rooted in the human capacity for consciousness, and this is made possible through interaction with others. The process by which the self is constructed is one of reflexive self-perception. During our early years, we present rather loose, unstructured images of self to others, whose perceptions and responses flow back to us and work towards the shaping of our self-identity. This process takes place mainly within primary groups, those with whom we have immediate and intimate relationships (specifically, the family). So, the self is constantly being reconstructed within the flow of interaction, and the normative world of expectations, we experience with others. One is not *born* a criminal, one becomes one through interaction with others and 'learn-ing the ropes', just as one *becomes* a student, an employee, a friend, or whatever (Becker, 1963). Thus, for Cooley, and by extension for later interactionists, the self has two primary qualities: first, it is fluid, rather than fixed according to some innate biology; second, it is inherently social, which is to say, it does not 'exist' outside of social relation-ships, it is constructed through interaction with others and through our reading of their perception of us. I 'become' that which I am by *internalising* my perception of how others see me (and this in turn sparks off a process of labelling about which I will say more below). Who I am, then, depends very much on my audience, the people I am present-ing myself to, a point made most lucidly by the Canadian sociologist **Erving Goffman**.

Goffman's body of work is often held up for special praise among those in the interactionist tradition, and with good reason, although it is debatable whether it can actually be said to fall within this tradition *per se*. Usually referred to as 'dramaturgy', the perspective pioneered by Goffman clearly owes as great a debt to Durkheim as it does to Mead, perhaps even a greater one (not so much, though, the Durkheim revered by the functionalists for his work on differentiation, but more the Durkheim of social anthropology, the student of rituals, celebrated by the structuralists we turn to in Chapter 9). In my classes, I prefer to locate Goffman outside the narrow definition of interactionism, and closer to the more recent eclectical work of Pierre Bourdieu and Anthony Giddens which I will come to in the final chapter. But in so far as Goffman presents an extension of Mead's theory of the self, it can be legitimately situated here. Mead focused on the *construction* of the self through social interaction, the internal process of social psychology. Goffman leaves this largely unchallenged and adds to it an external dimension, a kind of social anthropology, focusing on how the self is then *presented* to others and *maintained*. In his first major work, *The Presentation of Self in Everyday Life* (1959), Goffman introduced us to the metaphor with which he is most closely associated – that of society as a *theatre*, and of the self as a *performance*. 'All the world's a stage,' wrote William Shakespeare in *As You Like It*, 'and all the men and women merely players. They have their exits and their entrances, and one man in his time plays many parts.' Quite so, says Goffman, who proceeds to describe the performative dynamics of social interaction in rich detail. Each of us does indeed play many parts – employee, mother, friend – and each such part is performed on a different stage – at work, at home, in a social setting – to a different audience. In each case, the performance needs to be credible in the eyes of its audience, just as a comedian on stage, desperate that the audience finds her funny, has to convince them to like her. All performances begin with rituals of bargaining and negotiation between performer and audience, based on common expectations and desires – Goffman calls this 'role expectation'. If the actress forgets her lines, the audience will react negatively, and she will be embarrassed. To make her performance as convincing as possible, she learns those lines carefully, and makes use of various masks, costumes, signals and props. A successful performance relies upon a shared understanding of the particular context between performer and audience. It must be appropriate for that particular setting. The same is true in all social interactions. Learning how much space to allow a passer-by on the street is just one example of 'learning one's lines'. And clearly, the performance you put on at work, and the one you put on when you are with friends, are very different – there are different expectations of how you will behave, and a performance that is appropriate in one may not be appropriate in the other.

In Goffman's theatrical world, the social actor is clearly performing in a very strategic way, in that she or he is playing out the role based on what they think the audience is expecting, and with a view to eliciting a desired response from that audience. This is called **impression management**. A famous example Goffman gives is of the American high school girls who play down their intelligence or athletic skills in order to make themselves more appealing to boys – these girls are clearly putting on a performance inspired by their perception of what the boys expect. *They* know that the performance does not reflect their 'true' self. When they are 'front-stage', in front of their audience, they put on the show, but 'backstage', they can be very different people (some of the world's greatest comedians were, apparently, severe depressives 'backstage', but the audience would not know this from their onstage performances, and indeed would not want to know it). But herein likes the disturbing subtext to Goffman's work and, indeed, the interactionist theory of the self, more broadly – my audience can never *know* the 'real me'. In true pragmatist fashion, it is impossible to actually *know* such a thing. You can't get inside my head to see what I am thinking. You can't *know* if I am being 'sincere' or not. You can only give your best guess, your *account*, of what you *think* I am thinking. In other words, we are always just putting on a show. All social interaction is just an act, a performance for the benefit of others, and this is a pretty cynical view of the world – some have drawn parallels between the social actor in Goffman's view and the 'con man' (Messinger, Sampson and Towne, 1975: 38).

---

### EXERCISE 7.2 The roles you play

Think about some of the different roles you play, for example at college, at work if you have a job, at home, with your friends and so on. Think about the different expectations each audience might have of you in that role. Try to be as creative as you can – think about the different costumes, props, signals and so on you make use of. Now list some clear examples of impression management in respect of performing the role of student!

---

Goffman's work on the *presentation* of self thus extends the idea of the relational, reflexive self that develops through social interaction initially presented by Cooley. And his metaphor is extremely useful when it comes to describing the behaviour of actors in particular settings, be they medical professionals at work (Haas and Shaffir, 1982), spectators at a sporting event (Snow, Zurcher and Peters, 1984), military leaders displaying their authority in public settings (Kithahara, 1986), or politicians performing on television (Meyrowitz, 1995). But so far in this section we have discussed the theory of the *construction* of the self by Cooley and Mead, and examined its *presentation* via the work of Goffman. To conclude, we should consider how we come to *maintain* our sense of self, and for this, again, Goffman is a useful guide.

In a sense, it is in 'extreme' situations (unlike most that we have already discussed) that the ultimate test of 'the self' resides. How do we maintain our sense of self in environments designed to change or even destroy it? In his book *Asylums*, Goffman (1961) studied the asylum as a kind of 'total institution', a place where strict rules about wearing uniforms, about using numbers instead of names, about having personal property removed, and so on, were very much designed to suppress

Source: American Sociological Association

Erving Goffman

individuality and enforce conformity (what he called the 'mortification of the self'). From his observations he listed a series of responses inmates had to this brutal process, which I list in Table 7.1. The point is, the total institution is an extreme form, but also to a degree a microcosm, of wider society – so do any of these seem familiar to you?

A wonderful representation of this comes from *One Flew Over the Cuckoo's Nest*, a book by Ken Kesey made into a film by Milos Forman. In it, a rebellious character, MacMurphy, enters into an asylum under the belief that by doing so he will evade a criminal sentence. MacMurphy plays the rebel – Goffman's 'resistance' – and incites others to do the same. Most of them, despite being volunteers at the institution, have withdrawn into it, become institutionalised. One character, 'the Chief', has played it cool, pretending to be deaf and dumb, such that the authorities consider him unimportant and unthreatening. While the attention is on MacMurphy, whose rebellious efforts depressingly lead to a forced conversion through lobotomy, the Chief breaks free of the institution.

**Table 7.1** Goffman's five identity adjustments in total institutions

| Response | Typical behaviour |
|---|---|
| *Situational withdrawal (retreatism)* | Reduce level of commitment and involvement in external activity; 'drop out' |
| *Resistance* | Refusal to co-operate; refusal to accept the rules of the institution |
| *Colonisation (institutionalisation)* | Modify behaviour to fit into the institutional rules; gain advantage from accepting the system; become reliant upon the rules and expectations of the institution |
| *Conversion* | Modify beliefs, values, norms, world-view to fit into the institutional view; accept the institutional view as one's own, replacing personal beliefs, values, etc. |
| *Playing it cool* | Modify behaviour to suit specific, pragmatic needs; utilise other forms of behaviour if necessary to suit situation; quietly maintain control over the situation rather than be controlled by it |

## The theory of labelling

At the heart of the interactionist perspective, then, is the insistence that 'meanings' – which as sociologists and as passers-by we often give to situations – are not fixed, but dependent upon context. Just as our sense of self-identity is constructed largely in response to how others perceive us, so is how we make sense of, and give meaning to, any particular situation. To 'know' the meaning is to understand the context of the situation and the motives of those involved in it. Herbert Blumer identified three basic premises of social action, which again provide a stark contrast to the premises outlined later by exchange theorists such as Homans:

1 People's actions in respect of things are informed by the meanings they ascribe to those things.
2 These meanings are themselves the product of social interaction between people.
3 These meanings are developed through a careful, internal process of interpretation and negotiation, through which actions and orientations in respect of those things are formed.

In other words, we ascribe a meaning to a situation that is produced by social interaction, and then perform an action that is driven by that

meaning – 'truth' comes from **interpretation.** According to the interactionists, in any social setting we are unconsciously contemplating how
our mannerisms, appearances and personality traits are being perceived
by the other people around us. For example, while he is chatting up a
woman at a nightclub, a man is privately trying to work out whether she
likes him or not. If he comes to the conclusion that she is not, in fact,
interested in him, he may decide not to pursue his seduction. In fact, at
this point he has no way of knowing for sure whether she is or isn't
interested – in true pragmatist fashion, he cannot actually 'know' the
'real' truth of the situation. She may very well be interested, but may not
be a very expressive person. In this situation, he is making a judgement
based only on how he interprets her responses. He thus provides a *definition of the situation*, and in doing so, turns this definition into a *truth*
– by abandoning his pursuit of the woman he makes real the assumption
that the couple will not end up together at the end of the night. Aggleton
(1987: 51) gives another example, which is no doubt familiar to more than
a few veteran lecturers: if we believe that we come across as boring to
other people, this belief may convince us not to speak in public settings,
but if we believe that others find us interesting, we may be encouraged
to act in a far more extroverted way. In either case, our own beliefs
about our self and our personality traits, defined solely according to
how we interpret other people's behaviour towards us, are ultimately
confirmed, even though they may never have been 'true'. In other words,
once a situation has been defined as 'real', it *becomes real in its consequences.* There is little doubt that this idea is inherited from the pragmatists' critique of 'absolute' truth and knowledge. It was developed by the
Chicago sociologist William I. Thomas (1923) in a famous ethnography
about a young woman who, desperately short of finances, came to the
conclusion that the only way she could make any money was to become
a prostitute, and duly did. Thus the 'definition of the situation' becomes a
'self-fulfilling prophecy'. Years later, Thomas's observations were cleverly
reworked by members of the 'next generation' of Chicago scholars –
and most especially by **Howard Becker** – into a theory of labelling.

Labelling is possibly the most popularly cited of all the contributions
interactionists have made to sociology. It is important because it not
only describes a process which goes on around us all the time, but
because it provides interactionism with an implicit theory of power

relations. Labelling is the process by which others – usually those in more powerful positions – come to impose an identity upon us. Or, rather, we impose it upon ourselves, by internalising the labels we think others attach to us. To show this, Becker famously studied teachers at a Chicago school. The majority admitted to measuring their students against some abstract notion of the 'ideal pupil' (which, of course, was itself entirely dependent upon the teachers' own definition). Students from higher middle-class backgrounds came closer to this ideal, so teachers were more positive and encouraging towards them. Those from working-class backgrounds were further removed from it, and teachers often saw them as troublemakers, or even dismissed them, without any evidence, as being disinterested in formal education.

Clearly, the implications of this process of labelling are damaging for the person who is being 'labelled'. If a teacher makes an initial judgement on a pupil which labels that pupil in a negative way – perhaps as a 'dunce' or a 'troublemaker' – then the pupil is likely to internalise the label (following Cooley's idea of the looking-glass self) and act accordingly. Meanwhile the teacher is more likely to invest her or his energies in those pupils she or he sees as more intellectually worthy, and, necessarily, the negatively labelled pupil fails owing to a lack of attention. Thus, the labelling becomes another kind of self-fulfilling prophecy. Moreover, even if the pupil resists the label, the teacher is still likely to interpret the future actions of the pupil from within the framework established by the existing label. For example, if a student who usually does badly in tests happens to register a particularly high score one week, the teacher is likely to presume that the student, being less than bright, has cheated, rather than imagine that she or he has actually studied extra hard. Needless to say, it is very difficult opposing this kind of institutionalised labelling, and many pupils negatively labelled by their teachers may retreat into a subculture of others like them, thus 'becoming' the rebels or outsiders they were labelled as in the first place (Hargreaves, 1967). So again, the 'reality' is actually the construct of a self-perpetuating process of labelling.

Let's take a step outside the classroom and consider another example of labelling, also provided by Becker. A fight between two young men in an inner-city ghetto, and one which takes place in a wealthy neighbourhood, both constitute the same act, and yet only one is likely to be labelled as 'delinquency' by the police officers and court officials. The young men in the inner-city area are more than likely going to be charged with a criminal act, and thus labelled criminal by the authorities, whereas the middle-class lads are more likely to be given a mild telling-off, their behaviour dismissed as 'high spirits'. The point is that *because* of this, the former are more likely to *see themselves* as criminals (with the record to prove it!), and actually *become* that which everyone seems to be telling them they already are. Edwin Lemert takes this point a step further when he distinguishes between *primary* and *secondary* deviations. The *primary* deviation may be a simple act of vandalism or rowdy behaviour (or it could be something *physical* which constitutes a mark of stigma), but that in itself does not launch the individual onto a 'deviant career'. That comes from the response of others *to it* – the labelling of the individual as a 'hooligan' or a 'thug' (or a 'freak'). When the individual internalises the label, believing that he or she has little choice other than to act the part, thus taking on the *identity of the deviant*, then secondary deviation occurs. Give some thought to what is being said here for a moment – Lemert is not only saying that deviance only exists where people perceive it to exist, but that criminality is caused *not* by the 'criminal' but by those *other people*. And the process does not stop there. Once 'society' reacts to what is perceived as a problem of 'deviance', then the authorities get involved to try to 'deal with the problem', which of course draws attention to it, creating 'moral panics', and giving rise to an 'amplification of deviance' (Cohen, 1972).

## EXERCISE 7.3 Experiencing labelling

Can you think of any examples of labelling from your own experiences? Try not to focus just on examples where you may have been the *victim* of labelling, but on where you have been involved in labelling others as well. Try to follow through the labelling *process* as a story, beginning with an initial act, developing through the reactions to that act and the subsequent response to those reactions, and if possible to the point of any wider consequences of it.

In this example, we have a rich blend of the key concepts in the interactionist tradition – Cooley's looking-glass self ('I see myself as others see me'), Thomas's 'definition of the situation' ('If I perceive something to be true it becomes true'), Becker's 'labelling theory', and of course, the view that labels and definitions are achieved through a process of 'becoming', and are akin to 'careers'. It also serves to reinforce the view that interactionists by and large – and in the true spirit of pragmatism – seek to champion the oppressed, the misunderstood, the 'outsiders'. Becker does not *judge* his 'deviants', his marijuana users and his jazz musicians, but rather provides a space for their stories to be heard. Goffman, similarly, has shown a particular interest in *unusual* inter-actions, such as how people react to other persons who are noticeably *different* from them – those who carry with them 'stigmas', symbols of what Goffman (1963) calls 'spoiled identities' (perhaps a scar or a burn-mark, perhaps a speech impediment, or any number of other examples you might think of yourself). For both Becker and Goffman, the label of deviancy or stigma is not an inherent property of the 'deviant' or the stigmatised person, but is constructed within the relationship these 'outsiders' have to others in 'mainstream' society. From such careful insights emerges a challenging sociological account not only of how such a process of social exclusion takes place, but how, in turn, it serves to reproduce the dominant social order, by excluding from its visible frame those which it considers to be 'different'. Social order is dependent upon inmates, stigmatised persons and other such 'deviants' exhibiting 'good adjustment' to their roles – 'fitting in', doing what soci-ety *expects* them to do – and not showing up the obvious contradictions inherent within the so-called 'tolerant' society. For Goffman, Becker and others in this tradition, this social order, with its pretence of toler-ance and plurality, is not only fragile, but is also deeply hypocritical, reliant as it is upon the 'hushing up' of deviants and voices of difference. Such deviants are kept safe and secure in their cells on the margins of society so as not to embarrass and disrupt the smooth flow of social reproduction.

There is clearly a strong *politics* to these ideas, but it is not one that is developed explicitly by the interactionists themselves. Instead, that is left to the structuralists, who we discuss in Chapter 9. There is a close affinity between interactionism and structuralism, and it is worth bear-ing this in mind when you come to read that chapter. On the whole, though, interactionists have dealt with these matters at the more descriptive level of the actors involved in the situations themselves.

A case in point is how Goffman describes the strategies used by 'stigmatised' persons to resist the process of labelling in difficult social interactions and thus 'stay in charge' of the situation: how they might, for example, either withdraw from such potentially embarrassing encounters, or make a special effort to conceal their stigma, or even turn the tables on the audience by being unexpectedly open about it (for example, the person with a speech impediment who consciously makes jokes about it when talking to others). In each case, the point is to minimise embarrassment. Another fine example is Goffman's (1963) analysis of how individuals exercise what he calls **civil inattention**, employing a range of strategies to cope with the severe complexity and unpredictability of modern life (as beautiful an example of Durkheimian sociology as has ever been produced!), so as to avoid being dragged into 'out-of-frame activity', a situation over which she or he has no control. Every person who has pretended not to see the homeless person asking for some small change, or buried herself in a newspaper so as not to have to engage with the overly chatty commuter on the train in the morning, will surely understand what Goffman means by this.

The theory of labelling, then, goes way beyond the simple description of a particular social relationship, say, between a teacher and a pupil or a police officer and a teenager. It defines a process that carries on deep into our mundane, everyday experiences, in how we react to the world around us. It is as much about what we *don't* see as it is about what we do see, about the places we *avoid* as much as about where we go. It is about how we exclude that which we perceive to be threatening, that which brings unwanted complexity into our lives. It is, in effect, nothing less than *how we define our worlds*. And although in sociology those in the interactionist tradition have tended to focus on labelling as a process of interaction between people, there is nothing inherent in the idea that demands this. For example, Alexander Wendt (1999) has made use of it as a method for interpreting interactions between entire states in the international political arena, suggesting that relations between states are the product of perception, such as whether one state perceives another to be a threat and engages with it accordingly.

## Summary and final thoughts

So, the point of this chapter has been to introduce you to a perspective unlike any other we have so far encountered. While functionalists, Marxists, conflict theorists and even feminists tend to focus on the *bigger* picture, the invisible processes that drive society, and exchange theorists adhere to a heavily scientific approach to what people do, interactionists prefer to go about the business of finding out (and taking seriously) what people think, feel and believe about the world around them. It tells us, in a nutshell, that the world really is what you make it!

There is little doubt that interactionism is *exciting*. It approaches society from the 'bottom up', from the point of view of those *involved* in it, who give meaning to it. It speaks for, and to, the underdog, who has been otherwise marginalised by society and by sociology, dismissed as a 'deviant' or reduced to being the 'product' of something else. It takes seriously those little things, those 'ways of life', that *matter to us*. It strolls into our social worlds, which mean little in the great scheme of things but for us are full of passion and meaning, and it does not try to judge us, or 'explain' us, but rather to tell our stories.

As a perspective in sociology, interactionism seems a world away from all the other perspectives we have so far covered. While it overlaps to some extent with functionalism, both being normative approaches that discuss such terms as 'role' and 'socialisation', how these two approaches go about such a discussion is markedly different – functionalists start from the top (social structure) and work down to the level of the individual, while interactionists start with the actor as a creative and intelligent agent. And while it has common ancestry with exchange theory, its insistence upon the fluid and unpredictable nature of the self detaches it entirely from that particular tradition, with its scientific pretensions.

But is it useful? All in all, the extent to which one is convinced by the interactionist argument depends largely on how one takes the suggestion – from Mead and Cooley – that the self is socially produced in this way, and how one feels about the pragmatic methodological claim that social researchers can never 'know' the truth of any situation. Many of my students thus seem drawn to interactionism precisely because it seems to speak to us as people – it respects us for our creativity, it pays attention to the meanings we give to our situations. They may also be drawn to its simplicity, its refusal to impose big theoretical schemes upon how we live our daily lives. And, of course, many are drawn to it because it seems to speak on behalf of those 'little people', the deviants and outsiders, the repressed and misunderstood, and because its research is somehow 'sexy', akin to the work of a private investigator messing around in hip and seedy environments. All of this adds to its charm, and there is no doubt that it carries an implicit politics, especially in its work on labelling, which appeals to anyone who has ever challenged authority. In fact, many Marxists turned to labelling theory to help them better understand the dynamics of criminality within the capitalist structure. However, its critics would point out that its simplicity is actually its weakness, because, appealing though it is, interactionism is actually of only limited use. On its own, it cannot help us understand social change or large-scale power structures. Curiously, one critical voice, which emerged out of the interactionist tradition itself, states that for all its glorification of subjectivity and meaning, the interactionist tradition is actually rather tame and mainstream, it still takes certain things for granted in its approach to the world, and doesn't go far enough to show how even the most basic things we do involve negotiation and the social production of understanding. Such a perspective is ethnomethodology, and we turn to it now.

## Key terms

*Definitions for the key terms listed below can be found in the Glossary on page 227.*

- Behaviourism
- Civil inattention
- Ethnographic methods
- 'I' and 'me'
- Impression management

- Interpretation
- Labelling
- Looking-glass self
- Pragmatism
- Socialisation

# Biographies

*Short biographical descriptions for the names listed below can be found on page 240.*

- Howard Becker
- Herbert Blumer
- Charles Horton Cooley
- Erving Goffman

- George Herbert Mead
- Robert Ezra Park
- Georg Simmel

# 8 | Ethnomethodology

In this chapter we will be:

- discussing the innovative sociological perspective called ethnomethodology;
- summarising the criticisms ethnomethodology makes of all other sociological perspectives;
- pointing out the similarities, and differences, between ethnomethodology and interactionism;
- showing how ethnomethodology derives from a philosophical approach known as 'phenomenology';
- giving examples of where even sociologists take 'common sense' for granted;
- looking at how ethnomethodologists take a particular interest in studying everyday conversations between people.

## The social construction of reality

In this chapter, I want to introduce you to a sociological perspective known as ethnomethodology. Don't confuse this with 'ethnography', a term we came across in the previous chapter (many students do – and I once sat in on a colleague's class and heard him unduly conflate the two, so nobody is perfect!). Ethnography is a qualitative research method, whereas ethnomethodology is a very distinctive way of approaching the idea of society, a radically subjectivist theory which first emerged in the 1960s (see Turner, 1974, for a good collection of essays). The very name seems rather intimidating, and be warned: this is not an easy perspective to grasp – which is rather ironic, really, because the whole point of ethnomethodology is to bring 'common sense' to the foreground of sociological analysis. In order to try to make sense of ethnomethodology, we need to touch on a whole range of complex philosophical ideas, and in particular something called **phenomenology**. Probably the best way to off-set any potential confusion here is to imagine a single, broader school of thought across philosophy and the social sciences which we can call **social constructionism**. This broad school of thought is concerned first and foremost with how people *experience* the world. Rather than take for granted that a world 'out there' exists independently of our perception of it, which we as social scientists can therefore 'study' (the approach taken by most of the perspectives we have covered so far), social constructionists argue that this reality is the product, not the producer, of human perception – it is *socially constructed*. 'Phenomenology' is the name given to a philosophical tradition which interrogates human consciousness, and provides the foundations for the *sociological* theory of ethnomethodology (in much the same way as exchange theory derives from the psychological theory of behaviourism, or interactionism is the sociological manifestation of the philosophy of pragmatism). They overlap, as part of the broader movement of social constructionism, but ethnomethodology addresses distinctly sociological concerns. You may also find, as you work your way through this chapter, that ethnomethodology bears a striking resemblance to interactionism, and you may find it difficult to distinguish between the two. This is understandable, because at a superficial level they are very closely related, so try your best to understand the differences between them, and what makes ethnomethodology distinct.

So, the core concept underpinning ethnomethodology is of the social construction of reality, and the best way of explaining this is to go back to the work of our old friend Emile Durkheim, whose famous work *Suicide* (1897) is taken as the complete opposite of such a social constructionist approach. From here, we can move to the ethnomethodological critique of Durkheim, and that should provide us with a way in to understanding what ethnomethodology actually *is*. But first, here is a little exercise for you – an unusual one, perhaps, but one which will make sense later.

**EXERCISE 8.1 Take some time out...**

Enjoy a movie and a book. Take some time to watch the classic film *Twelve Angry Men*, starring Henry Fonda, and list the reasons the different jury members have for reaching their initial decisions about the case. Take some time as well to read the classic novel by Albert Camus, *L'Etranger*, which is usually translated into English as *The Outsider*, and pay attention to the changes in how the central character, Merseult, is perceived as the book progresses. Hopefully these exercises will make more sense to you later on!

Now, back to the chapter. As we have already mentioned, when Durkheim wanted to prove that sociology was a legitimate discipline, he did so by setting it up against a rival voice, that of psychology. He then chose a subject matter that appeared, on the surface, to be the most personal and intimate subject matter he could have chosen – suicide. His point was simple – ostensibly, suicide is a matter of one's individual psychology, one's state of mind, but, if we examine it more closely, we can see that suicide can also be the result of social and structural factors, pertaining to the extent to which the individual is integrated into the norms and values of the wider society. Sociology, then, has something distinct to offer even to the study of this most personal of subjects.

Nobody would deny that Durkheim's project – his defence of sociology – was undertaken with the best of intentions. But how did he go about proving his case? Quite simply, he took countries with high suicide rates as his starting point, and proceeded to explore the socio-cultural factors associated with those societies. But how did he know that those suicide rates, taken from official statistics, actually represented 'real' suicides? The answer is he didn't – there was no way he could have known this, and it was not important for him to question the validity of those statistics. The suicide rates he based his study on were, for him, 'social facts', 'truths' external to individual perception or interpretation. It is this assumption, which underpins his methodology, rather than his noble attempt to champion the cause of sociology against other disciplines, that has been subjected to intense criticism, not least by the ethnomethodologists.

Of course, the case against Durkheim and his legacy of structural sociology had already been made long before this, and was already a mainstream voice within the sociological canon, thanks to the efforts of the interactionists who we discussed in the previous chapter. For such scholars, schooled in the Chicago tradition, we can never really know the truth of a situation, we can only discover the meanings given to it by its participants, and from there conduct our research. Ethnomethodology is also concerned with understanding meanings, but wants to go even further into investigating precisely how these meanings are produced. If ethnomethodology splintered from interactionism with the publication in 1967 of **Harold Garfinkel**'s *Studies in Ethnomethodology*, it did so precisely because interactionism did not go far enough – it recognised the impossibility of 'knowing' the truth, but proceeded none the less to produce research based on observations that were still, to some extent, taken for granted. Let us imagine that the subject matter of sociological enquiry is an iceberg. Durkheim's critique of psychological accounts only examines the tip of the iceberg – the rest is left unexplored so, for example, it is taken for granted that suicide rates reflect real suicides. Interactionists reveal half the iceberg – they warn us that there is more to the story than we had hitherto imagined, that such statistics are problematic, but they do not give us the tools to examine what lies beneath the surface, they merely tell us that it is there. Ethnomethodologists would dive to the bottom of the ocean if necessary, to study the foundations upon which the iceberg is built, to examine how it is that the things we take for granted as social facts are actually produced. In short, ethnomethodologists are interested in carrying out rigorous scientific explorations of how the world in which we live – a world which necessarily has to be full of things we take for granted – is, in fact, produced and reproduced through the most mundane and banal of everyday actions and interactions. Suddenly, thanks to ethnomethodology, those everyday activities which sociology, even in its interactionist form, had hitherto not deemed worthy of academic interrogation – from how we get out of bed in the morning to how we speak to each other and how we make decisions at home or at work – are legitimate objects of enquiry, because only by understanding those can we honestly have anything meaningful to say about the broader society we all share. Ethnomethodologists study people and the methods they employ as they go about their daily lives – indeed, ethnomethodology literally means the study of the methods (-*methodology*) of people (*ethno-*).

This is precisely what ethnomethodologists such as Garfinkel (1967), J. Maxwell Atkinson (1978) and Jack Douglas (1967) sought to do when they undertook research into suicide rates. For them, a suicide statistic was not a social fact, but rather the outcome of a *social process*. Processes are always fragile and arbitrary – there is no singular set course that a process takes, but rather the course is dependent upon a variety of situations that could happen along the way. History tells us that Christopher Columbus 'discovered' the new world by setting sail westwards with a view to reaching Asia. A ship can set sail on a predetermined course but any number of factors, from heavy winds to a drunken steersman, can force it to deviate from that path. So, in the case of suicide, the ethnomethodologists asked how it is that some deaths become categorised as suicides, while others do not. What are the processes and circumstances at play in producing the social 'facts' that Durkheim took for granted? It is important to note that this has nothing to do with whether a death was actually the result of a person taking her or his own life. This is a reality that can rarely be known. The best we can do is piece together the evidence surrounding the death and come up with our own conclusion. Two bodies can be found in almost identical situations, yet one can be categorised as a suicide, while the other is not. Rather than being a foregone conclusion, a straightforward journey to a preset destination, it is quite an *accomplishment* for a death to be categorised as a suicide, because to be labelled thus is subject to all manner of metaphorical heavy winds and drunken steersmen. Think about the process a death has to go through before it is officially defined as a suicide. First of all, a body has to be found. The police officer on the scene has to make an initial judgement. A suicide note may or may not have been found. A coroner is brought in to lend her or his scientific 'expertise' to the situation. The coroner considers first of all the type of death – some, such as drug overdoses, are more commonly associated with suicides than others. Then the coroner considers the way the death was carried out, including the location and the degree of planning – suicides tend to be deliberately planned. The mental and personal state of the victim is also taken into consideration. The coroner makes a final assessment that is presented to a courtroom, largely based on how the death in question compares with a 'typical' template for a suicide. The moods and prejudices of the coroner and others on that day are quietly influential in determining the outcome of the process.

Ethnomethodological claims that official statistics do not represent 'actual' events thus make use of '**labelling** theory' (which we covered in the previous chapter as an aspect of interactionism) to show how prejudicial assumptions about 'causes' and official statistics are actually used to provide justification for each other. According to Atkinson (1978), coroners and others concerned with labelling deaths as suicides begin with certain pre-conceptions about what constitute 'typical' suicides, and these preconceptions duly 'become' scientific facts that are then used to *explain* a death as a suicide. When the 'common sense' preconception and the causal factor become interchangeable, the situation becomes tautological. Aaron Cicourel (1968) gives another example of this in the case of juvenile justice. According to his study, officials involved in making decisions about juvenile crime begin with the presumption that delinquency is more commonplace among youths from 'broken homes', which results in unequal treatment and statistical misinterpretation. The tautology is that while, on the one hand, the police records that show how juvenile delinquency is often caused by this particular family background are validated on the basis of these prejudices, on the other, the unfounded assumptions themselves are given legitimacy on the basis of these police statistics.

Another good example of how social 'facts' are instead constructed through social processes comes from Sidney Lumet's classic film, *Twelve Angry Men*, based on a play by Reginald Rose (which I asked you to watch in the previous exercise, for the following reason). In this case, the 'fact' that is subjected to scrutiny is the guilt associated with a young man on trial for murder. As with the example of suicide, we cannot 'know' whether a person is guilty or not, we can only evaluate the evidence and come up with a tentative definition of the situation. However, many factors are at play between the discovery of a crime and the announcement of a guilty verdict, not least those that influence the decision of the jury. Indeed, it is in the study of court-room behaviour – of how judicial decisions made by judges, juries, coroners and others were produced and how they were subsequently interpreted by others such that they formed the basis of law – that the perspective that would become known as ethnomethodology was first formulated (Garfinkel, 1949; see also Cicourel, 1968; Atkinson and Drew, 1979), and the term itself was first used by Garfinkel during the famous Chicago jury project, in which a jury room in Wichita, Kansas, was 'bugged' to allow researchers to analyse the methods used by jurors to make their decisions (Kalven and Zeisel, 1967). The film is a good representation of these concerns. It is set in a jury room, where at the beginning eleven men seem convinced that the young man accused of the murder is guilty. Guilt as a social fact is about to be constructed, but one juror, himself not overly committed to the innocence of the young man, asks for more time to discuss the case. As the story progresses, and the jurors examine in greater detail the evidence, one by one they convert to his cause, and the various reasons for their hasty decision of earlier are made apparent. The film shows just how arbitrary as important a decision as whether a man is guilty of murder or not, whether or not someone is to be sentenced to death, can be, dependent as it is on the whims, moods and prejudices of those people involved in making the decision.

So, these are examples of how 'reality' as we know it is socially constructed. As I have already indicated, the concept of the *social construction of reality* pre-dates Garfinkel and his associates, rooted as it is in the philosophical tradition known as phenomenology, upon which ethnomethodology clearly draws. Phenomenology is the study of how people experience the world, how we make sense of and engage with it. Although in philosophy, following the inspiration of the nineteenth-century scholar Edmund Husserl, phenomenology has tended to be detached and objective in its analysis of how the world is experienced by people, in sociology – which was introduced to phenomenology thanks largely to the efforts of the mid-twentieth-century Austrian theorist **Alfred Schutz** – the emphasis has very much been on the ways in which an actor not only comes to 'know' the social world, but through her or his actions, is actively involved in constructing it. It was Schutz who emphasised that, in going about our everyday lives and making sense of the things around us, we routinely make use of a particular stock of knowledge, common sense, which we do not subject to theoretical scrutiny. Probably the most famous example of this approach to sociology is the classic work by Peter Berger and Thomas Luckmann (1966), simply and directly called *The Social Construction of Reality*. In this ground-breaking text, the authors distinguished between the 'formal' knowledge held by academics and 'experts' who use complex theoretical models to 'explain' and 'make sense of' the world, and the 'everyday' knowledge held by the lay practitioner, which emerges from experience and practice, and is largely taken for granted. Berger and Luckmann argued that if we are to understand 'knowledge' at all, we must take seriously this subjective 'everyday' knowledge that is crucial in the definition and construction of social reality.

Indeed, Garfinkel wanted to go even further to show that what we 'know' about situations is very often invented by ourselves, based on the assumptions we make derived from the context in which the situation occurs, rather than from the information we are given *per se*. This emphasis on context is linked to what ethnomethodologists call **indexicality**, about which we shall say more below. To show this, Garfinkel encouraged his students to carry out what he called the *documentary method*. An example of this is the famous 'counselling' experiment. Garfinkel persuaded his students to communicate with a 'counsellor' using what was claimed to be a new form of psychotherapy. In the experiment, the students were to describe a particular trauma they might be experiencing, and proceed to ask the counsellor questions, to which the 'expert' would give only yes or no answers. The expert was, in fact, nothing of the sort, and was responding yes or no according to a random order, wholly unrelated to the questions. Even so, the students drew meaning and order from these responses, and invented a pattern to them. Garfinkel wanted to show that, by using existing patterns to give order to the situation, we 'invent' meanings presented to us by others, that is to say we imbue what others say with meanings derived from those patterns and the contexts they take place in.

In Berger and Luckmann's phenomenological analysis, the process through which individual members of society construct reality can be broken into three parts, or 'moments'. The first involves what the authors call 'externalisation'. This is where individuals are in a position to make sense of the world around them due to prior experience, and work to sustain and reproduce the 'reality' they create. The second part of the process is 'objectivation' in which this 'reality' is given some kind of order, as if it exists as a thing in itself. Finally, through the process of 'internalisation', this ostensibly objective reality acts back upon the individual, influencing her or his subsequent actions. According to this scheme, individuals are both the producers and the products of their social worlds.

As a distinctly sociological variant of phenomenology, ethnomethodology is therefore intensely subjectivist and individualistic – it is concerned with how individual people shape the world around them, and is littered with illustrations of the process outlined by Berger and Luckmann. In contrast to other perspectives in sociology, including interactionism, ethnomethodology does not presume the existence of a **social order**, of whatever kind, but rather begins with the view that the social world *appears* to be orderly from the point of view of the individual. In almost all sub-branches of sociology, ethnomethodologists invert the standard sociological method of beginning with social structures and working down to individuals, by adopting instead an extreme version of the 'action frame of reference'. In the sociology of organisations, for example, ethnomethodologists and their fellow travellers reject the traditional model of treating organisations as systems with rules and functions, beginning instead with the notion that organisations are nothing more than the sum of individuals who have to go about *making* the decisions, *inventing* or *adapting* the rules which then become formalised. Rules are used by members to make sense of, and in some cases justify, their activities, even when they are bending or breaking those rules to reach a desired goal (Zimmerman, 1971). Even more radical than, say, Goffman's interactionist view of the organisation as a total institution within which an actor's performance is framed and to some extent constrained, the ethnomethodologist would view the organisation as nothing less than the construct of the actions and orientations of its members. The difference between an *actor*, in the interactionist sense, and a *member*, a term preferred by ethnomethodologists, is significant in understanding the difference between the two related approaches. An actor is defined by the existence of an *other*, an 'audience' with whom he or she *interacts*. A *member* is defined by her or his role within the broader organisation, which in a sociological sense can be society itself. The relationship between a member and the organisation she or he is a member of can be studied in isolation from other members, but what is key is that a member has a voice in how the organisation operates; she or he contributes towards the rules of the organisation. For the ethnomethodologist, we are all *members* of society.

---

**EXERCISE 8.2  The social construction of a student's grade**

Remember what the ethnomethodologists said about suicide, and why they were critical of Durkheim's famous study? Durkheim had taken the suspicious leap from looking at a set of statistics supposedly reflecting suicide *rates* to assuming the reality of suicides as *social facts*. The ethnomethodologists questioned whether those statistics actually reflected real suicides by drawing attention to the arbitrary and unpredictable series of events which may have led to them. Try doing the same for student grades. I'll start you off. Standing in for Durkheim, I might say that certain universities produce 'better' students, and my evidence for this is the set of statistics produced every year detailing grades. Take the ethnomethodologist position and show how these grades may be unreliable indicators of 'actual' student achievement.

---

Back in the first exercise, I asked you not only to watch a movie, but also to read a book, namely, Albert Camus's masterful work of fiction, *L'Etranger*, which is published in English as *The Outsider*. Now is a good time to explain why – the book serves as a fair introduction to how another aspect of our social reality is 'constructed', namely, our self-identity, our perception of who we *are*. In this book, Camus tells the story of a man named Merseult, who is for all intents and purposes an ordinary, unspectacular individual. Early on in the book, Merseult attends his mother's funeral, and no doubt like many of us finds that on that occasion he is unable to cry for his deceased parent. Little is made of this until, later on, he is involved in a violent incident, and implicated in events over which he had no control. It is because of his accidental involvement in these later events that even his closest friends start to suddenly doubt him, and from that judgement, they recall his inability to cry at his mother's funeral, and begin to wonder whether he may have been involved in the earlier incident after all. Merseult's entire identity, his biography, is duly reconstructed due to a singular, quite ordinary, occurrence – not crying at his mother's funeral – once he is taken on a journey that deviates out of control.

Inspired by a similar view of the world, Garfinkel and his associates sought to show how identity is neither fixed in biology or psychology, nor purely something internal to an individual, but is – rather like the ship that reaches its destination – an *accomplishment*, the result of a negotiation between an individual and society itself. Self-identity, claimed the psychologist R.D. Laing, is formed by individual responses to particular social contexts. Like Cooley's looking-glass self, or Goffman's dramatic performer, both of which we met in the previous chapter, an individual has to learn how to behave in that identity, how to convince others of its authenticity, and how to satisfy the criteria other people attribute to that identity, so as to avoid the pitfalls that befell Merseult. An ethnomethodologist might say that Merseult lost control of his situation, and in doing so allowed his identity to be reconstructed for him by others.

One of the most enduring accomplishments documented by Harold Garfinkel in *Studies in Ethnomethodology* is his account of Agnes, the transsexual. Garfinkel describes Agnes as, in many respects, a 'perfect' woman. Her features, her bodily shape and poise, her mannerisms, all were 'quintessentially' feminine and female. However, Agnes had been born male, and until the age of sixteen appeared to act like a boy. At that point, she grew concerned about her identity, and, after leaving home, began to dress in female clothes. This, though, did not satisfy her need to be seen as a woman. She had to learn how to act like a woman. Agnes was, at the time of the encounter with Garfinkel, hoping to arrange a full sex-change operation.

Agnes was an 'ideal' woman but she was not born that way. Being a woman was, for her, an accomplishment. Garfinkel points out that gender identities are not biologically fixed, but accomplished through a process of learning. This applies not only to those who wish to change, or challenge, their sexual definition, but to all of us. I may have been born a man, but that alone does not make me the man I am now. Learning how to behave as a man is an accomplishment.

The story of how Agnes negotiates her self-identity – in this case, her gender identity – is applicable to other areas of identity as well. In each case, the bottom line, from an ethnomethodological perspective, is that there is no 'true' self, just as there is no 'true' reality, but a negotiated self, a constructed reality, that is the achievement of a process. Perhaps at this point the reader is starting to feel a little disconcerted – we rely so heavily on the assumption that some social order exists, that to challenge it in this way, to question its existence, is no easy thing. But that is precisely the point of ethnomethodology – how do we make sense of a world that is so fundamentally unpredictable?

## Making sense of the world

Garfinkel's *Studies in Ethnomethodology* was received not only as a radical and important critique of existing, 'mainstream' sociology, but also as a call to rethink the entire premises and foundations of social science. Rather than engage in polemical debates (such as, for example, between functionalists and Marxists over the pros and cons of Western society), Garfinkel and his followers wanted to take these debates to a different level. But, instead of simply analysing social structures and social 'facts' from a different perspective, the ethnomethodologists challenged the very existence of these structures, these 'facts'. They criticised social scientists for 'taking for granted' the existence of whatever phenomena they were studying. The task of sociology, they suggested, is not to provide a critical or analytical commentary on the structures themselves, but to study in focus the delicate processes which give 'life' to the structures in the first place; in other words, they should focus on how these everyday things become taken for granted. They should concentrate on what Aaron Cicourel – who often defined his own branch of ethnomethodology as 'cognitive sociology' (Cicourel, 1974) – referred to as *interpretive procedures*.

Ethnomethodology may have succeeded, to some extent, in shifting the attention of a lot of sociological inquiry towards these micro-procedures and away from hasty assumptions about the 'real' existence of social facts, but in doing so they necessarily provided an implicit theory of social structure. Social structure is a negotiated order, rather than a pre-existent one, a set of rules and expectations, which can be defined in terms of its instability. This invented social order, for the ethnomethodologist, is a fragile construction, constructed through a process of interactions, negotiations and often misunderstandings, dependent upon a multitude of unforeseen circumstances and accidents. It is rather like a house of cards or a row of dominoes which appears to be stable but the stability of which is contingent on numerous unpredictable factors – it is ready to collapse at any time. Society is comprised of people and institutions in which we invest considerable amounts of trust – and in the ever-complex modern world, these institutions and people have become increasingly detached from the daily lives of individuals (Tiryakian, 1968).

Remember that it was Alfred Schutz, the unofficial 'godfather' of ethnomethodology, who recognised the extent to which common sense dictates how we routinely go about engaging with the social world. To prove his point on the extent to which society itself is dependent on these taken-for-granted assumptions that are liable at any point to crumble, Garfinkel asked his students to carry out a series of *breaching experiments* (if you recall, Garfinkel was rather fond of experimenting with his students!). Breaching experiments are experiments specifically designed to upset the social order in any given situation, so as to reveal the fragility of that order and the preconceptions that underpin it. In one such experiment, Garfinkel asked his students to consider the relationships they have with their parents. In many respects, these relationships are based on a particular set of ordinary, 'stock knowledge' as described by Schutz. He then asked his students to try to breach this stock knowledge by going home and, for a short period of time, to behave at home as if they were lodgers. So, the obedient students (or, at least, some of them) went home and behaved in an unusually formal, detached way around their parents. At first, many of the parents thought that a joke was being played on them, but as the deception continued, they grew more and more frustrated. Everything they assumed they knew about their offspring was suddenly put into question – much like Merseult in Camus's classic. An everyday situation over which they had always had comfortable control – how to interact with their nearest and dearest – had suddenly been thrown into a mess of complexity, unpredictability and discomfort, and most upsetting of all, they were unable to impose any order upon the situation. To cope with the uncertainty, they sought to rationalise the behaviour – they would assume something had gone wrong to have caused this strange behaviour, such as flunking an exam or breaking up with a partner, or they would blame drink or drugs or something else which they could at least make some sense of. Even when the students revealed the truth to their parents, in some cases hostility remained. The parents felt somehow violated, such is the faith we place in our stock knowledge of particular situations. Rest easy, though, as I won't be adding this to your list of exercises – it is unlikely that a university ethics committee would give permission for a breaching experiment like this to be undertaken today!

This scenario, writ large, is precisely the model of society espoused by advocates of ethnomethodology. Inspired as they are by phenomenology, ethnomethodologists implicitly reject the 'pathological' model of society promoted by functionalists and others (that is, the idea that society, like the body, might have problems which can be 'cured'). Social 'problems' cannot simply be 'fixed' at the structural level in order to put society 'back on track' in some kind of healthy state. The increasing complexity of modern society makes it all the more frightening and alienating, all the more uncontrollable, such that the best any individual can do is try to 'deal' with the complexity as best she or he can. Life is a struggle through a jungle of emotions, norms and values which have to be engaged with head on by individuals, who then have to relate their own actions in accordance with these external complexities and expectations (Tiryakin, 1968). A contradiction often exists between an individual's desires and expectations and those of wider society. Jean-Paul Sartre famously said that 'Hell is Others' – we are not free to do as we like, rather, we are trapped by our duty to recognise the existence of others and by the expectations others have of us. Tolstoy captured it perfectly in *Anna Karenina*, when he suggested that every experience of unhappiness is unique. The psychologist Laing made a similar claim when he suggested that 'madness' has to be understood in its social context, and that 'insanity' often seems to be a perfectly rational response to 'insane' conditions.

Coping in such a complicated world of mixed expectations and moral demands often means developing strategies to legitimise our actions. This is precisely what ethnomethodology preaches as central to its understanding of the role of sociology: what are the strategies individuals employ in specific situations in order to go about living their daily lives, in order to 'cope'? We have already come across Zimmerman's (1971) claim that 'rules' in organisations are largely just guidelines for members to utilise in order to justify their actions. If our actions are 'deviant' or 'immoral', and go against the norms and values of wider society, how do we deal with them? In criminology, David Matza and

Gresham Sykes have written about the *techniques of neutralisation* employed by delinquents to distance themselves from the consequences of their actions and legitimise their activities (Matza and Sykes, 1961; see also Matza, 1964, 1969). In social psychology, Leon Festinger has discussed how we experience *cognitive dissonance*, the situation of holding conflicting values at the same time, such as when we feel compelled to do something which we know deep down is wrong, and how we employ strategies to help us cope with such contradictions, namely, *retionalisations*. For eample, the torturer rationalises his actions when he dismisses his victims as 'subhuman' or 'an enemy of the state', or claims that he is acting for the good of national security, or even in some cases blames his victim for forcing him to do what he has to do. All of these strategies help him sleep at night. These are extreme examples of otherwise everyday processes, the methods employed by people as they go about their daily lives.

At this point, we should recognise a similarity between ethnomethodology and the Durkheimian tradition, including functionalism, it otherwise opposes. Both are interested in the idea that there is a single *conscience collective*, a set of values which we are all supposed to share. By contrast, conflict theory, Marxism, feminism, interactionism and exchange theory all challenge that to different degrees by highlighting competing *differences*. But while the Durkheimian, including the functionalist, emphasises the 'normality' of this shared system, and insists that it exists as a thing in itself, beyond the individual, the ethnomethodologist is interested in how you and I go about *living within it*. How do we negotiate our lives against this value system, not least when we might privately feel that we disagree with it? In other words, while grand theorists such as Parsons tell us what the system looks like, ethnomethodologists carry out detailed studies of how it is produced, and for this reason they have sometimes been called Parsons's 'storm troopers'. That Garfinkel wrote his doctorate under the supervision of Parsons at Harvard, and cites him as a major influence on his theoretical thinking, is hardly surprising.

## Conversation analysis

As we've seen, ethnomethodologists are interested in the most routine and ordinary of activities, because it is through these activities that the things we take for granted that constitute social structure are constructed and negotiated. It is hardly surprising, then, that a lot of time has been spent by ethnomethodologists studying everyday conversations. More so than anything else, the conversations we have with other people carry a lot of taken-for-granted knowledge, yet it is in the shared understanding of these conversations that social order is successfully reproduced.

Consider a very simple and everyday example. You contact a friend and convey the very straightforward message: 'I'll meet you in the bar at 9 o'clock'. Your friend turns up, and you have an enjoyable evening. This is obvious, common sense, and not worthy of sociological investigation, surely? The ethnomethodologist would disagree. She or he would suggest to the contrary that the fact that you and your friend actually managed to be at the same place at the same time was, in fact, quite an achievement, an accomplishment. Quite a lot in that innocuous phrase uttered by you to your friend could have been open to misunderstanding. It was taken for granted that your friend knew which bar to meet you at. This is because the two of you share a history, a stock of knowledge unique to your relationship, which means that certain things can be taken for granted. Similarly, when you arranged to meet at 9 o'clock, why was your friend so certain that you meant 9 o'clock in the evening, rather than in the morning? There is nothing inherent in the words themselves that convey that information, rather, it is written into the context of the utterance.

Let us take another example. When a man and a woman drive home from a bar, and one invites the other for a coffee, there is an implicit suggestion in the utterance lying behind the words themselves. When the same individual invites his or her work colleague for a coffee, there is no such implicit suggestion. Imagine the confusion to social order if a man innocently invites his workmate to join him for a mid-morning cup of coffee only to be given a polite brush-off amid confusion over the sexually suggestive nature of the invitation. You may laugh, but earlier on I suggested that Garfinkel was rather fond of conducting experiments with his students. How did *you* read that potentially ambiguous statement?

Social order is built upon such everyday activities as talking to one another, but it is not the words themselves but their social context that needs to be understood. Ethnomethodologists refer to this as indexicality or *situational contextuality*, meaning that in everyday conversation, each word or phrase is indexed to a meaning that is contextual to that particular situation. Contextual terms relating to persons ('me', 'you', 'them') or places ('here', 'there') or times ('now', 'then') anchor conversations in particular contexts, and it is only within these contexts that the meanings of conversations can be ascertained. The art of conversation involves a hidden process of negotiation. Whether he or she knows it or not, a speaker begins a conversation by drawing on common sense, the stock knowledge he or she feels they share with the other participant in the conversation. From that initial assessment, the speaker proceeds to converse in shorthand, the choice of words and intimations dependent upon the nature of the relationship between the participants. To a close friend who shares this stock knowledge, the speaker does not need to spell out the location of the bar in any detail – it is taken for granted. If, however, the other participant is less well-known to the speaker, he or she may feel the need to be more specific, to speak in more detail. The use of shorthand in routine conversations is a matter of convenience, of common sense, but in fact each such statement on the part of the speaker can be unpacked to reveal a great deal of complexity which often goes unrecognised. Garfinkel famously asked his students (here we go again!) to consider the common expression, 'How are you?', and how it is not supposed to elicit a particularly detailed response. It is stock knowledge that when someone asks 'How are you?' you are supposed to respond in a brief and banal way, rather than go into rich detail about the current plagues upon your life.

The examples I have just used will no doubt strike the reader as ludicrous, and they are intentionally so. They do, however, highlight the extent to which a lot of how we live our lives, and thus reproduce the social order Durkheim and Parsons took for granted, is based around common sense and supposed understandings, grounded in language, which are easily open to misinterpretation. The academic study of these shared understandings in everyday language is associated with the practice of **conversation analysis** pioneered by ethnomethodologists such as Harvey Sachs, Emanuel Schegloff and Don Zimmerman, although we can trace it back to the 'ordinary language philosophy' developed by members of the 'Oxford School' of linguistic philosophy such as John

Austin, John Searle and Gilbert Ryle, and in a marginal sense the later work of Ludwig Wittgenstein at Cambridge (don't worry at this point too much about these names, I throw them in to give you some context, but you might want to check out more about them later). These 'ordinary language' philosophers had been heavily critical of such concepts as 'truth' and 'essence' in language (rather like the earlier pragmatists). They made the (similar) claim that the meaning of a word resides in its use. Influenced by this tradition, Peter Winch (1958), following Wittgenstein, points out that linguistic terms often have multiple uses and there is rarely a single definition capable of covering all these meanings. Winch adds – in much the same way as Berger and Luckmann had advised us to take seriously the forms of knowledge expressed by ordinary people – that we can only make sense of society if we look at language in the way that it is used by its members, to avoid imposing meaning upon a situation using the formal language of the detached observer, because it is through the use of language that a situation becomes 'real' to its participants. Indeed, it was the German philosopher Martin Heidegger who stated that our sense of being-in-the-world (*dasein*) is ordered through language, thus extending Husserl's earlier phenomenology which was rather objective and detached.

The point of conversation analysis – or what Deirdre Boden (1990) prefers to call 'interactional analysis' to give due regard to non-verbal communication – is to show how complex and ordered even simple, apparently random conversations actually are. The first 'rule' of conversation is *turn-taking*. Turn-taking is negotiated using strategies for opening and closing conversations (Sacks, Schegloff and Jefferson, 1974). Consider, following Schegloff (1979), the different ways telephone conversations are opened up, how the caller comes to identify himself or herself (explicitly or implicitly) to the receiver, and how then the conversation progresses. There is clearly an order and an organisation to such exchanges, even those which seem at first to be incomprehensible, suggesting that ordinary people in everyday settings are far more 'knowing' than one might assume. Consider also how, after making a 'gaffe' in a correspondence, the implications are immediately recognised by the speaker and the strategy for correcting the mistake, for 'repair', is already being devised in time for the speaker's next 'turn' (Schegloff, 1992; Schegloff, Jefferson and Sacks, 1977).

The analysis of such conversations, and the shorthand used therein, tells us a lot about the power relations inherent in society. West and Zimmerman, for example, have used this method to look at the power dimensions between men and women (West and Zimmerman, 1977, 1983), while West has also examined the relationship between doctors and patients in this vein (West, 1984), and Cicourel has looked at the role of language use in school performance (Cicourel *et al.*, 1974). The method also allows us to understand how individuals use particular speech forms to manage social interactions, including efforts to generate laughter in complex conversations (Jefferson, 1979, 1984), or how news interviewers and politicians manage their speech to play to audiences, for example to generate applause (Atkinson, 1984; Heritage, 1984; Heritage and Greatbatch, 1986). These are not random outbursts, but strategic responses, guided by the speaker.

## EXERCISE 8.3 Conversation analysis

Try a little exercise in conversation analysis of your own. Transcribe an ordinary, everyday conversation (nothing too controversial please, and make sure you follow all the right ethical guidelines). Look for examples of how mutual understanding is reached in the exchange based on the kind of 'stock knowledge' and 'common sense' we have discussed. Think about how these may have led to *mis*understandings. Also look for examples of turn-taking and how specific responses are elicited during the conversation.

## Summary and final thoughts

In this chapter we have looked at a quite peculiar school of thought in sociology. On the one hand, ethnomethodology is the natural extension of interactionism – like it, it wants to take seriously how you and I *perceive* the world. But it isn't interested, as is interactionism, in merely understanding the actor's point of view. Rather, it is more concerned with completing the project started by Durkheim and continued by Parsons. It is concerned first and foremost with this idea of social order. It shows us, quite convincingly, that this social order, the easiness with which we get up in the morning and go to school or work and talk with our friends and then go to bed, is actually possible due to an awful lot of complex stuff that other sociologists just take for granted and thus miss.

Ethnomethodology is a peculiar but significant addition to the sociological canon. On the one hand, it launches a radical assault on existing 'mainstream' sociology, by pointing out the deficiencies in its methodology. It also makes important contributions to the various subfields of sociological enquiry – to the sociological study of education (Cicourel and Kitsuse, 1963; Cicourel *et al.*, 1974), gender (Kessler and McKenna, 1978; West and Fenstermaker, 1993; West and Zimmerman, 1987), work and organisations (Zimmerman, 1971), health and medicine (Ten Have, 1995; West, 1984), politics (Atkinson, 1984), and law, crime and deviance (Atkinson and Drew, 1979; Cicourel, 1968). I won't go into detail about these projects here – check them out for yourself.

On the other hand, though, in its apparent lack of a politics, in its failure to provide any critical appraisal of the social structure it analyses in rigorous detail, it is susceptible to accusations of implicit conservatism. But while its biggest strength appears to be that it enlightens sociologists to the need to take seriously those everyday, mundane things it had otherwise ignored, and relegated to the intellectually inferior category of 'common sense', its biggest weakness may very well be the same – that is to say, while it makes interesting revelations about everyday life, exactly how useful these revelations are in the pursuit of knowledge remains open to judgement. Ethnomethodology reveals the weaknesses of sociology as a discipline, and sets itself the task of investigating the things sociology had not previously had the tools to investigate, but its criticism of sociology remains somewhat negative. It does not, ultimately, provide sociology with the tools it needs to incorporate that knowledge into the broader body. What does that say about sociology as a discipline? Can sociology make any valid claims to knowledge in the light of the ethnomethodological critique? Perhaps the bottom line is that sociology continues to make significant contributions towards our understanding of the world despite its limitations, made so apparent by ethnomethodology, and we should not be so ready to throw the proverbial baby out with the bath water. Rather, we should recognise the limitations to our knowledge, while at the same time respecting the usefulness that this knowledge still has.

## Key terms

*Definitions for the key terms listed below can be found in the Glossary on page 227.*

- Conversation analysis
- Indexicality
- Labelling

- Phenomenology
- Social constructionism
- Social order

## Biographies

*Short biographical descriptions for the names listed below can be found on page 240.*

- Harold Garfinkel
- Alfred Schutz

# 9 | Structuralism

In this chapter we will be:

- introducing the broad theoretical movement known as structuralism;
- showing how it emerged from the writings of a linguist, Saussure, and was adapted to become a model for analysing society by an anthropologist, Lévi-Strauss;
- showing how structuralism provides a semiotic theory of society, i.e. one based on understanding signs and their meanings;
- distinguishing between the signifier and the signified, and, beyond that, the possible deeper, more ideological, meanings of a sign;
- showing how, according to structuralists, social order is a convenient fiction, the outcome of a system of classifying things according to binary opposites;
- showing how structuralists focus not on the subject as such, but on the wider text, the system of signs, that constitutes society;
- showing how from structuralism emerged a new radical approach in the 1970s which became known as 'post-structuralism', and comparing the two.

## From structuralism to post-structuralism – and beyond

If sociology is about anything, it is about challenging essentialist assumptions about human behaviour. That is to say, it is about making the claim that human actions are not the result of biological or psychological predispositions, or the will of God, or any other such pre-social explanations, but of factors created by society itself. It is curious, perhaps, that we have to be reminded of this in Chapter 9, but it may not have been evident from reading the previous chapters. For sure, we discovered in Chapter 8 that Durkheim sought to challenge essentialist – i.e. psychological – explanations of suicide in order to give sociology its legitimacy. But although that critique has been at least implicit since the beginning of the book, the truth is, many of these sociological theories have remained to some extent dependent upon pre-social factors. Marxism, for example, was initially grounded in human nature, or 'species-being'. Functionalism remains largely grounded in biological theories of evolution. In some of its classical forms, conflict theory presumes a 'realist' perspective on human nature, which treats actors as if they are engaged in some inevitable pursuit of power. Exchange theory is rested upon psychological premises. Even some forms of feminism presuppose an 'original position' of patriarchy. Only interactionism and ethnomethodology – the so-called 'social constructionist' perspectives – seem untouched by this. But there is another perspective in the social sciences that can be termed 'constructionist' – the perspective known as structuralism, and this provides us with our eighth and final sociological theory.

First of all, let me explain precisely what I mean by the above, because it may seem like an odd thing to say, and might give cause for concern should anyone already familiar with structuralism be present when it is said, but it is true. Structuralism *sounds* as if it follows the ultimate Durkheimian line – the determinacy of external 'social facts' or 'social structure' upon the individual's capacity for creative agency. To some extent this is true. But beyond this, structuralism is about the way that the things we take for granted as 'real' – be they philosophical 'truths' or social institutions – are, in fact, constructed through social relations. It is about the way that 'meaning' is constructed in the cultural realm, particularly through language.

Back in Chapter 7, I suggested that there were close parallels between interactionism and structuralism. In both traditions, there is a tendency to use ethnographic research methods (although with noticeably different conclusions). Both are equally concerned with the quest for *meaning*, to which end both adopt *semiotic* approaches – meaning they see the world as a gallery of *symbols*, things that represent meanings. But if, for the interactionist, meaning is something that is *attributed* to a situation by the participants themselves, for the structuralist, that meaning exists independent of any participant's understanding of it, within the situation itself, according to the relationship between the various symbols that comprise it. Nothing about this is particularly easy to grasp at this point, which is why I want to spend a fair amount of time in the next section explaining precisely what I mean here by 'symbols' and how they 'relate' to one another. Suffice to say at this point that it will be necessary to try to understand this difficult concept, because from it flows a vibrant and, at times, politically challenging theory about how 'the way the world is', the *order of things*, is presented as if it derives from some essential 'truth' but is, in fact, an arbitrary construct, mythological, perhaps even ideological.

But first, a word or two about structuralism itself and its place in the social sciences may be in order. First of all, structuralism is not so much a coherent *theory* of society as it is a *methodology* informed by *epistemology*. At its crudest level, a structuralist approach requires the investigator to look *beneath* the surface, beyond the obvious, and uncover the hidden meanings, the *deep structures*, which might be found there. Second, this is a curious addition to the list of sociological viewpoints because precious few of the key names associated with it are actually sociologists. It is commonplace to identify **Ferdinand de Saussure**, a nineteenth-century Swiss linguist, as the 'founder' of structuralism, but Saussure was not trying to apply his ideas about the structures of language (his distinction between language as it is performed, and language as a set of rules, which we will come to below) to anything directly sociological. In the twentieth century, structuralist thinking entered into the discipline of psychology through the celebrated works of Jean Piaget, and into social anthropology through the contributions of the Belgian-born French scholar **Claude Lévi-Strauss**, who not only explicitly saw his work as an extension of Saussure's, but who also found similar inspiration from the later writings of **Emile Durkheim**. Structuralism became a crucially important school of thought in anthropology, and Lévi-Strauss's insights were taken forward by an army of major writers, even if not all of them explicitly identified with the label: those in the ranks included Marshall Sahlins, Louis Dumont, Victor Turner and **Mary Douglas**. Another area where structuralism has been prominent has been in the field of what we now call 'cultural studies', the study of media and of representations. **Roland Barthes** in particular has made huge contributions to this field, but others of note have included Vladimir Propp, Umberto Eco and Will Wright. In the 1960s and 1970s, structuralist ideas were so popular in certain circles that scholars sought to blend them with other, more established schools of thought – **Louis Althusser** brought structuralism together with Marxism in a bid to rescue Marxism of some of its perceived weakness, as we saw back in Chapter 4, while Jacques Lacan merged structuralism with psychoanalysis. Around this time another controversial scholar was beginning to make his name in philosophy and the social sciences generally through his innovative approach to the history of ideas – the scholar in question is **Michel Foucault** and his work largely defies disciplinary classification.

Each of these writers had something to say about society, but they were not producing work that was noticeably or self-consciously *sociological*. And even if they had been, it would no doubt have caused much confusion in the dominant English-speaking circles of the discipline. From Saussure and Durkheim through Piaget and Lévi-Strauss to Barthes, Althusser, Lacan and Foucault, structuralism was always a peculiarly *French* thing. The 'structures' they were describing were not at all the holistic, social totalities referred to in anglophone sociology, but rather those deep, hidden structures, those secret meanings and rules, which exist beyond the surface of a language, or an advertisement, or even the human mind. If Parsons thought of **structure** as akin to the anatomy, or constitution, of society, and associated it with function (and later writers such as Merton opted to divorce the two and concentrate on understanding social structure almost as a physical thing), then the French structuralists were interested in something altogether different.

Having said that, structuralism itself imploded at some point in the 1970s and created its own *antithesis*. The movement was so closely associated with an anti-humanist, overly deterministic view of the world, that much dissatisfaction resulted. Meanwhile, from the political upheavals of 1968 came a fresh radicalism concerned with the 'politics of identity' instead of the conventional Marxist concern with social class. This new radicalism emphasised the *plurality* of factors which give rise to our identities and by extension their politicisation – gender, ethnicity, sexuality, the environment, and so on. Out of the ashes of structuralism thus grew the movement unhelpfully called 'post-structuralism', which speaks of multiple competing structures, fluent and often untraceable, influencing social action. The prominent 'post-structuralists' are ex-structuralists themselves, such as Foucault, Barthes, and the French philosopher and literary theorist Jacques Derrida. More recently, these writers have been associated (loosely, sometimes unfairly, and in most cases inappropriately) with the concept (some call it a movement, but this is also inappropriate) of *post-modernism*. I'll say more about this in the concluding chapter.

## Signifier and signified

Structuralism sees society as a system of signs, a *text*. Let us backtrack for a minute – the concept of system here seems reminiscent of the functionalist perspective, discussed in Chapter 2, and there are overlaps, but there are significant differences. A system of signs has less to do with the functions and roles of parts of the system, than with the way in which each sign, which is representative of something else, interplays with other such signs to form the bigger picture. This is the point at which the structuralist makes a concerted assault upon the interactionist position – the *meaning* of any given situation is not produced by the participant or observer, but by the way in which *all* the components in the 'bigger picture' come together.

Let us use an appropriate analogy. You are reading a short story. The short story is a *text*. The text is a system of words, which only produces meaning when read in context, by which read *order*. If you jumble the words around, re-order them, you will lose the meaning. So, the meaning of a short story – the point that it tries to convey to the reader – is not resident in the words themselves, for the same words can be used in a rearranged version, but in the way they are forged in a particular order. The meaning of the text thus resides in the *relations* between the words, how they relate to one another. Let us consider another text – I send you a photograph from my holiday in the Caribbean. I am seated on a beach chair, grounded in sand, with a blue sky and the bright sun behind me. I am wearing only beach shorts and sunglasses, and holding a cocktail drink. There is a tropical lizard on the sand. I send this to you with the view of conveying some meaning, but how do you ascertain that meaning? Clearly, the meaning of this text is that I am enjoying myself on holiday in a sunny climate, but what actually gives this meaning away? My presence in the picture alone is clearly not enough

– remove everything that surrounds me, and the meaning is not evident. The meaning of the picture, as presented to the viewer, comes from the interplay between all the component parts – the body of me, the sun, the sand, the lizard, and so on.

Equally, like any other text, the meaning of a *social* situation resides not in any particular actor, but in the interrelationship between the component signs. While at university, you notice a particular activity taking place in one of the teaching rooms, and you ascertain that there must be a lecture going on. What is it that gives this meaning away? Surely it isn't just the presence of the bearded man at the front waving his arms around and talking – if he was doing that alone in the room, you would derive quite a different meaning from the situation. Rather, you know it is a lecture because he is standing in front of an audience of seemingly less-than-interested people who have note pads and pens at the ready, because the chairs are laid out in a particular way, because certain props are prominent, such as the overhead projector (let us assume the professor in question has not quite grasped PowerPoint but has at least moved beyond the use of the chalk board).

In Chapter 7, we discussed the claim made by interactionists that actors can never know the true meaning of a situation, they can only present their particular interpretation, or definition, of it. Structuralism – which as I have already said actually shares many kindred ideas with interactionism, insofar as they are both interested in the symbolic construction of meaning – provides us with an alternative to this account. For the structuralist, the 'agent' is just another sign in the system, no more or less important in the production of meaning. Suddenly, from such a perspective, I am no longer the conveyor of meaning in my own world, I am no longer the centre of my own picture! Instead, to understand meaning, we should look at the relations between signs, rather than focus on human actions and their intentions. Structuralists – and so-called 'post-structuralists' – speak of 'de-centring the subject' and of the 'death of the author' to describe such a perspective on human agency, and it is for this reason that structuralism, unlike interactionism, is wholly *anti-humanist*.

So far, so good, but what exactly is each one of these words, or images, within the text? Each word is a *sign*, which signifies some concept or material object. For example, the word 'chair' signifies the material object we use to sit down on, but the word 'chair' is not, in itself, that object. We cannot sit on the word 'chair'. Even so, when we use the word 'chair', we take it for granted that its meaning is already known to our audience. The word 'chair' is a **signifier**. The physical object it stands in for is the **signified**. We take it for granted that there is a natural relationship between the two – but there isn't. It is just an arbitrary label. We could just as easily have used the word 'spoon' to signify the object in question. Indeed, if we were to invent a language among ourselves, isolated from the rest of the world, we may very well decide to do this, and among ourselves, it would make perfect sense to ask for a spoon to sit on.

The origin of this way of thinking resides in the insights of the linguist Ferdinand de Saussure who, as stated earlier, is considered to be the founder of structuralism. Saussure wanted to develop a scientific study of language. He was quite aware that the object we, in English, call a chair is called something else in other languages, but for him, that was not the issue. The fact is, there is still something being represented, a signified object, that is true to any society, regardless of the arbitrary label they attach to it. Thus, there is a difference within the study of language between the actual act of speech or communication, which is subjective and arbitrary, and not useful for scientific purposes, and the underlying meanings, especially the structure of a language, such as the grammar or syntax, which is universal. Words differ, but the laws upon which they are aligned to form sentences and present meaning do not. For Saussure, the act of speech is a performance, *parole*, but the structure of it is a universal rule, *langue*.

On the face of it, Saussure's distinction between the contextually relative surface-level *use* of language and the underlying, fixed *rules* of it seems acceptable, although subsequent linguists have gone to great lengths to critique it. Alternative perspectives on this abound, from those placing greater emphasis on interpretation, such as that of Charles Sanders Pierce (a pragmatist we came across briefly in Chapter 7), to those more sympathetic critiques from within structuralist linguistics itself, such as that of Noam Chomsky (who may be better known to you as a radical political activist but who is also a highly celebrated linguistic theorist). We are not so interested here in whether Saussure's version of structuralism works as a framework for understanding language, or any other cultural form which clearly falls within the broader discipline of semiotics, the study of signs. The real concern is whether there is any value in applying this model to the study of human society and behaviour. At one, quite crude, level, there clearly *is* a case to be made for treating society in such a way. Clearly, like any such text, society is also a system of signs – each sign being an indicator which directs us to a deeper meaning. An obvious example is a driver who knows that the sign of a red light carries the meaning that she has to stop her car. And again, like a text, these signs are arbitrary labels, not natural ones. Why should a red light indicate the need to stop? This is simply a convention of culture – in another culture, a green light might mean the same thing, just as the word 'spoon' may indicate a chair. But the concept of 'stopping' is universally shared.

So, there is a social dimension to this model, but the real challenge is not to apply it to the subject matter of what we might term 'social semiotics' – the study of those signs we encounter in our daily lives. Rather, the question is whether we can actually read those lives in a semiotic fashion, and thus apply the principles of structuralism to the subject matter of sociology and social anthropology. Claude Lévi-Strauss firmly believed that we could. It was Lévi-Strauss who most convincingly applied Saussure's model to the study of social relations and in doing so paved the way for the structuralist dominance of social anthropology in the second half of the twentieth century.

So, what does Lévi-Strauss tell us? As an anthropologist, he is interested in studying cultural practices and institutions, for example religion and kinship. As a structuralist, he treats these as part of a cultural system, a broader system of signs. Lévi-Strauss makes the distinction between the practice of a cultural institution like kinship or religion, which of course is different everywhere you go, and the underlying logic of the institution itself. On the surface, kinship takes many forms – patriarchal and matriarchal, monogamous and polygamous, gay and straight, extended and nuclear family systems. Similarly, people and communities 'practise' religion in an incredibly diverse range of forms, some involving ornate buildings and colourful ceremonies presided over by appointed leaders, some in much more humble surroundings, some in total privacy. For some the practice involves dance and celebration, for others sombre self-reflection, for others still perhaps sacrifice is involved. Some worship a single supreme God, others a range of deities, others nature itself. There is no one way of *doing* kinship or religion. These cultural practices are akin to *parole*, entirely dependent on context, but underpinning them, Lévi-Strauss tells us, is the universal need for kinship or religion, which is equivalent to *langue*. Furthermore, recalling as we must that the meaning of something is not what we see on the surface, and that there is no natural link between the sign and its meaning, that we can only understand the sign in relation to other signs, these surface-level cultural practices and visual images are not necessarily what they appear to be, but rather signifiers representing deeper meanings, and we should look beneath the surface, beyond the practices themselves, to uncover these 'deep structures'.

So, structuralism views the social world as a wholly symbolic order, and we can hardly deny the symbolic nature of the world around us. As Durkheim told us, all societies have their rituals – the 'rain dance' to celebrate the coming of the rainy season, the coronation of a new monarch, the President's 'state of the nation' address, and so on. These rituals serve to uphold the established cultural values of the society. Such 'rites of passage' as graduation ceremonies at universities or the ordeals undertaken by boys in some tribal societies to achieve manhood carry significant symbolic value, in much the same way as familiar symbols such as flags and passports are far more than *just* flags and passports. The structuralist anthropologist Victor Turner (1969) has provided us with the definitive account of how such rites of passage are of crucial importance in reinforcing social solidarity – how very Durkheimian!

At this point, let me remind you that back in Chapter 3, I mentioned W. Lloyd Warner's work on the relationship between American racial segregation and the caste system that is prevalent in the Hindu culture in India. Warner identified the similarities between the two systems – both were closed stratification systems, and so on. I suggested reflecting on this in the light of Louis Dumont's structuralist approach to the problem. In many respects Dumont's take on this is an excellent illustration of what structuralism actually tells us about local cultures and their symbolic qualities. Though often dismissed as a cultural relativist position, this view actually sits somewhere between relativism and universalism. For Dumont, there would be a very good reason why the caste system has to be treated in a way different from segregation in the United States – it is a positive reflection of the dominant norms and values of its host society, whereas the other, rather like apartheid in South Africa, is an inversion, a corruption, of the dominant value system of liberal Western societies. For the structuralist, the focus is on how the surface practice relates to the underlying 'deep structure' of norms and values. While this can clearly be read in relativist terms, in its recognition that different societies have different cultural systems, in much the same way as they have different languages, it does not detract from those underlying similarities, those rules of behaviour, that are common across cultures.

## EXERCISE 9.1 Reading the signs

In your everyday life, you are surrounded by signs of the kind mentioned in the text above. The fact of the matter is, though, you probably just don't notice them. They tend to become very much 'taken for granted'. Try to keep a log book charting one ordinary day in your life, making a note of just some of the signs you encounter. Try not to look for just the obvious – like the red traffic light. Think in more complex ways about your different social situations as whole systems of signs generating meaning. Look for how different parts of those systems relate to one another to produce those meanings.

The more contemporary French philosopher and literary theorist Jacques Derrida (often called one of those 'post-structuralists') has upheld the structuralist claim that the social world, like language, is a text, a system of signs, and that, given that we all operate *within* language and cannot exist outside of it, we are bound by it (more anti-humanism – more on this later). But Derrida points out that it is not the bearer of hidden truths and meanings, but rather of *differences*. It could be argued that Derrida, who suggests the 'deconstruction' of such texts to reveal their ambiguities, is doing to structuralism what conflict theory did to functionalism – invert its core assumption while operating within its perimeters. But from Derrida's insights comes a very important development within the structuralist tradition. We can, in fact, go back to the work of the Canadian media theorist Marshall McLuhan, who, in commentating on the rise of new media technologies in the second half of the twentieth century, famously said that the 'medium *is* the message', suggesting (before there was such a thing as post-structuralism) that the signifier and signified had become blurred, distorted. McLuhan's insights should seem remarkably familiar to the current reader, bound as you are within a world in which the way something is represented seems so much more important that what it actually means – 'style over substance', so to speak. Seriously, just think for a minute about the idea of celebrity. Fame used to be a signifier that represents success in a particular field. But in a world of reality TV shows, media gossip obsessions and the like, we seem to be all too familiar with the concept of celebrities being famous for just being famous. There are signifiers without anything to signify. Contemporary theorists often labelled 'post-structuralist' or 'post-modernist' refer to these as 'free-floating signifiers'. One of the strengths of the 'post-modernist' argument is that the world today is dominated by these free-floating signifiers – for example, the idea of 'human rights' is supposed to signify a particular moral and political project, human freedom and equality and all that, but as the brilliant post-structuralist scholar Costas Douzinas (2000) points out, it has become separated from that project, emptied out of its politics, and turned into a concept easily appropriated by all sorts of political actors to legitimise their own particular ideologies. There is a clear *politics* to this approach – which we turn to now.

## The construction of social order

So, structuralism distinguishes between surface practices and deeper meanings. Hopefully that much is clear. But so far, we have concentrated solely on describing this important distinction. To fully understand the potential structuralism has to offer us as sociologists, we need now to address a more political question: what this means for the production, and reproduction, of **social order**.

What does this mean? Following Freud, Lévi-Strauss tells us that the deepest of these deep structures of meaning exist in the human mind. Jean Piaget, the celebrated Swiss psychologist, has shown us how our *moral consciousness*, our appreciation for the 'social rules' of right and wrong, emerges in stages during childhood, reflecting the logical, innate and relatively stable structures which underpin the various stages of child development. Lévi-Strauss tells us that these deep mental structures manifest themselves as classification systems, which are, in essence, ways of *ordering* the world. That is to say, when faced with uncertainty, we give meaning and order to a situation by locating it within some hypothetical 'filing system' in our heads. It's a bit like you, the reader, trying to make sense of what you are discovering through this book or any other. You can't just internalise some understanding of an alien concept such as functionalism or Marxism or indeed structuralism. In order to process it you first need to classify it according to some scheme you are already familiar with. Your understanding of sociological theory comes from relating it to other things which you may understand (perhaps you already were familiar with psychological theory so the best way for you to grasp sociological theory is to compare and contrast it with that). This is another example of that structuralist favourite, the system of signs, where the meaning is ascertained only in respect of the relations between the signs and not in any single aspect of it. Describe 'pink' to someone who has never heard of the colour and you will find yourself doing so through precisely such a system of classification. First, it is a colour (and not a farm animal). That cuts things down quite a bit. But what kind of colour is it? Are you familiar with red? Well, it is similar to red, but not the same . . . You could say that throughout this book, I have tried my best to apply structuralist reasoning to my subject matter. When I have asked you to try to understand one perspective, I have tried to do so by relating that first to those other perspectives that we have already come across, which it is not. If you can first locate each new perspective within the relational matrix of sociological theory in general, to see how it is similar to but different from something you already know, then hopefully you will be in a stronger position to start understanding what that perspective actually *is*.

According to Lévi-Strauss, this is what the mind does – it *structures* (i.e. gives order to) the world through classifying it within such a system of signs. The most natural way to classify something is by using *binary opposites* (relating one sign to another, its 'opposite'). Edmund Leach provided a famous example of this. He suggested (incorrectly, as a matter of fact) that all traffic light systems posit red and green at either end of the continuum, with yellow in the middle. This is because our minds classify yellow as residing somewhere between red and green on the spectrum. In other words, we turn this continuum into an arrangement of binary opposites based on our mental structures. Similarly, Lévi-Strauss (1969) famously discussed the distinction between the 'raw' and the 'cooked' to show how such distinctions have profound effects upon our cultural practices. And, taking this argument a step further, Marshall Sahlins (1976) has shown that once things are ordered into convenient relationships, *status distinctions* emerge. Using the example of food practices in America, Sahlins shows how *meat* is first classified according to the *edible* (e.g. cattle and pigs) and the *inedible* (e.g. horses and dogs), and then, within each category, according to *preferences* (such that beef is more desirable than pork, and so on). All of this has its origins in Durkheim's later work, particularly on religious practices and the different forms they take.

This seems innocuous enough. But it is worth reminding ourselves at this point that so often these binary opposites represent socially con structed assumptions about what is 'good' and what is 'bad'. That is to say, in surface-level practice, binary opposites carry a deeper meaning, a normative, ideological (and thus entirely arbitrary and socially constructed) dimension. It is only a short step to go from such an understanding of how the mind works, to a much broader, quite radical critique of how dominant power structures are successfully reproduced because a single idea can tap into such assumptions and prejudices. Take those definitive binary opposites 'black' and 'white'. They are colours (well, sort of), nothing less than shades of light, they are not inherently good or bad. So why do we so often associate white with purity and goodness, and black with evil and chaos? Furthermore, how do such associations impact upon issues of race relations in society?

An excellent example of how this process works is provided by Mary Douglas, a prominent British anthropologist. Douglas (1966) makes a very straightforward observation – that conventionally the pig is considered to be something of a dirty animal – and proceeds to dig beneath the surface of this ostensibly trivial observation in brilliant fashion. To this end, Douglas revisits the Old Testament of the Bible, Leviticus, Chapter 11:

> And the LORD said to Moses and Aaron, 'Say to the people of Israel, these are the living things which you may eat among all the beasts that are on the earth. Whatever parts the hoof and is cloven-footed and chews the cud,

among the animals, you may eat . . . (T)he swine, because it parts the hoof and is cloven-footed but does not chew the cud, is unclean to you.'

Therefore, according to this sacred writing, the pig is unclean because it does not exhibit the characteristics of 'proper' livestock (this, of course, is the source of how *kosher* food, especially important to those of the Jewish faith, is defined). A simple set of binary opposites is duly constructed, in which the pig is relegated to the realm of the unclean and comes to represent the disorder and chaos of the natural world against the ordered world of 'culture' or 'civilisation' (Table 9.1).

**Table 9.1** Classifying the pig as a dirty animal

| Good | Bad |
| --- | --- |
| 'Proper' livestock | Pig |
| Order | Disorder |
| Clean | Dirty |
| Culture | Nature |

In other words, the poor old pig upsets the order of things. If Douglas concentrates on how a sacred and ancient text provides the source for a significant polarisation of 'good' and 'bad', other writers have shown how this distinction is similarly reproduced through more contemporary popular cultural texts. Take, for example, the set of binary opposites offered by the cultural commentator Will Wright (1975) in his analysis of the common structure of western movies (Table 9.2).

**Table 9.2** Binary structures in Western movies

| Good | Bad |
| --- | --- |
| Hero | Villain |
| Inside society | Outside society |
| Strong | Weak |
| Civilisation | Wilderness |

It is from these insights into the construction of binary opposites that we arrive at one of the most important and convincing aspects of the structuralist contribution to social theory: how social order is constructed, and how this social order, which is arbitrary but 'made real', reproduces *power*. Make no mistake – what Douglas is saying is that taken-for-granted, stereotypical forms of classification, such as that of the 'dirty' pig, are based not on *actual* truths, but originate from particular dominant cultural systems. Dumont says something similar when he suggests that students of Hindi caste society should focus not on the practices of specific caste groups but on the dynamics of the all-inclusive caste *system*. There is a journey here that takes us from Lévi-Strauss through Douglas, to the radical French theorist Michel Foucault, and connects to the contributions of the radical semiotician Roland Barthes and extends even into Marxism through the writings of the philosopher Louis Althusser.

Let us return to Mary Douglas and her fascinating insights into the world of dirt. Douglas asks us to consider another, seemingly trivial question: when is a wellington boot *dirty*? The truth of the matter, she points out to us, is that the boot in question is not considered dirty when it is in the garden, but it is most certainly considered dirty when it is brought into the nice 'clean' kitchen! In other words, the muddy boot has its designated place. 'Dirt', Douglas asserts, is merely 'matter out of place', something which belongs somewhere else. Here, once again, 'cleanliness' is clearly intertwined with 'order', in so far as everything, proverbially, must have its place. Significantly, it is *all about the construction of social order*.

It seems a radical jump to go from Douglas's anthropological insights into the meaning of dirt to the unorthodox but undeniably brilliant observations of the French historian of ideas Foucault and his account of the origins and purposes of such institutions as asylums and prisons. Yet, if one strips away the historical interrogation Foucault gives his subject matter, one can see that he is asking a very similar question, namely, 'what *is* mental illness?' or 'what *is* deviance?' Foucault wants us to challenge essentialist assumptions about these categories or labels and treat them in historical context. Effectively, 'deviant' behaviour such as mental illness can be described, to borrow liberally from Douglas, as *behaviour* out of place; behaviour which does not conform to the 'acceptable' codes of society. Behaviour, in other words, which upsets the *order of things*.

When faced with dirt in the kitchen, most houseproud people would probably sweep it up and dispense with it in the bin, or else return it to

Source: Getty Images/AFP

Michel Foucault

the garden where it belongs! Perhaps the more unscrupulous among us, or those of us in a particular hurry, might resort to brushing it under the carpet. In either case, it is important to remove it from sight. This, Foucault suggests, is precisely why we have institutions such as asylums and prisons; we need places to which we can relocate those who do not fit, who need to be removed from sight because they do not fit neatly into our classification systems and upset the 'clean' and 'ordered' world of our society. Such places are on the margins of society, conveniently closed off, internally ordered, subjected to specific kinds of disciplinary regulation. But the Polish-born sociologist **Zygmunt Bauman** takes this analogy, derived from Douglas, further and into even darker territory (and here, my use of language reproduces the same distinction I pointed out earlier on) in his account of the horrors of the Nazi Holocaust. He shows how the segregation of the Jews, first into ghettos and then concentration camps, was a manifestation of precisely this struggle for maintaining some dominant and 'pure' social order, and that the 'extermination' of the Jews in the gas chambers was treated as an exercise in cleansing society of its 'Others', akin to removing a cancer from the body or disposing of unwelcome vermin, rather than an act of punishment. After all, punishment implies guilt and thus confers on the subject some legal protection, some acknowledgement of humanity. The Jews had committed no crimes, but were, like Foucault's deviants, the dirt in need of removal.

Such chilling accounts remind us of the price that is paid for the maintenance of social order, but it is important not to lose sight of the core claim of structuralist theory: that the order itself is not 'natural' but arbitrary, and reflective of *power relations*. This claim is at the heart of the writings of Roland Barthes. Following Lévi-Strauss, Barthes is quick to point out that in society, as in language, we take much for granted, assuming some things to be natural when they are, in fact, arbitrary. They become **mythologies**. Lévi-Strauss himself insisted on the importance of understanding mythologies in cultural context: they give meaning to so much of the world we live in. According to Lévi-Strauss, myths are localised representations of the universal rules which govern all cultural systems, which are built around binary opposites – the hero and the villain. The function of the myth is to brush aside the complexities, conflicts and contradictions inherent in societies and to render the world *knowable* in its simplistic form. Douglas illustrates this clearly in her analysis of Leviticus. Barthes, however, takes the debate down a slightly more radical path, by equating mythologies with the reproduction of dominant *ideologies*.

To this end, Barthes returns us to the origins of structuralism in Saussure's two-level account of language, and to the distinction between the signifier and signified. For Barthes, these represent different levels from which the meaning of a particular sign or situation is discerned. The signifier represents the *first order meaning*, namely, what something actually *is*. Thus, the red light is just that, a red light. The signified represents the *second order meaning*, namely, what something *represents*. Thus, the red light represents the command to stop. To these he adds a *third order meaning*, the level of **ideology**, namely, the underlying politics being reproduced in the process of constructing meaning. As an example of this, Barthes famously used the front cover of an edition of the Parisian magazine, *Match*, which showed a black soldier saluting the French flag. The first order meaning of this image, of course, is that it is

Source: PARIS MATCH/SCOOP/IZIS

The *Paris Match* cover used by Barthes

a photograph of a black soldier. The second order meaning, though, is that it represents multiculturalism in French society. The third level meaning, though, is the history of French racism and colonialism from which it cannot be dissociated. In a similar vein, Will Wright's account of the binary structure of the western movie, introduced earlier, includes a third order meaning, namely, the representation in simplistic terms of a particular myth, and the reproduction of a particular set of American social beliefs and values.

The point to all of this should be abundantly clear. Structuralism provides not so much a normative theory of society (it makes no suggestions, explicit or otherwise, about how society works and thus how it should be managed) as it does a method of looking for and at how the world works in a more systematic way. Structuralism does not demand, nor does it require, a political theory of how power reproduces itself, or a theory of how entire genocidal policies emerge from strategies of dehumanisation which are themselves made possible because of processes of classification and 'Othering', but a structuralist perspective makes it possible for us to see things in this way. It allows us to recognise in the world the subtle ways in which power is reproduced, and the role played by cultural forms, such as books, films, fairy tales, advertisements, religious texts, and so on, in making this possible. One of the most famous and celebrated examples of this is Edward Said's groundbreaking work *Orientalism* (Said, 1978), which precisely shows how the 'East' has been *constructed* through Western representations of it.

---

### EXERCISE 9.2  Binary opposites

Will Wright's analysis of the binary structure of good old-fashioned westerns should inspire you to look for these in other media. But let's stick with movies. Watch a few traditional films and note some similar examples. Then watch either Ridley Scott's *Blade Runner* or Quentin Tarantino's *Pulp Fiction* and note how certain binary opposites – such as nature/culture, good/bad, beginning/end – are *subverted*. These are examples of 'post-structuralism' in cinema. Enjoy!

---

## Decentring the subject

One of the key points made earlier is that structuralism does not carve out any special role for the actor within the context of the production of meaning. The basic societal premise in structuralism is that our identities are constructed within a broader system of signs, which we call social structure, and each person is another part of that system, understandable only so much as he or she makes sense within this broader context. Who 'I' am depends not so much on what 'I' 'think' as on how I relate to the world around me. Individual identities are not, then, personal constructions, but social constructions. The Oscar-winning film *Crash* provides a wonderful example of this. *Crash* is about twenty-four hours in the lives of an ensemble of people, from different ethnic backgrounds, in Los Angeles, and how they overlap. The film is constructed around narratives of race and ethnicity, but it is not about racism in any simple way. Rather, it is about *race relations*, the way in which identities and interpersonal relationships are racially constructed within a broader social structure. Each individual – black, white, Persian, Chinese – identifies himself or herself in relation to a broader system of signs, a set of assumptions, about themselves and others, none of which are necessarily real. There are no 'good' people or 'bad' people, there are simply people engaging with one another in ways that cannot be divorced from this broader set of social relations.

The assumption underpinning structuralism, then, is that there is no such thing as human *subjectivity* per se. Like meaning in a text, the subject is *produced* in relation to the external system of signs. It is grounded in language and cannot exist outside the text. The construction of the self in this fashion is what the psychoanalyst Jacques Lacan, who was deeply influenced by structuralism, termed *interpellation*. This is not an easy concept to grasp, by any stretch of the imagination. Nor, one would imagine, is it a welcome one, for most readers, for it challenges the belief that we are endowed with creativity and vitality, and presents us with a wholly pessimistic reading of the human condition. The capacity of humans to be *agents* inspires not only the philosophy of the 'constructionist' traditions, such as interactionism, but also underpins many of the 'radical' traditions such as Marxism and feminism. In denying subjectivity, structuralism appears to deny any possibility that human actors can change the world. This point is directly taken up by Louis Althusser, the French philosopher we encountered back in Chapter 4, whose often brilliant insights blended a Marxist concern with the oppressive nature of **capitalism** with a structuralist account of the constitution of society. Althusser sought to rid Marxism of its *humanism* – its belief in the working class as an historical agent of change – and re-present the Marxist project in wholly structuralist terms, as the study of capitalism as an entire social system, a *social formation*. Once you get through this chapter, and have grasped the decidedly anti-humanist and relational themes that are central to structuralism, you may wish to revisit that chapter and take another look at what Althusser says, this time reading him as a structuralist rather than a Marxist.

Its pessimism notwithstanding, by shifting the focus of attention from the 'subject' to social *relationships*, i.e. relations *within* the text, the structuralist tradition is capable of producing some radical and quite brilliant observations on the dynamics of society, an excellent example of which is the theory of *power* derived from the writings of Foucault. Traditionally, most theories of power had treated it in *instrumentalist* terms, as a resource or an instrument which is *used* by an agent, such that, in a given situation, 'I' have power *over* 'you'. We came across an example of this back in Chapter 6, under the banner of exchange theory, although it was also there in Chapter 3, when we discussed conflict theory in terms of competing interest groups pursuing their own goals sometimes at the expense of one another. Within the structuralist tradition, though, and drawing on Foucault's insights, power is cleverly redefined as a kind of energy that runs through social practices and is inherent in all social relationships. For Foucault, power is intrinsically linked to *knowledge* (such that from Foucault, we speak of **power/ knowledge**), which is objective of individual intentions but at the same time *defines* a social interaction and *constructs* the subjects involved in it. In other words, recast in more familiar structuralist language, 'discourses' produce their own subjects and render those subjects subservient to the knowledge they present.

There are numerous examples of this which we could turn to. For example, consider how medical discourse constructs the power relationship between the doctor and the patient. Clearly, there *is* a power dimension to such a relationship, but it has nothing *per se* to do with *intention* or indeed with *agency*. It is embedded in the *social relationship* that exists between the two participants. The doctor *relates* to the patient in a dynamic defined objectively by the discourse of medical knowledge. The relationship between a lecturer and a student exists in a similar dynamic. Indeed, *all* social relationships contain such power dimensions. Power is thus an inescapable feature of social life. This is clearly a radical departure from those approaches which locate power in terms of inequalities and control: from Foucault, the focus shifts away from the study of how power is exercised, sovereignty, towards how power dynamics produce dominant and subordinate subjects, *governmentality*. This is all a bit detailed for a book like this – but I hope you are sufficiently interested to pursue it subsequently.

## Summary and final thoughts

I have tried, in this short chapter, to give you a flavour of structuralism and post-structuralism as distinctive approaches within sociological theory. It is probably fair to say that of all the perspectives discussed in this book, this is the most difficult tradition to grasp. By comparing it to interactionism I have tried to show how structuralism is in the first instance about the relationship between what something *is* and what it *means*, so it is about the production of *meaning*. But I have also suggested that if we take its core assumption, which is that while the meaning may be absolute the thing that stands in for it, the *sign*, is entirely arbitrary, then we can develop from that a powerful account of how social order is reproduced, and how it reflects dominant power relations. But if we hold structuralism up, like Marxism, as a kind of radical sociological theory, heavily critical of how society *is*, we need also to be aware that, unlike Marxism, it is entirely pessimistic when it comes to talking about *change*. After all, power is everywhere, inevitable, bound up in social relations, and everything is just part of the text, which is inescapable.

The eminent British sociologist **Anthony Giddens** once began a useful survey of structuralist thinking with the somewhat dismissive observation that 'structuralism, and post-structuralism also, are dead traditions of thought' (Giddens, 1987: 195). He went on to explain why, citing the tradition's failure to live up to its promise to revolutionise social theory.

Giddens is rarely wrong, and in this respect, as ever, there is method in his madness. Structuralism is 'dead' because ultimately it cannot account for human intuition; it presents us as little more than puppets in a show. Post-structuralism is 'dead' because at the end of the day, it goes nowhere. It presents the world as a mass of contradictions, a plurality of possibilities but all trapped within an inescapable system of signs, in which 'anything goes'. In fact, in structuralism, the entire world is just an inescapable system of signs. Many accuse structuralists and post-structuralists of surrendering to a moral and cultural relativism (not entirely fairly, as suggested earlier). Depressed yet? You should be. This is a social world entirely devoid of choice, of freedom. But, depressing or not, is there any truth to it? Try to imagine a new colour. You can't, can you? Every one you come up with is not new at all, but the combination of existing colours you are already familiar with. You and your imagination cannot exist outside the system of signs within which they are already existent, and constructed. And that is what the structuralists have always told us about language – everything we think we 'know' and all the things we think we create are ultimately bound up within it, including our own identities and personalities. And that is what they tell us about the social world in all its glory.

So, on the one hand, we have a perspective which denies us **agency**. That hardly makes it popular. But then again, if you think about it, and try not to get carried away by the understandable reactions we all have when we are accused of lacking agency, the basis for this seems undeniable – just think about the example of colours. Can we accommodate agency within a theory of society as a system of signs? Post-structuralism sought to address exactly this question, and remains popular to this day, despite its tendency to slip into relativism. But there is surely a theoretical brilliance to the way structuralism allows us to address certain political questions – such as the way that the concept of 'humanity' is itself a free-floating signifier, capable of being redefined so as to legitimise particular ideological projects.

## Key terms

*Definitions for the key terms listed below can be found in the Glossary on page 227.*

- Agency
- Capitalism
- Ideology
- Mythologies

- Power/knowledge
- Signifier and signified
- Social order
- Structure

## Biographies

*Short biographical descriptions for the names listed below can be found on page 240.*

- Louis Althusser
- Roland Barthes
- Zygmunt Bauman
- Mary Douglas
- Emile Durkheim

- Michel Foucault
- Anthony Giddens
- Claude Lévi-Strauss
- Ferdinand de Saussure

# 10 | Conclusion: The present and future of sociological theory

In this concluding chapter we will be:

- returning to the classic debate in sociological theory, between approaches that emphasise structure and those that emphasise agency, and suggesting how recent theorists have sought to overcome this problem;
- evaluating the claim that we have moved into a 'post-modern' era, and looking at the 'post-modernity' critique of mainstream sociology;
- considering another important contemporary claim, that the contemporary world is undergoing a process of 'globalisation', and suggesting that this term might actually refer to a whole bunch of different things;
- asking what the future might hold for sociological theory.

## Recent developments in sociological theory

The purpose of this book has been to introduce the reader to a range of perspectives employed by sociologists over the years. These perspectives are ways of defining the core concept in sociology – society itself.

For much of the twentieth century, the discipline of sociology was dominated by this kind of approach, which resulted in the formation of the major 'schools of thought' outlined in this volume. Towards the end of the century, though, a number of major writers abandoned this approach in favour of developing more eclectic, multidimensional perspectives. Such writers were largely of the belief that the dominant schools of thought were too restrictive, and merely served to reproduce classic dichotomies – such as between prioritising **structure** over **agency** or vice versa – which were unhelpful. At the same time, a re-interest in the idea of social change, which after all had inspired the classical sociological theorists of the nineteenth century, ignited by debates around **post-modernity** and **globalisation**, called for new theoretical tools. Not that the perspectives which dominated the century merely faded away – far from it. Today there are still numerous contributions to sociological theory which sit firmly within the Marxist camp, the feminist camp, or the interactionist camp, for example. Functionalism has been revived in the form of neo-functionalism, exchange theory goes from strength to strength in the form of contemporary rational choice theory, and the influence of the structuralist perspective is still clearly there in the writings of the numerous contributors termed 'post-structuralist'. The conflict theory tradition has been quieter but remains present, especially in British sociology, while ethnomethodology may not be as popular as it once was but continues to enjoy plenty of support.

In this conclusion, I want to move beyond thinking about sociological theory in terms of *schools* and concentrate on some of these key debates which usually cut across these existing definitions, and fuel much current thinking in sociology. Many of the most important theorists of the turn of the millennium – **Pierre Bourdieu**, **Jürgen Habermas**, **Anthony Giddens**, **Zygmunt Bauman** – have engaged in each of these debates, although the limitations of space mean I have to be a bit selective on which contributions to include here. Treat this conclusion more as a *taster* of these debates, and take the time to explore them further afterwards.

## Structure and agency

One of the dominant features throughout the history of sociological theory has been the sometimes implicit debate over structure and agency. For *structure*, read those factors external to the individual which determine her or his actions. For *agency*, read those characteristics of the individual which serve to *construct* the world around them. Therein lies the old sociological version of the chicken and the egg – do we make the world, or does it make us?

When **Emile Durkheim** set about trying to prove the legitimacy of sociology as a discipline, he was in no doubt over the answer to that conundrum. He argued explicitly when defining his *Rules of Socio-logical Method* that the 'determining cause of a social fact should be sought among the social facts preceding it and not among the states of the individual consciousness'. We are born into a world which determines who we are, what we become. But **Max Weber** disagreed. For him, as stated in his *The Methodology of the Social Sciences*, his role as a sociologist was defined by the need to dispose of the use of collective and structural concepts and begin with the actions of individuals. And as for **Karl Marx** – well, Marx was rather ambivalent on the subject, his most famous contribution to the debate being something we will discuss shortly, but in a nutshell it has been subsequent Marxists rather than Marx himself who took a strict position. But in the twentieth century sociological perspectives became defined by their take on this thorny issue. By emphasising the way the **social system** operates beyond the individual, functionalists clearly take a structural line, and so do the structuralists (unsurprisingly), who tell us that meaning exists within the relational aspects of the wider text and not within the consciousness of any individual. Clearly some Marxists veer towards a similar position, by suggesting that the economy drives history and exercises control over our lives, and some feminists do as well, by emphasising the way the ideology of **patriarchy** structures social relationships. Interactionists, by contrast, focus on how the world can only be studied in respect of our perception of it, and thus individual meanings given to situations have to be taken into consideration. Ethnomethodologists take this interest in how people *interpret* the world even further. Conflict theorists also take agency into account – after all, **interest groups** are viewed as actively seeking to promote their respective interests. Also, many feminists are concerned with the *experiences* of women, and many 'humanist' Marxists focus on the human capacity to change the world through political action. Exchange theorists, of course, focus on the individual but treat that individual as predictable and determined by factors such as **conditioning**, and perhaps are neither structure-oriented nor agency-oriented. In a nutshell, we can summarise the classical debate between structure and agency in table form, as in Table 10.1.

**Table 10.1** The structure–agency debate in sociological theory

| Structure | | | Agency |
|---|---|---|---|
| Determinism | | | Free will |
| Objectivity, fact | | | Subjectivity, meaning |
| Collective | | | Individual |
| Macro-approach | | | Micro-approach |
| Durkheim | Marx | | Weber |
| Functionalist theory of social order (Parsons, Merton) | | Ethnomethodological theory of social order (Garfinkel) | |
| Structuralist theory of meaning (Lévi-Strauss) | | Interactionist theory of meaning (Mead, Becker) | |
| Structural-Marxist theory of domination (Althusser) | | Humanist-Marxist theory of domination, e.g. critical theory (Marcuse) | |

Think for a second about this in respect of the concept of **social class**. What does class mean to you? Do you think of yourself as working class, or middle class, or something else? Why? For most Marxists, class is an objective category. It is defined by factors external to you, by your relationship to the means of production. You either work, or you own. It has nothing to do with what your job actually is, or which newspapers you read, or which leisure pursuits you enjoy. But others talk about working-class (and middle-class) *culture*, a way of life which incorporates holding certain values and tastes. It involves an element of choice which doesn't feature in the earlier definition.

## EXERCISE 10.1 A question of choice

Why did you come to university to study for this degree? Try to think of answers to that question which sit on the continuum between structure and agency. What factors influenced, or even determined, you being here? To what extent did you exercise choice in the matter? Once you have come up with a list of reasons which fit into one side or the other in the debate, try to counter each one from the other side. In other words, to what extent might the choices you made have been determined by other factors, and to what extent might the factors determining your decision have resulted from your own actions?

In Table 10.1, however, Marx himself sits nicely on the fence. This is not just because his later acolytes took it upon themselves to *read* him either as a scientific theorist of structure, or as a revolutionary theorist of agency, but because he himself came up with the definitive account of how *both* positions are to some degree correct. In *The Eighteenth Brumaire of Louis Bonaparte*, he famously wrote that: 'Men (*sic*) make their own history, but they do not make it as they please; they do not make it under circumstances chosen by themselves but under circumstances directly encountered, given and transmitted from the past'.

Contemporary sociology has sought to rescue this little insight from Marx and use it as a way of overcoming our chicken and egg scenario, by emphasising what Anthony Giddens, a prominent British sociologist, refers to as the *duality* of structure and agency. In what he calls his theory of **structuration**, Giddens looks at the way individuals make choices and perform actions within structures. These structures, he says, are 'rules and resources' which give meaning to and shape the situations we find ourselves in. By being knowledgeable about these structures, we are able to exercise agency, which means we can find ways of doing things. Agency is impossible without structure, the present impossible without the past, yet structure itself is determined by what people actually *do* in the present.

Giddens is not the only sociologist to have theorised a way of overcoming the structure–agency divide – far from it. For a start, he acknowledges his own debt to **Erving Goffman**'s work. We have already seen in Chapter 7 how Goffman focuses on social interaction not from the purely agency-oriented perspective of social psychology, in which the individual *perceives* and thus *constructs* the world, but from the view that the individual is an actor who performs a prewritten script to an audience. The stage on which the actor performs is a structure, it provides the rules and resources which make it possible for the actor to properly perform her lines and legitimise her performance. In fact, Goffman's theatrical metaphor is merely a wonderful way of showing how the choices that an individual makes, which she or he is perfectly 'free' to make, and which result from human *agency*, are in fact confined within an existing set of expectations. This is to some degree reminiscent of how the Frankfurt School neo-Marxist **Theodor Adorno** dismissed the choices we make when we come to select our musical preferences as false choices, 'pseudo-individualisation', because the *real* choice has already been made for us; we exercise choice, or agency, only within limited confines. As a voter you have the choice between political parties, but is this really a choice between genuine alternatives?

In his later work, Goffman found himself more and more inclined towards this position, that individual actions were *framed* within socially defined situations. But the seeds of this are then in his earlier work as well – the entire metaphor of the stage is nothing more than a frame which defines and gives meaning to performances. An almost identical account is provided by the French sociologist Pierre Bourdieu. Little has been made of the similarities between Goffman's work and that of Bourdieu but they are quite striking, except that Goffman was schooled in the North American tradition while Bourdieu is European and shows a more explicit engagement with issues of class and power. In Bourdieu we find one of the most influential and important attempts to overcome the old structure versus agency problem.

Bourdieu is an interesting sociologist for many reasons, and possibly the eclectic theorist *par excellence*. He is clearly influenced by Marx, because his work is about social class and capitalist reproduction, but he is no conventional Marxist. He is equally clearly influenced by Weber, given that he writes about status groups and social closure (which he calls *distinction*), but he is hardly a Weberian. He is certainly influenced by Durkheim, given his fascination with social structures and the rituals of everyday life, but he cannot be called a typical Durkheimian. Instead he develops a theory – which has been called his 'theory of practice' – which like Goffman tries to understand our actions and choices within pre-given frames.

Bourdieu's theory is relatively straightforward and rather difficult to disagree with, at least on a certain level. But sometimes he intimidates students owing to his use of particular bits of jargon: 'habitus', 'field', **'cultural capital'** and 'distinction'. These need to be understood but thankfully they do not refer to anything too complicated to grasp. Let us start with the most difficult – *habitus*. For Bourdieu, this is an individual's disposition towards the world, a kind of personal culture, a stock of sedimented knowledges, histories, experiences that we acquire over the years and carry with us, which makes us who we are. Our habitus influences how we see the world, our preferences and *tastes*. As we go through life, we acquire new *habitus*, but we never lose any of it.

By *field*, Bourdieu refers to those settings external to the individual which equate to structure. Fields can be quite general, like the economic, cultural or political fields, or specific, like the university, your workplace, your social club, the football terrace, and so on. Fields are all regulated by specific norms, rules, expectations of behaviour, and to be accepted in a field, one has to learn these rules, but of course they differ between fields – the rules of behaviour in a posh club are quite different from those on the football terrace. Success in any field is defined by how much of the appropriate *capital* you possess. In an economic field, your success is measured by how much economic capital, or money, you have, but in a cultural field, it is measured by how well you know the rules, by what Bourdieu calls cultural capital. Your success at university, for example, is measured by your ability to *know* things, not by the money in your pocket, however hard you try to bribe your professor!

So far, we have from Bourdieu a fresh take on structure and agency, but the brilliance and simplicity of his account lies in how these are linked, and how in that linkage dominant power structures are reproduced. Our cultural capital, what we *know*, is intrinsically connected to our habitus. Different types of cultural capital are related to different social classes. Compare, for example, clever mechanical skills with knowledge of fine wine. There is nothing inherently *better* about the latter compared with the former, and in certain fields, your ability to tell a Chablis from a Chardonnay would mean very little indeed! I often ask my students how familiar they are with the rules of polo, and unsurprisingly, very few of them have ever given this a second thought. Not that they have any fierce dislike of the game, it's just not something they have ever really encountered in their everyday lives. On the football terrace and in the working-class pub, in the nightclub or at your part-time workplace, your success is defined by altogether different forms of knowledge. But – and it is a big but – these are rarely spaces where the 'big decisions' are discussed. Access to *that* kind of power requires more middle-class forms of cultural capital. Herein lies Bourdieu's major contribution to the structure–agency debate: all fields enforce a kind of social closure, which Bourdieu calls *distinction*, which separates the 'outsiders' from the 'insiders' based on their cultural capital. Why bother learning about polo or fine wine if it serves no practical purpose? Far better, you might feel, to revel in the things you *do* know, and the status that knowledge gives you in your own social circles. That is an understandable *choice* we all make, which is inevitably influenced by our knowledge and our tastes, and by our social class, but in making that choice, we are helping to reproduce dominant power relations in society. Paul Willis described this beautifully in his classic book *Learning to Labour* (1977), an ethnographic study of how kids from working-class environments often have little interest in the kind of cultural capital considered important at school: the result is captured neatly in the book's subtitle – *How Working Class Kids Get Working Class Jobs*.

## Modernity and post-modernity

For much of the 1980s and 1990s, the 'post-modern' debate found itself centre-stage in the arena of sociological theory. This was largely sparked by the publication in 1979 of **Jean-François Lyotard**'s *The Postmodern Condition*, and provoked contributions from a wide range of major scholars in the discipline, not least Zygmunt Bauman, Anthony Giddens, Jürgen Habermas, **David Harvey** and Frederic Jameson.

In truth, the 'debate' was a bit of a non-starter, mainly because of a confusion over what was actually being discussed. All too frequently, post-*modernity* and **post-*modernism*** were being readily conflated. Scholars such as Harvey and Jameson (both of whom belong broadly to the Marxist tradition we discussed back in Chapter 4) were rather lazily listed as 'post-modern theorists' or 'post-modernists' as if there was a single school of thought, 'post-modernism', to which they adhered. What these and others had actually done was to take on some aspect of what was being termed 'the post-modern' and interrogate it within the framework of sociological theory (in this case, Marxism). Meanwhile the French post-*structuralist* writer **Jean Baudrillard**, who had been schooled in Marxism, structuralism and semiotics, was developing a very distinctive *style* of writing to describe an increasingly confused and superficial world which others took to be the definitive account of post-*modernity* (although Baudrillard himself was never keen on this association). On the face of it such writers were engaged in quite different projects.

So, what do, or perhaps *did*, these terms mean? Post-modernity clearly suggests a phase in history, one which comes *after* **modernity**. Actually, it is not even that clear cut, but let us presume it is for the time being. To understand this term, then, we need to understand what it means to speak about historical phases in the context of social change, and specifically to understand what we mean by 'modernity'. Of course, the classical sociological theorists seem to understand this well enough. Marx, Durkheim, Weber and most of their contemporaries were all writing against the backdrop of major social changes in the nineteenth century. We listed some of these changes back in Chapter 1. They each tried to identify the main causes of these changes, and in doing so provided us with comparative accounts of the main *features* of the transformations. In other words, they contrasted 'how things are now' with 'how things were back then'. In some cases, it was possible – such was the grandness of the transformations – to speak of 'then' and 'now' as entirely different *stages* in history ('epochs'). If we return to Marx, we have already seen how he described the *capitalist* stage replacing the earlier *feudal* stage. Marx of course had his own language, and he called these stages *modes of production*. That is because for him, their defining feature (the 'engine' of change) was their form of economic organisa-tion. It's a logical sequence for Marx – the driving force in history is the economy; historical epochs are defined by their distinctive way of organ-ising economic activity, the production of goods and so on; so, *logically*, when one such form of organisation is replaced with another, then it signals the shift from one stage in history to another.

Now, neither Weber nor Durkheim accepted Marx's view of histor-ical stages being defined solely by their form of economic organisation, but they did to different degrees accept the idea of transformation. But it would not be impossible to imagine some forgotten scholar, one of Marx's contemporaries, agreeing with him entirely on the theory of historical stages and modes of production, but disagreeing with him on whether a new stage had actually been entered into. Such a person would be operating from within the same framework as Marx, using the same tools to describe how the world works at a theoretical level, but questioning a specific observation that has become central to his account of capitalism's emergence. We will see similar confusions arising when we come to discuss the different accounts of post-modernity.

But first, what is modernity? That would seem crucial, if we are to seriously interrogate the claim that we have moved beyond it. According to Steven Best and Douglas Kellner:

> Modernity, as theorized by Marx, Weber and others, is a historical perio-dizing term which refers to the epoch that follows the 'Middle Ages' or feudalism. For some, modernity is opposed to traditional societies and is characterized by innovation, novelty and dynamism . . . The theoretical dis-courses of modernity . . . championed reason as the source of progress in knowledge and society. (1991: 2)

So, modernity as a historical period was closely associated with industrialism and **capitalism** and the Enlightenment project of 'truth' and 'reason'. From this sprang the artistic and literary movement of **modernism**, which sought 'to transform culture and find creative self-realization in art' (*ibid.*). Furthermore, 'the dynamics by which moder-nity produced a new industrial and colonial world can de described as "modernization" – a term denoting the processes of individualization, secularization, industrialization, cultural differentiation, commodifica-tion, urbanization, bureaucratization, and rationalization which together have constituted the modern world' (*ibid.*: 3). Thus, the 'modern' has been used to define a historical period, an artistic style, and a form of knowledge, a way of seeing the world. The *post*-modern can also be defined in respect of these three categories (*ibid.*: 164).

Now, you may be wondering, if modernity and modernism were such progressive forces, surely any suggestion that we have moved beyond them or indeed that they should be abandoned as projects, should be met with some resistance. However, in truth, the concept of modernity has always been somewhat two-faced. On the one hand, it offers progress, but on the other, it delivers excessive regulation and control. This was the image of modernity so brilliantly captured by the Frankfurt School writers we came across in Chapter 4, and it was echoed by post-structuralists such as **Michel Foucault**, who we met in Chapter 9. You should know by now that in sociological theory it is not easy to clearly identify the good from the bad! Many people champion the positive benefits of capitalism (one of the key components of the modern world), but that did not stop Marx providing a trenchant critique of the system as alienating, exploitative and oppressive. And this is precisely what

Lyotard and others do when they champion the post-modern *contra* the modern. For Lyotard, modernity was always bound up in oppressive claims about absolute truth. The application of scientific method in the pursuit of truth and knowledge was always contained within totalising accounts of how the world works, of which Marxism is a classic example. These are called *meta-theories* or 'grand narratives' – stories that seek to explain everything. What is lost is any sense of difference, relativity and opposition. Just as Foucault emphasised the dynamics of resistance at a local level to the grand and absolutist power structures which serve to categorise everything, Lyotard champions an end to all-assuming modernist reason and all-encompassing modernist politics in favour of new forms of knowledge and *micro-politics*, the politics of identity, if you will.

It may be helpful to think about the distinction between the 'modern' and the 'post-modern' in tabular form. There are numerous rather complicated examples of this, and Table 10.2 is a very slimmed-down summary of some of the key differences in emphasis.

**Table 10.2** Modern and post-modern characteristics

| The modern | The post-modern |
| --- | --- |
| Industrialisation | Post-industrialisation |
| Capitalism as political economy | A cultural economy of signs and space |
| The Enlightenment project of truth and meaning | A celebration of image and diversity |
| Science and 'absolute' knowledge | Relativism |
| Grand narratives | Multiple narratives |
| Bureaucracy and rationalisation | Organising through networks |
| The nation state | Separation of nation and state, globalisation |
| Urbanisation and the city | Suburbanisation and the margins of the city |
| Production | Consumption |
| Class and party politics | Identity and 'life politics' |
| Universal morality | Pragmatic ethics |
| Agency and subjectivity | The decentred subject |
| Functionality | Aesthetics |
| The signified, the message | The signifier, the medium |
| Linear structures | Bifurcation and dislocation |

At this point, it may also be helpful to think about these different applications of the label 'post-modern' in terms of films (because film critics are quite fond of using the language of post-modernism in reference to cinema). Journal articles abound on why Ridley Scott's *Blade Runner*, David Lynch's *Blue Velvet*, Spike Lee's *Do the Right Thing*, or Quentin Tarantino's *Pulp Fiction* (to use just four obvious examples) are 'post-modern' films. It seems to me that there might be many reasons why a film could be so labelled. It may adopt a style or an approach that consciously subverts the *modernist* obsession with structure and narrative. It may provide a commentary on the world which challenges 'modernist' assumptions about who we are and how we live. Or it may deal with something distinctive to the current period of history – like information technology or the so-called 'slacker' generation. Films in the first category might be described as exhibiting an *artistic* post-modernism. The structure of a film like *Pulp Fiction* is clearly intended to subvert those old modernist rules (that a film should have a beginning, middle and end, ordered in a sequence; that is should have goodies and baddies, clearly defined, and so on). But post-modernism as a style need not actually have anything to say about the actual world we live in nor less about what's new about it. The French 'New Wave' were doing this long before anyone in sociology started talking about post-modernity, and in mainstream Hollywood cinema, it has been a feature of Robert Altman's work for decades. Films in the second category can perhaps be assembled together under the banner of a *sociological* post-modernism (although some may also be of the artistic variety). In *Blade Runner* we are asked to question assumptions about particular *binary opposites* (human versus non-human). In *Do the Right Thing* specific assumptions surrounding ethnicity and identity are clearly challenged. Neil Jordan's *The Crying Game* challenges similar assumptions about **gender identity**. Films in the third category which address themes considered central to the idea of post-*modernity* (any number of 1980s films cashing in on the sudden obsession with an associated paranoia about computers and artificial intelligence, or films like *Reality Bites* documenting the experiences of the late twentieth-century's 'Generation X') might of course be very *modernist* in their style.

We can use a similar scheme to discuss sociological debates around post-modernity and post-modernism. In some of his more celebrated writings, Baudrillard's *style* is 'post-modernist', and so is the world he is describing. However, many writers have sought to challenge 'essentialist' assumptions about identity, gender, ethnicity and so on without specific reference to post-modernism as a style or claims about historical change. Foucault and Lyotard clearly both fall into this camp, although the latter is distinguished by his unapologetic use of the term itself. Furthermore, writers such as Harvey and Jameson, who we touched on in Chapter 4, have engaged with both post-*modernity* as a historical phase and post-*modernism* as an artistic style, but firmly within the framework of a modernist perspective (Marxism). There are significant differences between them, but for our introductory purposes we can summarise their take on the 'post-modern question' in simple terms: following Marx and subsequent Marxists, *culture* is the ideological aspect of the superstructure which is dependent on and reflective of the *economy*, the base; *modernist* culture was thus an ideological reflection of the dominant *capitalist* economy; *post-modernist* culture is an ideological reflection of a *later stage* of the capitalist economy. For example, if modernism was relatively structured, reflecting capitalism during its industrialised, Fordist, organised, centralised, nation-state phase, *post-modernism* is highly unstructured and reflects a capitalism that is *post*-industrial, *post*-Fordist, *dis*organised, *de*-centred, internationalised (Harvey, 1989; Jameson, 1992; Lash and Urry, 1987). But it is *still* capitalism, and so while the condition of it may have changed, it is still driven by the same basic principles and can still be subjected to the same tools of analysis.

It is at this stage, in the debate around the contemporary condition of the world, that the British sociologist Anthony Giddens enters the debate. As we have seen above, Giddens was already well known during the 1980s for his theoretical work on the structure–agency problem. In 1990, perhaps as an extension of his work on structuration, he set himself the task of addressing the two most controversial issues within sociological theory at the time – post-modernity and globalisation. He did so within a single package, his theorisation of the contemporary global condition as one of 'late modernity'. Giddens wanted to neither accept uncritically the shift from modern to post-modern conditions, nor did he want to dismiss entirely the post-modern claims. To find a middle ground, he returned to the definition of modernity, which, he claimed, was characterised by four principal dimensions: *capitalism* as an economic system; *industrialism* as a system of production; the rise in *military power* focused around the nation-state system; and the increasing use of *surveillance* within the centralised bureaucracy of the state. Clearly, his definition is explicitly indebted to Marx and Weber, and also to the post-structuralist Foucault. Giddens then asked, what has happened to these four dimensions? They are still prevalent, he suggested, and so *logically* we cannot say we have moved beyond modernity *per se*, but in a radically altered way. The logic of modernity, manifested in these four central dimensions, has been speeded up, extended across the globe, creating a *new* kind of modernity in which individuals and institutions act in increasingly reflexive ways – thus, *late* modernity.

So, how should we assess this 'debate that never was'? It seems to me that one need not 'buy into' the idea of epochal change to critically accept post-modernity as a *concept*. Like all concepts, one can either accept wholeheartedly that it exists, or accept why some people might think it exists, or show how it doesn't exist. That's what sociological theorists *do*. But just engaging, whether critically or affirmatively, with post-modernity as a concept does not make someone a post-*modernist*. Rather confusingly, as we have already seen, post-*modernism* as a movement already has an accepted definition (albeit a rather vague one), which is as a kind of artistic *style*. There is clearly no reason why adopting a particular style has to tie someone in to accepting a whole series of assumptions about historical change. In fact, post-*modernism* as an artistic style is defined in relation to the earlier style of *modernism*. Modernist artists were not necessarily doing sociological theory; ditto *post-modernist* ones. What links them is their critique of a particular form of reason, a particular set of assumptions about knowledge – what it is, and what we should do with it. That is precisely what Lyotard tried to draw attention to, and that is also why the 'debate' was a bit of a nonstarter, because very few people actually read it specifically in terms of historical change. For most, it was a discussion about the claims we make as theorists. Broadly speaking, the post-modernists, following Foucault and Lyotard, wanted to warn us of the dangers of the so-called 'Enlightenment project', the search for 'reason', while others, most notably Habermas, urged us not to give up on modernist knowledge and the Enlightenment project, stating that, for all its oppressive characteristics so acutely observed by the post-modernists, it still contained within it the potential for *true* freedom, and that to abandon it would be to abandon the radical quest for a 'better world'. Can you appreciate the complexity? The very idea of a 'better' world is a consummate 'grand narrative', yet if we abandon it, we surrender to a rather 'anything-goes' kind of relativism.

---

### EXERCISE 10.2  Identifying the modern and the post-modern

Fill in the following table, in which you are asked to identify an example of 'modern' and 'post-modern' forms of each of the listed categories. Then explain why they satisfy the definitions of the modern and the post-modern respectively.

|  | Modern | Post-modern |
|---|---|---|
| Music |  |  |
| Architecture |  |  |
| Television programme |  |  |
| Theory of society |  |  |
| Form of religious practice |  |  |

---

## Globalisation and the nation state

The debate around post-modernity has in some quarters become interwoven with another, equally controversial, debate within sociological theory (and beyond): that of globalisation. Globalisation is something which not only seems to mean different things to different people, it has also incited heated arguments within virtually all the disciplines of the social sciences. Naturally, we only need to concern ourselves here with the way sociology has engaged with it. So far, the major contributors to the *sociology* of globalisation have been **Roland Robertson, Immanuel Wallerstein**, Anthony Giddens, Martin Albrow, **Ulrich Beck**, and the various contributors to the journal *Theory, Culture and Society* who draw heavily on post-modernist insights.

But first of all, let us think for a minute about what this term might actually mean. We hear it used all the time, by politicians and journalists as well as academics and also activists. Many use it to describe the global reach of the capitalist economy, the so-called 'free market' of a world without borders. Some champion it as a thing of good, while others protest against it, claiming that it causes great misery in the world. I have always found such accounts frustrating in their simplicity. When I teach about globalisation, I begin by urging my students to try to see beyond what they *think* it means, what perhaps they have been told by commentators on the news, and by extension to move beyond any prejudices they may have about its inherent 'value'. I want us to go back to basics, and ask what 'it' actually *is*. What I am suggesting here is that we have all been guilty of *reifying* the concept of globalisation, giving it an essence, a legitimacy, as if it is a 'thing', an undeniable 'reality' which then has to be either opposed or endorsed. Good sociological theory should never fall into this trap. If we look at the word, it simply suggests a *process* – in this case, the process of 'becoming global'. As a process, it has no substance of its own, beyond that to which it is *applied*. We should talk about the globalisation *of something*. It may be legitimate to talk about this in some grand fashion, as the globalisation *of the world* (admittedly, an odd thing to consider, but one which hopefully will make some sense to you in a moment), but we can also talk about the extent to which more mundane, everyday aspects of our lives have themselves been *globalised* or not.

It seems to me – and here I owe a debt to the person most closely associated with introducing the term into sociology, Roland Robertson – that the *process of becoming global* can be measured by the extent to which something relates directly to the globe as a single place, unmediated by, for example, nation states. On the one hand, if the capitalist economy does indeed touch every corner of the world and is no longer respectful of nation-state boundaries (and there's no obvious reason to believe that it does), then we could legitimately call it a *globalised* economy, because it operates with nothing less than the single globe as its stage. But when a product is marketed as a brand designed to appeal to the whole world rather than just one part of it, it too is operating at this level, to a global audience, and when I recycle my papers because I am concerned for the future of the planet, I as an individual am exhibiting a direct relationship with the world itself.

Having said that, not everyone would agree with my definition (why should they?), and so as a student of sociological theory you will come across a number of books which look at 'globalisation' in a very different light. In a recent book co-authored with Alexander Hensby, I have tried to separate out some of the different *processes* different authors are alluding to when they write about 'globalisation'. My schema is summarised in the Table 10.3.

**Table 10.3** Eight models of global change, according to O'Byrne and Hensby (2011)

| Process | Characteristics and associated writers |
| --- | --- |
| Globalisation | The process of becoming or engaging with 'one world', in which the mediating role played by the nation state is diminished (Roland Robertson) |
| Liberalisation | The process by which the borders between nation states are loosened, allowing easier flows of capital, goods and people – but not necessarily *global* (economist Kenichi Ohmae and numerous other liberal and neo-liberal economists like him) |
| Polarisation | The process by which economic and political power are becoming concentrated in certain parts of the world, at the expense of others (Immanuel Wallerstein, a Marxian-inspired writer we met in Chapter 4, and more recently numerous commentators representing the 'anti-globalisation' (*sic*) movement) |
| Americanisation | The process by which the world is becoming culturally, politically, economically and militarily dependent on the last great superpower, a kind of new American 'empire' (various neo-Marxists, including Leo Panitch and David Harvey) |
| McDonaldisation | The process by which, across the world, in different nation states, the practices and institutions are becoming increasingly standardised (George Ritzer, a sociologist inspired by Weber's theory of rationalisation and its revision by the Marxian-influenced Frankfurt School, who we also met in Chapter 4) |
| Creolisation | The process by which different cultures intermingle to produce new hybrid forms of culture and identity (various post-Marxists, post-modernists and cultural anthropologists) |
| Transnationalisation | The process by which institutions, practices and people now operate on a level above that of the nation state – but not one that is inherently global as such; examples include transnational corporations or the United Nations (Leslie Sklair, a neo-Marxist we encountered in Chapter 4, plus various political theorists endorsing 'cosmopolitanism') |
| Balkanisation | The process by which the world is becoming increasingly divided into often conflicting cultural and political blocs (Samuel Huntington, author of *The Clash of Civilisations* (1996), and numerous neo-conservative foreign policy analysts in the United States) |

OK, so 'globalisation' can mean all sorts of different things to all sorts of different people. But as it remains a key issue in sociological theory, we have to address it here, and we have to start somewhere. So, if we take it to mean a process, and apply it to the way some of the major dimensions of society (such as but not exclusively the economy) are currently constituted, we should start by asking some core and perhaps basic questions. Is there actually anything going on worth talking about? If so, is there anything particularly *new* about it? If there is something we can identify as 'globalisation' occurring, when and why did it start? What are its principal features and characteristics, and what, if anything, is the engine that drives it? What does it tell us about the world we live in today? And, finally, what challenges does it posit to how we go about thinking and doing sociology?

That's a lot of questions to try to answer in a short space, but at least, after this basic introduction is digested, you can take advantage of whole libraries full of books on the topic, many quite accessible, to further feed your curiosity. But it may be that you find yourself agreeing with Paul Hirst and Graham Thompson, who tell us, in their *Globalisation in Question,* that today's capitalist marketplace is actually no more 'globalised' than it was back in the late nineteenth century. Not everyone readily accepts that 'globalisation' is some kind of new phenomenon, or indeed that it exists at all. In many respects, the idea of globalisation seems entirely incompatible with the ambitious theorisation of the 'world system' pioneered by Immanuel Wallerstein, which we came across in Chapter 4. If you recall, Wallerstein argues that the modern integrated world economy, which is defined by an international division of labour and by the relational power dynamic between the rich 'core' nations and the exploited 'periphery', has its origins in seventeenth-century Europe.

Roland Robertson does not disagree with Wallerstein's claim that the process we now refer to as 'globalisation' actually goes back hundreds of years, indeed to Europe in the early fifteenth century. But unlike Wallerstein, Robertson is clear that the process we are talking about is one of *globalisation,* the emergence and growth of the idea of, and recognition of, the world as a single place. This is defined by two major characteristics: objective, material processes of 'compression' which make the world seem smaller, and the subjective quality of 'globality', or consciousness of the world as one place. The twentieth century saw this process of globalisation reach new heights, although these should be understood, insists Robertson, as a continuation of a much longer-term process.

Anthony Giddens, Martin Albrow, and also David Harvey, who is better known as a critic of the theory of post-modernity, all to some extent begin their contributions to the theory of globalisation by focusing on this most recent phase identified by Robertson. For each of them, albeit for very different reasons and with very different implications, globalisation *is* a relatively new thing, a process resulting from the radical transformations of the twentieth century. Giddens and Harvey both address globalisation within their broader theories of late modernity and late capitalism respectively. Giddens draws particular attention to how post-war globalist attitudes and the revolution in communications and information technologies have served to 'speed up' modernity's logic. He uses the term *time–space distanciation* to refer to the way that the logics of *space* and *time* have been separated (in that, for instance, spatial distance is no longer a barrier for immediate communication), and the term *disembedding* to refer to how in such a globalised world, *place* loses its significance (in that, for example, companies, people, cultural festivals and so on have become detached from any specific association with place). Harvey also highlights the changing relationship between time and space, although for him, *time–space compression* refers to the 'annihilation' of space by time, which – remembering that Harvey is a Marxist – is tied in to new forms of capitalist production.

Albrow's account links this modern process of globalisation to an even more radical transformation in world history, and thus presents us with yet another theory of epochal change, quite different though from that discussed under the banner of 'post-modernity'. A disciple of Max Weber, Albrow is happy to concede that the *modern* age was defined by the centrality of the nation state in people's lives. Globalisation results in the *decentring* of the nation state, as the focus shifts towards the globe itself, and thus, necessarily, brings about the end of the *modern* age and ushers in the new *global* age. Whether or not we want to involve ourselves in big debates around epochal change, the suggestion that the nation state is no longer the focal point of our lives is crucial to our sociological understanding of globalisation. Giddens and Ulrich Beck are two writers who put this into context with the concept of *risk*. Giddens describes the project of modernity as akin to a juggernaut, speeding ever forwards. But what happens when the pursuit of scientific knowledge and progress has negative consequences? What happens when Giddens's juggernaut veers out of control? Beck speaks of the production of *manufactured risks*, and such risks have global implications.

The last theorist of globalisation I want to introduce you to here is Leslie Sklair. What is particularly interesting about Sklair is that while he openly identifies as a Marxist, and discusses globalisation in respect of capitalism, his theory is a world removed from Wallerstein's quasi-Marxism, and indeed he takes particular issue with it. If Wallerstein disregards globalisation and focuses on the power dynamics between countries, Sklair is adamant that global capitalism transcends the nation-state system, and is characterised by *transnational corporations* (shades here of Giddens and disembedding), *transnational practices* (in a similar vein to Harvey), and *transnational classes*. Sklair even gives his neo-Marxist theory of globalisation a normative twist and lays down a theoretical challenge to those who take to the streets in opposition to global capitalism: if capitalist globalisation is driven by a culture ideology of consumerism (which we all help to reproduce), then we need to push for an alternative, *socialist* globalisation driven by a culture ideology of human rights. There's no call for a return to the days of the nation state from Sklair!

## EXERCISE 10.3 Measuring globalisation

I want you to think about this idea that 'globalisation' is a process. What indicators would you look for to judge how far along that process something might be? For example, what would characterise an economy that is *non-global*? What would constitute an economy that is *fully* global? What would sit somewhere in between? Think of some examples of the things you think would indicate these different levels of globalisation in the following areas:

|  | Non-global | Partially global | Fully global |
| --- | --- | --- | --- |
| Economy? |  |  |  |
| Politics? |  |  |  |
| Culture? |  |  |  |
| Social networks? |  |  |  |
| You? |  |  |  |

I wonder whether you included the current influence of transnational corporations as evidence of a partially or a fully globalised economy. Perhaps you thought that a fully globalised economy would require a single market with a single currency and a single set of economic regulations. So, how far down the line are we in respect of *economic* globalisation? What about *political* globalisation? Would the 'end-point' be a single world state, with a single world government? This is what is most interesting about debates over globalisation – that there is either an awful lot of it going on, or not much of it at all, depending on your point of view. If we treat it as a process, then we can better see how some parts of our lives may be more globalised than others.

## Summary and final, final thoughts

Debates concerning the relationship between structure and agency, post-modernity and globalisation, will continue. New topics will emerge that divide the sociological community. Fresh contributions will rejuvenate old controversies. After all, there was a time when it looked as if any mention of society as a 'system' would have you dismissed as antiquated, at best, reactionary at worst – such was the general feeling towards any association with functionalism – but then Niklas Luhmann, a phenomenally productive German theorist whose ideas have yet to find their way into many English-speaking curricula, gave us an exciting new 'systems theory' which had elements of post-modernism, complexity and chaos, a world removed from the staid and conservative systems theory of **Talcott Parsons** and his students. There was also a time when any mention of Karl Marx would have you dismissed as a maverick: Marx was, if anything, a brilliant theorist of capitalism in his time, but what could he offer us in the twenty-first century? Even radical sociologists were questioning Marx, and happier to associate themselves more with the newer generation, the scholars of the 'new left' that emerged in the turbulent 1960s, such as Jürgen Habermas or Michel Foucault. Then suddenly, we found ourselves in a global economic crisis, and commentators dusted off their copies of *Capital* and realised there was still much they could learn from it.

Who can tell what comes next in the history of sociological theory? For sure, the issue of risk continues to be a major topic of discussion, and Beck's star will continue to rise. Since Sylvia Walby re-theorised patriarchy, there have been fascinating debates on the future of feminist theory. Some very exciting things have been happening in the sociology of science over what constitutes a 'human', inspired by the pioneering work of Donna Harraway. But this is all part of sociology's rich tapestry. And you are part of it. The subject matter of sociology is the world in which you live. As a student of sociology it is your duty to be curious about it. And that involves theory. Remember, theory is not something that *other* people do, often old/dead, white, male other people who you are forced to learn about in compulsory classes. It is what makes *you* a sociologist. It is your expression of what **C. Wright Mills** called the 'sociological imagination'. Theory is an adventure, and theorising about the world around you is what should inspire and excite you. Don't consign theory to the nominal theory class – use it in all your classes. Over a hundred years ago, various people showed just such a curiosity about the world around them. We venerate them, rightly, because of the sheer volume of their productivity and the complexity of their insights. You may never contribute as much as them, but few people ever will, and that is why they still provide the jumping-off point for our theory classes. But sociological theory is not just about Marx, Durkheim and Weber, never mind Parsons, Giddens and Habermas. It needn't require long words and jargon, although remember these are usually just shorthand for ideas. It is about looking at the world sociologically, asking questions about it, and keeping an open mind. In this book I have summarised how the journey has so far been travelled. The next step is yours to take. Enjoy!

## Key terms

*Definitions for the key terms listed below can be found in the Glossary on page 227.*

- Agency
- Capitalism
- Conditioning
- Cultural capital
- Gender identity
- Globalisation
- Interest groups

- Modernity/modernism
- Patriarchy
- Post-modernity/post-modernism
- Social class
- Social system
- Structuration
- Structure

# Biographies

*Short biographical descriptions for the names listed below can be found on page 240.*

- Theodor Adorno
- Jean Baudrillard
- Zygmunt Bauman
- Ulrich Beck
- Pierre Bourdieu
- Emile Durkheim
- Michel Foucault
- Anthony Giddens
- Erving Goffman
- Jürgen Habermas
- David Harvey
- Jean-François Lyotard
- Karl Marx
- C. Wright Mills
- Talcott Parsons
- Roland Robertson
- Immanuel Wallerstein
- Max Weber

# Glossary

**Agency** is the capacity to act in a controlled and knowing way. An agent is active, in the way that a patient is passive, acted upon. In sociology, agency is usually juxtaposed with structure, and used in the context of those theoretical perspectives that emphasise the way people actively create the world around them, such as interactionism, ethnomethodology, feminism and some forms of Marxism.

**Alienation** means something more specific in sociological circles than it does in its everyday use. Often when we say we are alienated from something, we mean we feel detached from it. But Karl Marx uses the term to refer to a very precise kind of detachment – the detachment a worker experiences in a capitalist society from their work. For Marx, people are by their very nature creative and industrious, but under capitalism, they effectively sell themselves for a wage and have no investment as such in their work process or the product of their labour. This is alienation.

**Anomie** means normlessness. Durkheim uses the term to refer to the condition of detachment one might have from the wider norms and values of society. It is often contrasted with alienation, a different form of detachment associated with Marxist thinking. Robert Merton took Durkheim's theory of anomie as the basis of his famous study of the causes of crime in America.

**Base** and **superstructure** are the two constituents of a mode of production, according to Marx. Base refers to the foundation upon which the rest of society is built – which is its system of production, its economy. Superstructure refers to the other aspects of a society – its culture, politics, laws, religion and so on – which according to many Marxists are dependent on and driven by the base. The base–superstructure model of society is often considered to be an example of economic determinism, in that the superstructure has little or no autonomy from the base.

**Behaviourism** is a popular theory in the psychology of child development. It is based on the idea that the infant begins as an empty vessel, with no innate knowledge of the world, and thus learns how to behave through experience, through trial and error. Behaviour is thus programmed in a relatively predictable way. Pioneers of behaviourism in psychology included Ivan Pavlov, John B. Watson and B.F. Skinner. In sociology, George Homans used behaviourism as the premise of his exchange theory.

**Capitalism** is an economic system characterised primarily by the concept of the market. In a capitalist economy, wealth is generated through the buying and selling of goods. These goods are assigned a market value, i.e. how much they are deemed to be worth for the purpose of buying and selling. This value is not the same as the actual value of the goods in production terms, i.e. how much it may have cost in materials and labour power to produce them. Rather, the market value is determined by such factors as scarcity of supply and consumer demand for the product. Thus, a product can be sold for considerably more than it might have cost to produce it, generating a healthy profit, which is returned to the owner. In its pure form, capitalism is about private ownership rather than state regulation, because, according to the nineteenth-century economist Adam Smith, the market works best, and generates most wealth, when left to its own devices. In a capitalist economy, some enterprising people – the capitalists – can make a sizeable profit for themselves, but as Karl Marx points out, capitalism cannot guarantee to generate wealth for everyone, because its fundamental premise is exploitation: that is to say, the capitalists or bourgeoisie make their money on the backs of the labour of others, the workers or proletariat, who receive fixed wages for their efforts rather than a share of the spoils. Marx understood capitalism to be a distinctive stage in history, a mode of production that at one point is radical because it overthrows the earlier feudal system (in which the distribution of wealth is fixed at birth). However, it inevitably creates its own inequalities and contradictions, born out of the considerable polarisation of wealth it creates, and is thus ultimately unfair. Marx called for its replacement by a socialist economy in which those who do the work also benefit from the fruits of their labour. Supporters of capitalism, though, maintain that it is a fair system as long as everyone has equal opportunity to benefit from it. Whether a system based on exploitation is or is not fair is a moral question, and much economic debate concentrates instead on the practical question of whether capitalism is capable of continuously generating wealth. Because capitalism is based on private ownership and the generation of wealth for individual owners and investors, it is closely associated with the individualistic ideology dominant in Western societies. In sociology, the Marxist definition of capitalism has been the most influential, although there have been numerous attempts by 'neo-Marxists' to update it based on changing practices and qualities (examples being the inclusion of cultural as well as material goods in the marketplace, or a recognition of new transnational practices). The most radical attempt to redefine capitalism was by Louis Althusser, for whom it represented an entire way of life, a 'social formation', and not just a system of organising the economy.

**Civil inattention** is one of Erving Goffman's most famous concepts. It refers to the strategies we employ to conveniently not see what is going on around us in the world. Very often, in a complex world, things happen around us which make us uncomfortable, because they render us powerless and vulnerable. They drag us out of our comfort zone. Naturally we wish to avoid this so we exercise civil inattention.

**Class, status and party** are, according to Max Weber, three distinct forms of power relation in society. Class refers to economic position (as it does for Marx), so that some people have more power because they have more money. Status refers to one's share of social honour – how one is perceived by others in the community. Party refers to one's political affiliation. For Weber, power doesn't just come from class position – it also comes from status position and from party position. Using this scheme, Weber is able to add complexity to the power dynamics of society – someone can have a relatively low wage, a low class position, but still have power because of their status in the community, for example.

**Commodification** is the process of ascribing a market value to something. A commodity is something that can be bought and sold on the marketplace, thus potentially generating a profit for its owner. For example, an object can be sold for three times what it costs to produce, because as a commodity the market has determined that it is worthy of such a high value. Neo-Marxists describe how the process of commodification occurs in every walk of life, and does not only apply to material goods. For example, the student experience in the UK may have been commodified, in that it is now reducible to a fixed price, its cost in the marketplace. When experiences like this become reducible to the laws of the market, it represents the successful intrusion of capitalism as a mentality into other areas of life.

**Conditioning** is a concept used within some branches of exchange theory which rely on the psychological premises of behaviourism, popularised by B.F. Skinner. The theory asserts that people's actions are largely predictable, driven by the desire to satisfy basic needs, and are influenced by external stimuli and conditions. Thus, if certain conditions are put into place, specific outcomes can be successfully achieved. Conditioning thus represents a form of programming.

**Conversation analysis** is a methodology used mainly by ethnomethodologists, who are interested in how ordinary, everyday and rather mundane things like routine conversations actually involve quite a lot of complexity. Pioneered by Emanuel Schegloff and Harvey Sachs, it involves a precise transcription of such ordinary conversations, and a rigorous analysis of how, throughout the exchange, meanings are produced and agreements reached, even if they are not obvious or explicit.

**Cultural capital** is a term used by Pierre Bourdieu to refer to the kind of knowledge that carries value in particular settings. Most people think of 'capital' in economic terms – money in your pocket! The more you have of that kind of capital, the more you are able to buy, and naturally, having money brings with it a certain kind of power and influence. But Bourdieu reminds us that money isn't the only form of capital that can open doors for us. Indeed, you might have plenty of material wealth and still not gain acceptance into the top clubs if you don't know the right etiquette! Bourdieu also tells us that cultural capital is heavily influenced by social class background – working-class people grow up acquiring a particular kind of cultural capital that serves them well in working-class environments, while middle-class people develop very different forms of knowledge, that suit middle-class settings. Compare, for example, mechanical skills with knowledge of fine wine.

**Cultural relativism** is the belief, popular in anthropology, that cultural forms and practices are different across societies, such that one cannot make generalised assumptions about 'how things are done'. It is the opposite of universalism, the idea that certain norms and values are 'universally held' by all people and transcend local differences. Cultural relativists are quick to criticise efforts to impose some understanding of local cultural practices which derives from an altogether different setting, such as the imposition of 'Western values' upon non-Western societies. Cultural relativists emphasise that cultural practices have to be understood in their own contexts. However, more recently the term has been inappropriately used to refer to a kind of *moral* relativism in which all judgements about 'right' and 'wrong' are to be suspended in favour of a respect for local difference. Critics of such an approach suggest that it leads into a theoretical abyss: if attempts to criticise a particular practice are inherently 'imperialistic', in so far as they represent an attempt to impose one set of values upon another, then all that remains is a kind of 'anything goes' scenario, in which any one action is as legitimate and acceptable as another. Post-modern theory has been accused of promoting such a relativistic position.

**Differentiation** is a term used in the biological sciences to refer to the specialisation that exists in more complex organisms. The human body is such a complex organism, which consists of a variety of component parts each of which performs a function for the body as a whole. The amoeba, by contrast, has a far more simplistic structure. Herbert Spencer and Emile Durkheim both introduced the concept into sociology, to show how more complex societies are characterised by more specialised divisions, of roles, functions and so on. Differentiation is heavily associated with evolutionist approaches to social change, such as some forms of functionalism.

**Economic determinism** is the suggestion that all other facets of the social world, such as culture, religion, politics, laws, morals, and the way we live our lives, are entirely dependent on the economy; in other words, we are shaped by our relationship to the economy, by the money we have or don't have, by the work we do, and wider society is merely a reflection of the kind of economic system in operation. Sociologists who subscribe to this view, many of whom are Marxists, would therefore look at how the capitalist economic system, for example, shapes the rest of society.

**Ethnographic methods** are research methods employed by some sociologists who are interested in finding out how and why people do things, rather than measuring general statistical trends. Ethnography is rather like hanging out with people in particular settings and keeping records of conversations, observations and interviews. Participant observation is a form of ethnography. Ethnographic methods are often employed by interactionists and some structuralists.

**Functional prerequisites** are, according to Talcott Parsons, the basic needs that any system has to satisfy in order to sustain itself. Parsons categorised the functional prerequisites of society using his famous AGIL scheme, in which he suggested that different parts of society, such as politics, the economy, culture and so on, serve to satisfy different functional prerequisites.

**Gender identity** is a concept popular within feminist theory to refer to the fact that gender is not fixed and biological, but rather socially constructed. It is part of the identity of a person, rather than a simple matter of their sexual physiology. It is negotiated in social interactions and acted out by people like a performance. It is also potentially heavily political, as part of the broader 'politics of identity' which emerged from the 1960s.

**Globalisation** is, taken literally, the process of becoming global. Presumably, then, it involves a start point, where something is not global at all, and an end point, where it is fully global. Of course, it isn't entirely clear what being 'global' actually means so different writers tend to mean different things when they use the term. In the language of many journalists, politicians, activists and even a few academics, globalisation refers not to a process at all but to a thing – namely, the contemporary world capitalist marketplace. You will therefore often hear people talking about 'it' either as a 'good' thing or a 'bad' thing, but this usage is misleading. The extent to which there is much 'globalisation' going on is the subject of much debate among social scientists. Different interpretations, accounts or explanations of globalisation have been offered by the likes of Anthony Giddens, Roland Robertson and David Harvey, to name just three.

**Historical materialism** is an approach to the evolution of societies over time which was popularised by Karl Marx and is central to Marxist theory. Marx suggested that we can categorise societies according to how their economies are organised. He listed various types of economic system, which he called 'modes of production'. Each is defined by its distinctive means of producing the goods needed to survive, and by the social hierarchy that emerges in each case between

231

those with and those without power. Historical materialism is Marx's way of looking at history as a sequence of such modes of production, each subsequent one emerging out of its predecessor. Marx suggested the following sequence: a primate communist system of shared ownership, an ancient mode of production based on slavery, a feudal system based on agricultural production, a capitalist system based on industrial production and private ownership, and finally an advanced communist system of shared ownership. Many subsequent Marxists rejected Marx's theory of historical materialism as being too fixed and teleological.

**I and me** are the two aspects of the self, according to George Herbert Mead, the founder of interactionism. The 'I' is the outward-facing self, which appears to others in social interaction. The 'me' is a more inward sense of self, one's perception of self-identity which is constantly being reshaped through interaction with others. While the 'I' is a kind of performance, the 'me' stores the responses of others to that performance and changes accordingly, and can never be known by anyone else.

**Ideology** means a system of ideas which, taken as a whole, provides the direction for a person, an organisation or institution, or society as a whole. For example, people may join a political party because they subscribe to its particular ideology. However, Karl Marx provides a more specific definition of the term – as the set of dominant norms and values which correspond to, and serve to reinforce, the economic base. For Marx, ideas are driven by material realities, not independent of it, and ideology amounts to a subtle form of brainwashing. A good example, provided by Leslie Sklair, is how the ideology of consumerism corresponds to and upholds the economic system of transnational capitalism.

**Impression management** is an important goal in the performance of the self. It is what makes each performance successful and convincing in the eyes of the audience. In short, we all have certain expectations of the roles people have in life, and these are often represented by such things as the clothes they wear, the way they carry themselves, as well as that they know what they are talking about. According to Erving Goffman, it is vital for each actor to match these expectations so as to achieve legitimacy in that role in the eyes of others.

**Indexicality** is a term used by ethnomethodologists to show that ordinary, everyday interactions between people often involve the taking for granted of shared knowledge or common sense. Communication between people does not require us to explain everything, we go about our lives assuming that much is already known, our conversations treating language rather like an index in a book, which makes reference to something else that is not explicitly said. Because of this, conversations need to be understood in their situational contexts.

**Interest groups** are groups of people united by shared goals or interests. Central to conflict theory, the idea of the interest group is a way of categorising people across a grid of overlapping and sometimes contradictory positions. Each person belongs to multiple interest groups, each of which is defined by its specific goals. For example, you may be a student, and also a woman. These are different interest groups, but not conflicting ones. In almost every case, though, an interest group has its complete opposite, that group which is defined by goals that are entirely incompatible with yours. Conflict theorists are interested in the power struggles that emerge between such conflicting interest groups in plural societies.

**Interpretation** is central to the method of sociological inquiry pioneered by Max Weber and later championed by interactionists and others. It is about trying to understand the meaning of something as ascribed by the actors involved. It emphasises subjective understanding, and is the opposite approach to that of the positivists who seek to explain phenomena according to objective, general laws.

**Labelling** has been a popular concept among interactionists, particularly Howard Becker. Labelling theory suggests that actors, particularly people in positions of authority, often unintentionally assign labels to people based purely on presumptions. Examples might include a teacher labelling a student as troublesome, or a police officer labelling a group of youths as delinquents. The point is two-fold: first, that the label is not based on any actual 'fact'; second, that the label is often internalised by the person being labelled, who comes to accept it and acts accordingly, thus making the label 'real'.

**Looking-glass self** is a term coined by Charles Horton Cooley, to describe how the 'self' is never fixed but rather constantly changing based on our perception of how others see us. It is rather like looking into a mirror, and seeing ourselves as we think others see us, and making adjustments on the basis of this. Thus, the 'self' is a permanently unfinished product of reflection. Cooley's ideas, similar to those of his contemporary George Herbert Mead, came to influence interactionism.

**Methodological individualism** is the belief that, when studying society, one should always start with the individuals who comprise it. In other words, one should not begin with the assumption that there is something called 'society' which is external to the individual, but rather with the actions, motivations or experiences of those individuals. Max Weber was an early champion of this approach. While methodological individualism is opposed to the doctrine of methodological holism (starting with society and working downwards), it should not be conflated with the concept of agency as opposed to structure. Exchange theory is the most overt form of methodological individualism in sociology, but it is not a theory which is at all interested in agency.

**Modernisation** is the name given to the process by which the 'natural' evolution of a society from a 'primitive' to a more 'complex' state can be speeded up. As a process, it assumes that there is an end-state, 'being modern', which is clearly (and controversially) defined as corresponding to Western societies, with democratic political systems, liberal social systems, and capitalist economic systems. During the 1950s a lot of effort was made by policymakers to develop strategies for 'improving' the social conditions of poorer countries through modernisation. In the sociology of development, modernisation theory was particularly associated with functionalists such as Talcott Parsons. However, modernisation theory was criticised both by traditional evolutionists who felt that it was not possible to 'jump-start' progress in this way, and more significantly by some neo-Marxists who suggested that the poverty of some countries was directly related to the wealth of others, such that development should be studied in structural terms. A further criticism was that the assumption that 'modern' Western societies represent some 'advanced' stage of development should itself be contested.

**Modernity** and **modernism** are not easy terms to define. Suffice to say that when one comes across a reference to something that is 'modern' in sociological theory, it rarely means 'current' or 'contemporary', as popular usage of the term might suggest. Instead, it refers largely to a period of history which is characterised by an associated way of seeing the world, expressed as culture, politics, economics and social relationships. There is no obvious point at which 'modernity' began, although some accounts point to Europe in the fifteenth century. Modernity as an age encompasses the period from the Industrial Revolution in which industrial production methods went hand in hand with an emerging capitalist economy, democratic political structures, a liberal social philosophy emphasising the individual, and large-scale urbanisation. However, it also encompasses the so-called Age of Enlightenment, in which scientific reason came to replace traditional customs and religion as the dominant world view. Modernism is often used to refer to an artistic style (in, for example, paintings, literature, architecture and philosophy) which reflects these characteristics of modernity. In sociology, modernity is associated with attempts to impose scientific rationality upon the world, as in theories such as Marxism, functionalism or structuralism. So-called 'post-modernist' writers have suggested that we have moved beyond the restrictive shackles of modernity, but others, such as Jürgen Habermas, have defended the progressive qualities of modernity against such criticisms. Some sociologists, such as Anthony Giddens, have attempted to show that the world in which we live today is not 'post-modern' but rather an advanced, complex form of modernity.

**Mythologies** are stories about the world which, though not based on any 'fact', become taken for granted. Structuralists such as Claude Lévi-Strauss and Roland Barthes have shown how these myths serve to reproduce dominant ideologies.

**Patriarchy** is the name given to a system of male dominance in a society. Feminists have argued that social institutions such as religion, the family, education or the media serve to sustain patriarchy by reproducing positive roles for and images of men and negative roles for and images of women, thus keeping women subordinate. Patriarchy is thus a structural power relationship based on gender, not reducible to other factors such as social class position.

**Phenomenology** is the philosophy of perception, of how people see and experience the world. There are many forms of phenomenology, not least the existential phenomenology which was popularised in the twentieth century by the likes of Jean-Paul Sartre, which was about understanding the strategies employed by people to make sense of the world around them, which is both inhibiting and ridiculous. Phenomenology was brought into sociology by Alfred Schutz, and became the inspiration for the theory of ethnomethodology.

**Plural society** is a term popularised by writers in the conflict theory tradition, to describe any society which contains more than one cultural group, and thus often competing value systems, but in which one group has achieved a greater share of power and influence than its rivals.

**Positivism** refers to the belief that the methods and techniques employed in the natural sciences, like biology, chemistry or physics, can be employed in the social sciences. In other words, it is the assumption that one can study society scientifically. Natural scientists tend to seek factual explanations for things, and often use experimental methods to uncover the general laws about how something behaves. For positivists, what is true of biological bodies, or chemicals in a test tube, or electricity, is also true of the social world. There are two kinds of positivism in sociology. One reduces social action to some already existing natural science to explain it, such as using genetics to explain why some people do certain things and others don't. The other treats sociology as a science in its own right, and uses scientific method to explain how it works. This latter form of positivism was pioneered by Auguste Comte, the 'founder' of sociology.

**Post-modernity** and **post-modernism** are terms that need to be understood in relation to modernity and modernism. It is argued by some writers (such as Jean-François Lyotard) that Western society since the late twentieth century can no longer be described as 'modern' because it is no longer bound by the logic of modernity, such as the imposition of scientific reason upon the world and attempts to uncover objective truths. Post-modernism is an associated style, popular in the arts, which subverts the order and structure associated with modernism, seeking instead to deconstruct traditional binary opposites. Advocates of post-modernity and post-modernism champion freedom from fixed labels and definitions, and the end of the so-called 'grand struggles' in favour of more localised politics of identity, but their opponents suggest that they go too far in dismissing the 'big' issues of truth and justice and end up endorsing an 'anything-goes' kind of moral relativism.

**Power elite** is the name given to the coalition of interests who enjoy the greatest power and influence in society. While politicians hold official power over decision-making at the state level, and do indeed constitute part of the power elite, the radical American sociologist C. Wright Mills tells us that unelected business leaders and military leaders are also part of it, and very often the three groups operate as a kind of clandestine cabal, doing each other favours so as to protect their own interests. More recently, attention has been paid to the power wielded by global media tycoons as well as CEOs of major corporations, which is often more considerable that than wielded by the elected politicians who form the government of a country.

**Power/knowledge** is a term popularised by Michel Foucault. Foucault observes how power is inherently contained within all social relationships, and is embedded in the forms of knowledge which define those relationships. Examples include the doctor–patient relationship, or the teacher–student relationship.

**Pragmatism** is a movement that originated in the philosophy of knowledge, and came to be influential in moral philosophy, the philosophy of education, and, in the form of interactionism, in sociology. Founders of the movement include William James, John Dewey, C.S. Pierce and George Herbert Mead. Pragmatism maintains that we cannot actually know the meaning of any event, we can only inquire what it might mean to those involved. In other words, while there may be an objective 'truth', it is not something we can ever actually 'know'. Rather than seeking out general laws, knowledge should be understood in context, in terms of its practical uses and consequences. As a moral philosophy, pragmatism applies the same principle of doubt to questions of 'right' and 'wrong'. Modern pragmatists such as Richard Rorty assert that rather than trying to provide objective moral criteria we should ask whether an action is right or wrong in its particular context.

**Relations of ruling** is a term popularised by Dorothy E. Smith to refer to the complex way in which different forms of power relations, including gender relations, intersect. The term is intended to rejuvenate debates around patriarchy by focusing on processes and dynamics rather than simple institutions.

**Sexual division of labour** is a term initially used by anthropologists to show how some roles in societies are attributed to men and others to women, for example 'hunters' and 'gatherers'. Feminists have criticised assumptions that the sexual division of labour is somehow 'fixed' and 'natural', suggesting instead that it is socially constructed and reflective of power relations.

**Signifier and signified** are the two parts of a sign, according to structuralists. The signifier is the representation of something, the signified is the thing it represents. Simple examples include a red light, which signifies the command to stop in some cultures. Language itself is a collection of signifiers, words that represent things but are not those things themselves. A lot of work has been carried out on the media which looks for the meanings that are being portrayed by certain images, or signifiers. More recently, post-structuralists have suggested that contemporary society is increasingly dominated by 'free-floating' signifiers that are no longer attached to the things they are supposed to represent.

**Social class** is a form of classification system or hierarchy in society which categorises people according to their economic position. A common way of doing this is through occupation, so that certain managerial jobs are deemed 'middle class' while manual ones are considered 'working class'. However, such a system is unsatisfactory for many sociologists, especially Marxists, because it does not take into consideration the power relations between the classes. Karl Marx came up with a far more tightly defined approach to social class – he suggested that all people fit into one of two categories, depending on how they relate to the 'means of production': they either own it or they work it. Those who own (or in some more general cases exercise control over) the means of production generate wealth from it, and are the bourgeoisie, or middle class. Those who work it effectively sell their labour power for a fixed sum and do not reap the profits of their work; they are the proletariat, or working class. According to either definition, though, class is an economic category, and should not be conflated with other forms of stratification such as status. Nonetheless, some writers do introduce a cultural dimension to social class, suggesting that certain values, preferences and tastes constitute distinctly 'working-class' or 'middle-class' ways of life, which people often carry with them even if they move into different jobs.

**Social constructionism** is the umbrella term for those perspectives in sociology which suggest that the world is constructed by people, through their perceptions of it. This is not to suggest that there is no world outside of our perception of it, but that our knowledge of that world is defined by such perceptions. In sociology, it is usually used to refer to interactionism, ethnomethodology and phenomenology, and some forms of post-modernist social theory. However, the term more broadly refers to any approach which rejects non-social explanations for social phenomena (for example, approaches grounded in religion, or in some appeal to a pre-social 'human nature'). Such approaches constitute 'essentialism', which is the opposite of social constructionism.

**Social integration** is a term used by Talcott Parsons to refer to how, through socialisation, individuals are properly integrated into the wider social system. An example is how the formal education system serves to reproduce a belief in certain norms and values which are then internalised by a student. Successful social integration minimises the likelihood of deviance.

**Social order** is one of the fundamental problems that has intrigued sociologists since the dawn of the discipline. How is it even possible, they ask, that we live in a world that appears at least to be orderly? Most of us get up in the morning, carry out our morning rituals, then head off to work or school, and take for granted that this is the way the world is. Without this semblance of order, the world would be a wholly unpredictable, anarchic place, subject only to the self-serving laws of the jungle. While social order is formally maintained through regulatory institutions such as the law which seek to prevent us from violating it, for Durkheim and also Parsons, the most important means of maintaining order is the successful reproduction, via institutions such as the family and the school, of a shared set of values. Ethnomethodologists have subsequently extended this by showing that the appearance of order in society is due to the existence of a lot of taken-for-granted assumptions grounded in common sense. Structuralists have also suggested that social order is a reflection of power relations, such that that which is 'different' is marginalised, and the 'order of things' becomes taken for granted as the 'natural' way of the world.

**Social system** is a central concept in functionalist theory. It is suggested by functionalists such as Talcott Parsons that society operates as a system, comprised of multiple component parts each of which performs a necessary function for the wider system. Sociologists who use this approach tend to concentrate on identifying the specific functions performed by different aspects of society. The model of the social system is a holistic one, in that everything is studied in relation to the wider whole (so, rather than studying education, one studies the role of the education system within the broader social system). Very few people adhere to Parsons's theorisation of the social system today, but variations of it remain popular, not least Niklas Luhmann's version.

**Socialisation** is the process of becoming a 'fully social' person. In some psychological theories of child development, it is suggested that an infant goes through stages of socialisation, from an initial phase in which she is the centre of her universe, through to a recognition of how she relates to other people. Drawing on the work of Sigmund Freud, the functionalist Talcott Parsons treats socialisation as a process of social integration, in which an individual grows to internalise the norms and values of wider society. Thus, a 'fully socialised' person is one who has fully accepted and is compliant with these norms and values. Deviance is the result of incomplete socialisation. However, for interactionists, socialisation is *never* complete, because we are always learning new things about ourselves from interacting with others, so we are constantly in the process of 'becoming' complete but never actually achieve it.

**Structuration** is the name of the theory associated with Anthony Giddens, and of the process it describes. Giddens seeks to overcome the classic dualism of 'structure' and 'agency' in sociology, i.e. the schism between those theories which emphasise the impact of structural forces upon the individual and those which begin with human agents perceiving and thus creating the world. He suggests that, in fact, these are one and the same, our actions create the world but are at the same time constrained by it, given that we operate within predefined sets of rules and resources. This duality of structure and agency is dubbed 'structuration'.

**Structure** is a term which has long been a core concept in sociological theory, although it has multiple meanings. In functionalist thinking, it refers to the existence of a level of determining factors beyond the individual, embedded in society itself. A structural explanation thus emphasises the extent to which such external factors produce individuals. Not only functionalists, but also many Marxists, are accused of relying on such explanations. An alternative use of the term comes from structuralist theorists, who distinguish between the 'surface structure' of a social practice (such as a religious ceremony), and the 'deep structure' it represents (such as the human need for religion). For a long time it was believed that structural explanations were incompatible with those that emphasise human agency, but in recent decades there have been attempts to reconcile the two, such as Anthony Giddens's theory of structuration.

**Utilitarianism** is a theory in moral philosophy which claims that the 'rightness' or 'wrongness' of an act is dependent upon its consequences rather than any inherent property of the act itself. Utilitarianism emphasises that 'right' is determined by happiness, so that an act can be deemed right if it results in greater happiness – the classic utilitarian maxim is that the ultimate end should be 'the greatest happiness to the greatest number'. There are different versions of utilitarianism, but the broader movement is most closely associated with such philosophers as Jeremy Bentham, James Mill and John Stuart Mill. Critics argue that, as a theory of ethics, utilitarianism is flawed because it tries to reduce morality to quantifiable indicators, numbers. In sociology, utilitarianism was instrumental in the development of exchange theory by George Homans.

# Biographies

**Adorno, Theodor** (1903–1969) was a core member of the neo-Marxist Frankfurt School. Together with Max Horkheimer he wrote *Dialectic of Enlightenment*, which juxtaposed two competing forms of rationality. A musicologist and psychologist as well as a sociologist, he is best known for his work on the 'culture industry', in which he suggested that owing to commodification culture now formed part of the economic base rather than the ideological superstructure.

**Althusser, Louis** (1918–1990) was a French Marxist philosopher who blended Marxism with structuralism with a view to overcoming the perceived weaknesses in Marxist theory. He is best known for recasting capitalism as an entire social formation, which manifests itself in cultural and political as well as economic forms. In sociology, his theorisation of 'ideological and repressive state apparatuses' which serve to reproduce capitalism has been particularly influential.

**Barthes, Roland** (1915–1980) was a French cultural theorist who was schooled in the tradition of structuralism but moved beyond this and is considered to be one of the original 'post-structuralists'. Barthes took the structuralist interest in semiotics – in the relationship between the signifier and the signified – a step further by introducing a third level, of ideology.

**Baudrillard, Jean** (1929–2007) was a French philosopher and sociologist celebrated by many as the archetypal post-modernist. Influenced originally by Marxism and structuralism, Baudrillard found fame for his critical commentaries on the vacuous state of the contemporary world, which he saw as exhibiting 'hyper-reality'.

**Bauman, Zygmunt** (1925– ) is a Polish-born theorist whose work is eclectic in its nature. Influenced by structuralism and critical theory, he has written on globalisation, post-modernity and the horrors of the Nazi Holocaust. Underpinning his work is a concern with how knowledge and language are linked to power, and with the Weberian problem of rationalisation.

**Beck, Ulrich** (1944– ) is a German sociologist best known for his groundbreaking work on the *Risk Society*, in which he defined the contemporary condition of globalisation as one of manufactured risk.

**Becker, Howard** (1928– ) is an American sociologist who is one of the most famous exponents of interactionism, in the tradition of the Chicago School. His ethnographic studies of classroom interactions, workplace interactions, and the lifestyles of such 'deviants' as marijuana users are rightly feted. A passionate lover of jazz music, Becker is hailed as a champion of misunderstood underdog who sits on the margins of society. He is credited with developing the theory of labelling, and his most famous work is the collection *Outsiders*.

**Bernard, Jessie** (1903–1996) was an American feminist who played a major part in developing feminist sociology in the United States. Her most famous work is *The Future of Marriage*, and throughout her career she drew attention to how the institution of the family restricted the position of women in society.

**Blau, Peter** (1918–2002) was an Austrian-born American sociologist most famous for extending George Homans's exchange theory to accommodate issues of power and social structure. In his later career, he abandoned exchange theory to develop a purely structural form of sociological analysis.

**Blumer, Herbert** (1900–1987) was an American sociologist who studied at Chicago under George Herbert Mead, and was responsible for taking Mead's ideas and developing from them the theory of interactionism.

**Bourdieu, Pierre** (1930–2002) was a French sociologist whose major theoretical contribution to sociology was in the development of his theory of practice, which blended the influences of Marx, Durkheim and Weber, as well as structuralism, and which was hailed as a brilliant attempt to overcome the dualism of structure and agency in sociology. In this theory, Bourdieu showed how our tastes and dispositions, which are influenced by our class upbringings, impact upon our opportunities in life. He thus synthesised a theory of individual tastes and the choices we make that derive from our tastes with a theory of how dominant social structures are reproduced.

**Coleman, James** (1926–1995) was an American sociologist most famous for introducing rational choice theory into the discipline, in his massive work *The Foundations of Social Theory*. Coleman was a prolific writer who also served as a consultant on educational policy.

**Comte, Auguste** (1798–1857) is considered to have been the founder of sociology. A French philosopher, he believed that it was possible to study the social world in much the same way as one studies the natural world, through the discovery of the general laws that govern it. As a pioneer of positivism in sociological theory, he had a profound effect upon the later development of the discipline he inspired.

**Cooley, Charles Horton** (1864–1929) was an American sociologist and social psychologist who is most famous for his idea of the 'looking-glass self', which, together with George Herbert Mead's theory of the 'I' and the 'me' came to influence interactionism. He was also a pioneer of the use of case studies and of the 'introspective' approach to studying society.

241

**Dahrendorf, Ralf** (1929–2009) was a German sociologist and politician, one of the founders of modern conflict theory, who later became a British citizen and as a prominent member of the Liberal Democrats was elevated to a seat in the House of Lords. His academic work was largely driven by the desire to rethink the idea of social class beyond the narrow confines of Marxist theory, to take account of the multiple forms of conflict in late industrial society.

**Douglas, Mary** (1921–2007) was a British anthropologist and later a Dame of the realm. Influenced by Durkheim and by structuralism, Douglas's most famous work is *Purity and Danger*, in which she explored the cultural reasons why some things are considered 'dirty' and others 'clean'.

**Durkheim, Emile** (1858–1917) was one of the founding fathers of sociology. Inheriting the French tradition from Auguste Comte, he was responsible for setting up the first department of sociology in Europe, and throughout his works he emphasised the relevance and distinctiveness of sociology in uncovering the structural factors which influence social actions. His early work, especially *The Division of Labour in Society*, influenced functionalism with its emphasis on how modern complex societies are characterised by increasing differentiation and specialisation. His later work, sometimes co-written with his nephew Marcel Mauss, influenced structuralism with its interest in the forms of cultural practice. He also made significant contributions to sociological methodology, utilising comparative statistical research in works like *Suicide* and *Rules of Sociological Method*.

**Firestone, Shulamith** (1945– ) is a Canadian-born feminist sociologist who has been instrumental in developing a distinctive radical feminist movement in sociology. Since the publication of her major work, *The Dialectic of Sex*, she has also been hailed as a pioneering figure in the sociology of the body.

**Foucault, Michel** (1926–1984) was a French philosopher and historian of ideas who may rightly be hailed as the most influential social theorist of the late twentieth century. In his early work Foucault was heavily influenced by structuralism, but his career was defined by attempts to politicise the structuralist project by showing how the institutions of modernity, the asylum, the prison and so on, which ostensibly service the interests of a progressive rationality, are actually inseparable from power dynamics. Foucault's work is akin to an archaeology of power relations, uncovering how power is intrinsically connected to knowledge systems. Although recognised as a definitive 'post-structuralism', Foucault rejected this label and his library of works defies easy classification.

**Friedan, Betty** (1921–2006) was a leading American feminist theorist. Her book *The Feminine Mystique* is considered to be one of the most important contributions to liberal feminist sociology, although Friedan was also a dedicated activist for women's rights.

**Garfinkel, Harold** (1917– ) is an American sociologist most famous for being the 'founder' of ethnomethodology. His *Studies in Ethnomethodology* is still considered to be the definitive account of the perspective. His theory is seen as a synthesis of Parsons's functionalist interest in social order and Schutz's phenomenological interest in how people perceive situations. Garfinkel spent much of his career at the University of California, Los Angeles.

**Giddens, Anthony** (1938– ) is the most important and influential British sociologist since Herbert Spencer. His early work was largely metatheoretical, engaging with the legacies of Marx, Durkheim and Weber and critiquing the dominant sociological theories of the time, such as functionalism, Marxism and structuralism. In the 1980s he developed his own theoretical perspective, the theory of structuration, which was an attempt to reconcile the structure–agency dualism. In the 1990s he turned his attention to the controversial problems of globalisation and post-modernity, interpreting both within the framework of 'reflexive' late modernity. He then began to focus on political questions, seeking to develop a new political position beyond the old-fashioned left–right divide, which became known as the 'Third Way' and won him the endorsement of Prime Minister Tony Blair, to whom he became an adviser. He became a Labour peer in the House of Lords, having spent much of his academic career at Cambridge and the London School of Economics, of which he served as director.

**Goffman, Erving** (1922–1982) was a Canadian sociologist best known for developing the 'dramaturgical' approach, in which social interaction is viewed as a performance involving an actor and an audience. Goffman's work is distinctive because it blends Mead's social psychology with a Durkheimian social anthropology, an interest in the rituals and practices of everyday life. His major works include *The Presentation of Self in Everyday Life*, *Asylums* and *Stigma*.

**Gramsci, Antonio** (1891–1937) was an Italian Marxist philosopher and a leader of the Italian Communist Party who was famously imprisoned by Mussolini. He is considered to be one of the pioneers of humanist Marxism, blending the Marxist revolutionary project with an interest in how people relate to the dominant culture ideology of capitalism. He developed the concept of hegemony, the manufacture of consent, to show how the exploitative capitalist system sustains itself.

**Habermas, Jürgen** (1929– ) is a German social theorist who is the leading voice of the 'second generation' of the Frankfurt School. In his early career, Habermas developed an interest in the decline of the 'public sphere', and in the importance of open political debate. He developed this into his famous 'theory of communicative action', which explored the different ways in which communication can be hindered and infiltrated by power dimensions. In the tradition of critical theory, Habermas has presented the case that modernity is characterised by competing forms of rationality, associated with the 'system' and the 'lifeworld', and that the logic of the former, deriving from science and economics, is increasingly colonising the latter. This is basically an extension of the Marxian theory of commodification. Although Habermas's work is inspired by Marx, it is not conventionally Marxist, drawing heavily on other approaches in the social sciences. He has remained, though, the most outspoken disciple of Marx's revolutionary spirit, in his attacks on post-modernism and his defence of the 'grand projects' of modernity, such as the pursuit of social justice.

**Harvey, David** (1935– ) is a British-born social geographer who is one of the most influential living intellectuals working in the Marxist tradition. He has famously engaged in the debate around post-modernism, which he sees as a reflection of a particular stage of late capitalism. He has also attacked the logic of neo-liberal economics, and the project of American imperialism.

**Homans, George** (1910–1989) was an American sociologist who taught at Harvard University. He was the founder of exchange theory, which he developed from his interest in behavioural psychology and his concern that mainstream sociology, such as that championed by his colleague Talcott Parsons, was overly structural in its approach and had little to say about the role of the individuals who comprise society.

**Lévi-Strauss, Claude** (1908–2009) was a Belgian-born French anthropologist recognised as the founder of structuralism in anthropology. He applied the insights of the linguist Ferdinand de Saussure to social practices and institutions, focusing on the role of mythologies and binary opposites in producing a meaningful social order. He was one of the most influential academics of the twentieth century.

**Lyotard, Jean-François** (1924–1998) was a French social theorist whose opposition to the 'grand narratives' of the Enlightenment reached its high point with the publication of *The Postmodern Condition* in 1979, in which he celebrated the diversity that characterised this new phase in history.

**Marcuse, Herbert** (1898–1979) was one of the core members of the Marxist-inspired Frankfurt School of Critical Theory, a German intellectual who fled to America when the Nazis came to power and became a leading intellectual spokesperson for the New Left, including the radical student movement of the 1960s. His work is characterised by a blending of the ideas of Marx, Weber and Sigmund Freud. His project was to update Marxist theory to become a critique of all forms of domination and authoritarianism, whether articulated as Western capitalism, Soviet-style communism, or European fascism. In *One-Dimensional Man* he suggested that the working class could no longer function as the agent of revolutionary social change because it has been incorporated into the system, and so called upon other marginalised groups in society, especially students, to take up the banner.

**Marx, Karl** (1818–1883) was a German-born activist and theorist who is rightly hailed as one of the most important intellectuals of all time. His lifelong project was a critique of the capitalist economic system, which he showed to be exploitative and unjust. In his earlier work he demonstrated how it went against the basic principles of human nature, arguing that people are born to create and enjoy the benefits of their creations, but in capitalism, they are alienated from these efforts, while others get rich on the backs of them. He suggested that the exploited working class would eventually realise that it was being subjected to exploitation by the bourgeoisie and exhibit true class consciousness, overthrowing capitalism and replacing it with a fairer system, communism. In his later work he applied a more rigorous approach to analysing how capitalism actually operates. He provided a clear definition of social class as the relationship one has to the means of production, either owner or worker, and developed a theory of social change called historical materialism which was grounded in his belief that the driving force in any society is its system of production. His works range from politically motivated pamphlets and long essays to multi-volume academic treatises, of which the most significant is the three-volume *Capital*. Marx's ideas gave rise to the theoretical school of thought that bears his name, and much of the world has at some time or another been organised according to principles ostensibly inspired by him, although the extent to which Soviet-style communism was in any way Marxism remains debatable. For much of his life he lived in London and he often co-wrote with his sponsor, Friedrich Engels.

**Mead, George Herbert** (1863–1931) was an American sociologist, philosopher and social psychologist who taught at Chicago University and whose ideas inspired the theory of interactionism. Mead blended the insights of philosophical pragmatism and psychological behaviourism to develop a theory of the self as constantly evolving through social interaction, distinguishing between the outward- and inward-facing aspects of the self, the 'I' and the 'me'. His lectures on the topic were collected under the banner *Mind, Self and Society*, which is considered to be his definitive work.

**Merton, Robert** (1910–2003) was an American sociologist who began his academic career at Harvard University before moving to Columbia, and became, after Talcott Parsons, the most important figure in the functionalist movement. Unlike Parsons, Merton was not interested so much in developing grand all-explanatory theories as in working with 'theories of the middle-range', and he sought to apply the insight of functionalist theory to an understanding of deviance and social inequalities in American society. He extended functionalist theory beyond the limitations of earlier approaches, introducing such concepts as 'latent and manifest functions' and 'dysfunctions and non-functions' into the perspective, and also made a significant contribution to the sociology of science.

**Millett, Kate** (1934– ) is an American feminist writer whose major work, *Sexual Politics*, is considered to be one of the definitive accounts of the dynamics of patriarchy in society. Miller has also been an outspoken activist and journalist.

**Mills, C. Wright** (1916–1962) was an American sociologist who was considered to be a maverick and a thorn in the side of the mainstream sociological community, but who is now recognised as one of the greatest American sociologists of all time. Considered something of a radical by American standards, his work was actually inspired more by Weber than by Marx, and can be seen as an American version of conflict theory. Mills is best known for two works: *The Power Elite*, in which he suggested that power in American society was held by a coalition of three interest groups, the politicians, the military leaders and the leaders of big business; and *The Sociological Imagination*, which has inspired subsequent generations of sociologists for its celebration of the critical inquiry crucial to the discipline.

**Oakley, Ann** (1944– ) is a British socialist feminist theorist, the daughter of the celebrated sociologist Richard Titmuss, who taught for many years at the University of London. She is best known for her analysis of the unpaid work often carried out by women in their domestic roles, although she has also made contributions to medical sociology and is a successful author of fiction.

**Park, Robert Ezra** (1864–1944) was an American sociologist who taught at the University of Chicago and championed the use of ethnographic methods rather than detached statistical analysis, famously telling his students to go out into the city and 'get the seat of your pants dirty in real research'. Park's work blends a fascination with the micro-level webs of social interaction which he inherited from Georg Simmel, with an interest in real lives and real experiences, inspired largely by his previous work as an activist and secretary to the civil rights leader, Booker T. Washington. Although best known for his contributions to urban sociology, Park is considered to be a major influence on the development of interactionist theory.

**Parsons, Talcott** (1902–1979) was probably the most significant American sociologist of the twentieth century. He taught at Harvard University where he inspired a generation of scholars to adopt and develop the functionalist approach of which Parsons himself is seen as the chief theoretician. In his first work, *The Structure of Social Action*, he sought to blend the insights of four European theorists – Weber, Durkheim, Vilfredo Pareto and Alfred Marshall – to form a general voluntaristic theory of action. However, he quickly moved from focusing on action to concentrating on systems. In his major work *The Social System* he presented the most detailed account of the way society operates as a system, comprised of subsystems which perform necessary functions for the broader whole. In doing so he provided the framework within which most American sociologists and many others worldwide operated for decades. Although best known for his grand-scale theorising, Parsons also contributed specific analyses of social institutions, and became a prominent figure in the theory of modernisation which was influential in policy circles in the 1950s.

**Perkins-Gilman, Charlotte** (1860–1935) was an American feminist sociologist and writer whose work can be seen as an early example of that which would become commonplace in later feminist sociology, namely the analysis of how social institutions reproduce patriarchy. In particular, she turned her attentions to the study of religion and the institution of the family. She is usually considered to be an exponent of cultural feminism, concerned with women's experiences, and in addition to her academic publications she was a prominent novelist. Her writings have, however, been subject to controversy surrounding her alleged views on race relations.

**Rex, John** (1925– ) is a South African-born British sociologist whose work sits firmly in the camp of conflict theory, and is largely inspired by the ideas of Max Weber. Rex's major contributions have been to the study of race relations and to urban sociology as well as to the development of the conflict theory perspective.

**Robertson, Roland** (1938– ) is a British sociologist who taught for many years at Pittsburgh before taking up his current post at Aberdeen. In his early career he found fame as a sociologist of religion, but he is now best known for his theorisation of globalisation as a process of the long-term emergence of a global consciousness. Robertson's theoretical approach is broadly considered to be neo-functionalist.

**Saussure, Ferdinand de** (1857–1913) was a Swiss linguist who pioneered the use of structuralist analysis. He famously divided language into two component parts, corresponding to the performance of an utterance, including the words themselves, which he suggested is culturally relative and not useful for scientific analysis, and the underlying rules, such as the grammar, which are universal. This distinction inspired Claude Lévi-Strauss to develop structuralism as a theory of human societies.

**Schutz, Alfred** (1899–1959) was an Austrian sociologist who is best known for bringing the philosophical tradition of phenomenology – the philosophy of how people perceive the world – into sociology. He was actually a lawyer by profession, based in New York, yet his impact on the academic world has been significant, not least through its adoption by Harold Garfinkel who used it as the basis of his theory of ethnomethodology.

**Simmel, Georg** (1858–1918) was a German sociologist whose work was so eclectic it is hard to pin down in a single statement, which is probably why he has not endured the long-term recognition attributed to his contemporary, Max Weber. His fascination with social relationships and the webs of interaction influenced Robert Park and the later interactionist movement. However, his interest in the forms of social action marks him as a forerunner to structuralism. He is also celebrated as a major influence on conflict theory, and, through his work on money and on the philosophy of knowledge, on critical theory.

**Smith, Dorothy E.** (1926– ) is a Canadian sociologist best known for extending the traditional concerns of liberal feminist theory into new territories with her work on feminist research methods, her call for feminists to better understand the perspectives of their subjects using ethnographic methods and 'standpoint theory', and her concept of the 'relations of ruling', which helped move the debate about patriarchy beyond institutional analysis and into an appreciation of what subsequent writers have called 'intersectionality'.

**Spencer, Herbert** (1820–1903) was a British sociologist and liberal politician who was an outspoken advocate of the application of evolutionary theory to the social world. Not only did Spencer fiercely defend the idea that societies, like biological organisms, evolve over time, governed by the maxim of the 'survival of the fittest', he also applied this logic to questions of public administration, arguing that each individual should be left to fend for her- or himself and that the state had no role to play in providing welfare for the needy, in a manner that pre-dates the policies of the New Right by over a century. Spencer is considered to be one of the founders of sociology, and although his social Darwinism is no longer popular in the discipline, his chief legacy is in the functionalist movement, as it was Spencer who first spoke of society as a system, and who introduced the distinction between 'structure' and 'function'.

**Wallerstein, Immanuel** (1930– ) is an American historical and economic sociologist who was for much of his career director of the Fernand Braudel Center at the State University of New York, Binghamton. He is famous as the founder of world systems theory, and although his work has a distinctly Marxian flavour, he consciously subverts much of what Marx said about the nature of capitalism. Wallerstein believes that since the nineteenth century sociologists, including Marxists, have operated within a nation-state paradigm and have thus neglected the way in which capitalism has for hundreds of years operated as a world system. Wallerstein treats this system in much the same was as Marx treated social class, as comprising a dominant group (the richer 'core' countries) and a subordinate one (the 'periphery') and showing how the relationship between them is one of exploitation.

**Weber, Max** (1864–1920) was a German social theorist who, along with Marx and Durkheim, is credited with being one of the 'founding fathers' of the discipline of sociology. Weber's contributions to the discipline are immense, but because of their rather diverse nature, did not result in the emergence of a particular school of thought to carry on his legacy. For example, he was an advocate of an interpretive method in sociology, of understanding the motivations of participants, which later became the hallmark of interactionism (although in no other way is interactionism clearly derived from Weber's work). He was also interested in how different forms of rationality influenced different political, economic and legal systems, and was considered by some to be a cultural relativist. His most famous work was *The Protestant Ethic and the Spirit of Capitalism*, in which he suggested that capitalism as an economic system emerged from a dominant individualistic world view which he attributed to Protestantism. This was a deliberate inversion of Marx's materialist theory of history, and in many respects Weber can be seen as engaging in a dialogue with Marx's ideas. Whereas Marx prioritised economics, Weber looked at the multiple factors which direct societies. While Marx reduced conflict to the economic category of social class, Weber was concerned with class, status and party as different sources of power. His theory of social conflict came to influence conflict theory in the twentieth century, while his pessimistic concern with the increasing dominance of means–end rationality across society – including the reliance upon an increasingly dehumanising system of bureaucracy – influenced the Frankfurt School of critical theory among others. More so than any of his contemporaries, Weber theorised the emergence of the modern nation state, with its centralised system of social control. His legacy continues to be felt across sociology in all its forms.

# Bibliography

Afshar, H. (1985) *Women, Work and Ideology in the Third World*. London: Tavistock.

Aggleton, P. (1987) *Deviance*. London: Tavistock.

Atkinson, J.M. (1978) *Discovering Suicide: Studies in the Social Organization of Sudden Death*. London: Macmillan.

Atkinson, J.M. (1984) 'Public Speaking and Audience Responses: Some Techniques for Inviting Applause' in J. Maxwell Atkinson and John Heritage (eds) *Structures of Social Action: Studies in Conversation Analysis*. Cambridge: Cambridge University Press.

Atkinson, J.M. and Drew, P. (1979) *Order in Court: The Organization of Verbal Interaction in Judicial Settings*. London: Macmillan.

Bandura, A. (1973) *Aggression: A Social Learning Analysis*. Englewood Cliffs, NJ: Prentice-Hall.

Barrett, M. (1980) *Women's Oppression Today: Problems of Marxist–Feminist Analysis*. London: New Left Books.

Barthes, R. (1957) *Mythologies*. London: Paladin.

Barthes, R. (1964) *Elements of Semiology*. New York: Stanford University Press.

Bauman, Z. (1989) *Modernity and the Holocaust*. Cambridge: Polity.

Beauvior, Simone de (1973) *The Second Sex*. New York: Vintage Books.

Becker, G. (1968) 'Crime and Punishment: An Economic Approach' in *Journal of Political Economy*, 76.

Becker, G. (1976) *The Economic Approach to Human Behaviour*. Chicago: University of Chicago Press.

Becker, G. (1981) *A Treatise on the Family*. Cambridge, MA: Harvard University Press.

Becker, H. (1963) *Outsiders: Studies in the Sociology of Deviance*. New York: Free Press.

Benedict, R. (1934) *Patterns of Culture*. Boston: Houghton Mifflin.

Berger, P. and Luckmann, T. (1966) *The Social Construction of Reality*. London: Anchor Books.

Bernard, J. (1976) *The Future of Marriage*. Harmondsworth: Penguin.

Berreman, G. (1967) 'Stratification, Pluralism and Interaction' in A.V.S. de Reuck and J. Knight (eds) *Caste and Race: Comparative Approaches*. London: Churchill.

Best, S. and Kellner, D. (1991) *Postmodern Theory: Critical Interrogations*. New York: Guilford Press.

Blau, P. (1964) *Exchange and Power in Social Life*. New York: Wiley.

Blumer, H. (1969) *Symbolic Interaction: Perspective and Method*. Englewood Cliffs, NJ: Prentice-Hall.

Boas, F. (1940) *Race, Language and Culture*. New York: Macmillan.

Boden, D. (1990) 'People are Talking: Conversation Analysis and Symbolic Interaction' in H. Becker and M.S. McCall (eds) *Symbolic Interactionism and Cultural Studies*. Chicago: University of Chicago Press.

Bowles, S. and Gintis, H. (1976) *Schooling in Capitalist America: Educational Reform and the Contradictions of Economic Life*. New York: Basic Books.

Braverman, H. (1974) *Labor and Monopoly Capital: The Degradation of Work in the Twentieth Century*. New York: Monthly Review Press.

Brownmiller, S. (1975) *Against Our Will: Men, Women and Rape*. Harmondsworth: Penguin.

Buchanan, J. and Tullock, G. (1962) *The Calculus of Consent*. Ann Arbor: University of Michigan Press.

Butler, J. (1993) *Bodies that Matter: On the Discursive Limits of 'Sex'*. London: Routledge.

Caplow, T. (1959) 'Further Development of a Theory of Coalitions in the Triad' in *American Journal of Sociology*, LXIV.

Caudwell, C. (1946) *Illusion and Reality*. London: Lawrence & Wishart.

Chambliss, W. and Seidman, R. (1971) *Law, Order and Power*. Reading, MA: Addison-Wesley.

Cicourel, A. (1968) *The Social Organization of Juvenile Justice*. New York: Wiley.

Cicourel, A. (1974) *Cognitive Sociology: Language and Meaning in Social Interaction*. New York: Free Press.

Cicourel, A. and Kitsuse, J. (1963) *The Education Decision Makers*. New York: Bobbs-Merrill.

Cicourel, A. *et al.* (1974) *Language Use and School Performance*. New York: Wiley.

Clarke, R. (1992) *Situational Crime Prevention*. New York: Harrow and Heston.

Clarke, R. and Felson, M. (eds) (1993) *Routine Activity and Rational Choice*. New Brunswick: Transaction.

Cohen, A. (1955) *Delinquent Boys: The Culture of the Gang*. Glencoe, IL: Free Press.

Cohen, A. (1966) *Deviance and Control*. Englewood Cliffs, NJ: Prentice-Hall.

Cohen, S. (1972) *Folk Devils and Moral Panics*. London: Paladin.

Coleman, J.S. (1960) 'The Mathematical Study of Small Groups' in H. Solomon (ed.) *Mathematical Thinking in the Measurement of Behavior*. New York: Free Press of Glencoe.

Coleman, J. (1990) *Foundations of Social Theory*. Cambridge, MA: Harvard University Press.

Coleman, J. (ed.) (1992) *Rational Choice Theory: Advocacy and Critique*. London: Sage.

Collins, P.H. (1990) *Black Feminist Thought: Knowledge, Consciousness, and the Politics of Empowerment*. Boston: Unwin Hyman.

Collins, R. (1975) *Conflict Sociology: Toward an Explanatory Science*. New York: Academic Press.

Collins, R. (1994) *Four Sociological Traditions*. Oxford: Oxford University Press.

Conrad, J. (1981) *Justice and Consequences*. Lexington, MA: Lexington Books.

Cooley, C.H. (1964; original 1902) *Human Nature and the Social Order*. New York: Scribner's.

Cornish, D. and Clarke, R. (1986) *The Reasoning Criminal*. New York: Springer-Verlag.

Coser, L. (1956) *The Functions of Social Conflict*. New York: Free Press.

Dadrian, V. (1974–5) 'The Structural-Functional Components of Genocide' in *Victimology*, vol. IV.

Dahrendorf, R. (1959) *Class and Conflict in Industrial Society*. Stanford, CA: Stanford University Press.

Davis, K. (1937) 'The Sociology of Prostitution' in *American Sociological Review*, 2, pp. 744–755.

Davis, K. and Moore, W.E. (1945) 'Some Principles of Stratification' in *American Sociological Review*, 10, pp. 242–249.

Delphy, C. (1984) *Close to Home*. London: Hutchinson.

Douglas, J. (1967) *The Social Meanings of Suicide*. Princeton: Princeton University Press.

Douglas, M. (1966) *Purity and Danger: An Analysis of the Concepts of Pollution and Taboo*. London: Routledge & Kegan Paul.

Douzinas, C. (2000) *The End of Human Rights*. Oxford: Hart.

Downes, D. (1966) *The Delinquent Solution*. London: Routledge & Kegan Paul.

Dumont, L. (1972; original 1966) *Homo Hierarchicus: The Caste System and Its Implications*. London: Paladin.

Durkheim, E. (1947; original 1893) *The Division of Labour in Society*. New York: Free Press.

Durkheim, E. (1951; original 1897) *Suicide: A Study in Sociology*. New York: The Free Press.

Durkheim, E. (1964) *The Rules of Sociological Method*. New York: Free Press.

Dworkin, A. (1979) *Pornography: Men Possessing Women*. Harmondsworth: Penguin.

Eisenstadt, S. (1956) *From Generation to Generation*. Chicago, IL: Free Press.

Eisenstein, Z.R. (ed.) (1979) *Capitalist Patriarchy and the Case for Socialist Feminism*. New York: Monthly Review Press.

Elias, N. (1978) *What is Sociology?* London: Hutchinson.

Eysenck, H. (1970) *Crime and Personality*. London: Paladin.

Firestone, S. (1972) *The Dialectic of Sex*. London: Paladin.

Foucault, M. (1961) *Madness and Civilisation: A History of Insanity in the Age of Reason*. London: Tavistock.

Foucault, M. (1963) *The Birth of the Clinic: An Archaeology of Medical Perception*. London: Tavistock.

Foucault, M. (1966) *The Order of Things: An Archaeology of the Human Sciences*. London: Tavistock.

Fraser, N. (1989) *Unruly Practices: Power, Discourse and Gender in Contemporary Social Theory*. Cambridge: Polity Press.

Friedan, B. (1963) *The Feminine Mystique*. Harmondsworth: Penguin.

Friedl, E. (1975) *Women and Men: An Anthropological View*. New York: Holt, Rinhart & Winston.

Friedman, D. and Hechter, M. (1988) 'The Contribution of Rational Choice Theory to Macrosociological Research' in *Sociological Theory*, 6, pp. 201–218.

Garfinkel, H. (1949) 'Research Note on Inter- and Intra-Racial Homicides' in *Social Forces*, 27, pp. 69–81.

Garfinkel, H. (1967) *Studies in Ethnomethodology*. Englewood Cliffs, NJ: Prentice-Hall.

Giddens, A. (1985) *The Nation-State and Violence*. Cambridge: Polity Press.

Giddens, A. (1987) 'Structuralism, Post-Structuralism and the Production of Culture' in Anthony Giddens and Jonathan Turner (eds) *Social Theory Today*. Cambridge: Polity Press.

Gilligan, C. (1982) *In a Different Voice: Psychological Theory and Women's Development*. Cambridge, MA: Harvard University Press.

Glaser, B. and Strauss, A. (1967) *The Discovery of Grounded Theory*. Chicago: Aldine.

Goffman, E. (1959) *The Presentation of Self in Everyday Life*. New York: Doubleday.

Goffman, E. (1961) *Asylums: Essays on the Social Situation of Mental Patients and Other Inmates*. New York: Doubleday.

Goffman, E. (1963) *Stigma: Notes on the Management of Spoiled Identity*. Englewood Cliffs, NJ: Prentice-Hall.

Haas, J. and Shaffir, W. (1982) 'Taking on the Role of Doctor: A Dramaturgic Analysis of Professionalization' in *Symbolic Interaction*, 5, pp. 187–203.

Habermas, J. (1976) *Legitimation Crisis*. Cambridge: Polity Press.

Hargreaves, D. (1967) *Social Relations in a Secondary School*. London: Routledge & Kegan Paul.

Harvey, D. (1989) *The Condition of Postmodernity*. Oxford: Blackwell.

Hauser, A. (1951) *The Social Theory of Art*. London: Routledge & Kegan Paul.

Hauser, A. (1958) *The Philosophy of Art History*. Evanston, IL: Northwestern University Press.

Hawkes, T. (1977) *Structuralism and Semiotics*. London: Methuen.

Heath, A. (1976) *Rational Choice and Social Exchange: A Critique of Exchange Theory*. Cambridge: Cambridge University Press.

Heritage, J. (1984) 'Analyzing News Interviews: Aspects of the Production of Talk for an Overhearing Audience' in T. van Dijk (ed.) *A Handbook of Discourse Analysis*, vol. 3: *Discourse and Dialogue*. New York: Academic Press.

Heritage, J. and Greatbatch, D. (1986) 'Generating Applause: A Study of Rhetoric and Response in Party Political Conferences' in *American Journal of Sociology*, 92, pp. 110–157.

Hewitt, C.J. (1974) 'Elites and the Distribution of Power in British Society' in P. Stanworth and A. Giddens (eds) *Elites and Power in British Society*. Cambridge: Cambridge University Press.

Hirst, P. and Thompson, G. (1999) *Globalisation in Question*. Cambridge: Polity Press.

Holmes, O.W. (1920) *Collected Legal Papers*. London: Constable & Co.

Homans, G. (1960) *The Human Group*. New York: Harcourt, Brace and World.

Homans, G. (1961) *Social Behavior: Its Elementary Forms*. New York: Harcourt, Brace and World.

hooks, b. (1984) *Feminist Theory from Margin to Center*. Boston: South End Press.

Huntington, S.P. (1996) *The Clash of Civilizations and the Remaking of World Order*. New York: Touchstone.

Jameson, F. (1992) *Postmodernism, Or the Cultural Logic of Late Capitalism*. London: Verso.

Jefferson, G. (1979) 'A Technique for Inviting Laughter and Its Subsequent Acceptance Declination' in G. Psathas (ed.) *Everyday Language: Studies in Ethnomethodology*. New York: Irvington.

Jefferson, G. (1984) 'On the Organization of Laughter in Talk about Troubles' in J.M. Atkinson and J. Heritage (eds) *Structures of Social Action*. Cambridge: Cambridge University Press.

Kalven, H. Jnr and Zeisel, H. (1967) *The American Jury*. New York: Routledge & Kegan Paul.

Kessler, S.J. and McKenna, W. (1978) *Gender: An Ethnomethodological Approach*. Chicago: University of Chicago Press.

Kithahara, M. (1986) 'Commodore Perry and the Japanese: A Study in the Dramaturgy of Power' in *Symbolic Interaction*, 9, pp. 53–65.

Koedt, A., Levine, E. and Rappone, A. (eds) (1973) *Radical Feminism*. New York: Quadrangle.

Kuper, L. (1981) *Genocide: Its Political Use in the Twentieth Century*. New Haven: Yale University Press.

Lash, S. and Urry, J. (1987) *The End of Organised Capitalism*. Cambridge: Polity Press.

Lévi-Strauss, C. (1969) *The Elementary Structures of Kinship*. Boston: Beacon.

Lewis, O. (1959) *Five Families: Mexican Case Studies in the Culture of Poverty*. New York: Basic Books.

Lewis, O. (1961) *The Children of Sanchez*. London: Random House.

Lewis, O. (1967) *La Vida: A Puerto Rican Family in the Culture of Poverty*. London: Random House.

Llewellyn, K. (1960) *The Common Law Tradition: Deciding Appeals*. Boston: Little, Brown and Co.

Lovell, T. (2000) 'Feminisms of the Second Wave' in B.S. Turner (ed.) *The Blackwell Companion to Social Theory*. Oxford: Blackwell.

Lyotard, J.-F. (1979) *The Postmodern Condition*. Manchester: Manchester University Press.

MacKinnon, C. (1989) *Toward a Feminist Theory of the State*. Cambridge, MA: Harvard University Press.

MacKinnon, C. (1993) 'Crimes of War, Crimes of Peace' in S. Shute and S. Hurley (eds) *On Human Rights*. New York: Basic Books.

Malinowski, B. (1954) *Magic, Science and Religion, and Other Essays*. New York: Anchor Books.

Marcuse, H. (1964) *One-Dimensional Man: Studies in the Ideology of Advanced Industrial Society*. Boston: Beacon Press.

Marx, K. (2008) *The Eighteenth Brumaire of Louis Bonaparte*. Rockville: Wildside Press.

Matza, D. (1964) *Delinquency and Drift*. New York: John Wiley and Sons.

Matza, D. (1969) *Becoming Deviant*. Englewood Cliffs, NJ: Prentice-Hall.

Matza, D. and Sykes, G. (1961) 'Delinquency and Subterranean Values' in *American Sociological Review*, 26.

Mauss, M. (1965) *The Gift: Forms and Functions of Exchange in Archaic Societies*. London: Cohen and West.

Mead, G.H. (1962) *Mind, Self and Society: From the Standpoint of a Social Behaviorist*. Chicago: University of Chicago Press.

Mead, M. (1928) *Coming of Age in Samoa*. London: Cape.

Merton, R. (1938) 'Social Structure and Anomie' in *American Sociological Review*, 3, pp. 672–682.

Merton, R. (1957) *Social Theory and Social Structure*. Glencoe, IL: Free Press.

Messinger, S., Sampson, H. and Towne, R. (1975) 'Life as Theatre: Some Reality' in *Sociometry*, 25, pp. 98–110.

Meyrowitz, J. (1995) 'New Sense of Politics: How Television Changes the Political Drama' in *Research in Political Sociology*, 7, pp. 117–138.

Miller, W. (1958) 'Lower Class Culture as a Generating Milieu of Gang Delinquency' in *Journal of Social Issues*, 14.

Millett, K. (1970) *Sexual Politics*. New York: Doubleday.

Mills, C.W. (1956) *The Power Elite*. New York: Oxford University Press.

Mills, C.W. (1959) *The Sociological Imagination*. New York: Oxford University Press.

Modleski, T. (1986) 'Femininity as Mas(s)querade: A Feminist Approach to Mass Culture' in C. MacCabe (ed.) *High Theory/Low Culture*. Manchester: Manchester University Press.

Mohanty, C.T. (1988) 'Under Western Eyes: Feminist Scholarship and Colonial Discourse' in *Feminist Review*, 30, pp. 61–89.

Momsen, J. (1991) *Women and Development in the Third World*. London: Routledge.

Moore, B. Jnr (1966) *The Social Origins of Dictatorship and Democracy*. Boston: Beacon.

Moore, W.E. (1963) *Social Change*. Englewood Cliffs, NJ: Prentice Hall.

Morgan, R. (1970) *Sisterhood is Powerful: An Anthology of Writings from the Women's Liberation Movement*. New York: Vintage.

Mulvey, L. (1975) 'Visual Pleasure and Narrative Cinema' in *Screen*, 16, 3.

Murdoch, G.P. (1949) *Social Structure*. New York: Macmillan.

Oakley, A. (1974) *Housewife*. London: Allen Lane.

O'Byrne, D. and Hensby, A. (2011) *Theorising Global Studies*. Basingstoke: Palgrave.

Olson, M. (1965) *The Logic of Collective Action*. Cambridge, MA: Harvard University Press.

Ortner, S.B. (1974) 'Is Female to Male as Nature is to Culture?' in M.Z. Rosaldo and L. Lamphere (eds) *Woman, Culture and Society*. Stanford, CA: Stanford University Press.

Parsons, T. (1937) *The Structure of Social Action*. New York: McGraw-Hill.

Parsons, T. (1951) *The Social System*. New York: Free Press.

Parsons, T. (1959) 'The Social Structure of the Family' in R.N. Anshen (ed.) *The Family: Its Functions and Destiny*. New York: Harper & Row.

Perkins-Gilman, C. (1898) *Women and Economics*. Boston, MA: Small, Maynard and Co.

Perkins-Gilman, C. (1923) *His Religion and Hers*. Westport, CT: Hyperion Press.

Plummer, K. (ed.) (1991) *Symbolic Interactionism*, 2 volumes, Aldershot: Edward Elgar.

Plummer, K. (2000) 'Symbolic Interactionism in the Twentieth Century' in B.S. Turner (ed.) *The Blackwell Companion to Social Theory*. Oxford: Blackwell.

Posner, R. (1972) *Economic Analysis of Law*. Boston: Little, Brown & Co.

Posner, R. (1981) *The Economics of Justice*. Cambridge, MA: Harvard University Press.

Quinney, R. (1970) *The Social Reality of Crime*. Boston: Little, Brown.

Rex, J. (1970) *Race Relations in Sociological Theory*. London: Weidenfeld & Nicholson.

Rex, J. and Moore, R. (1967) *Race, Community and Conflict: A Study of Sparkbrook*. Oxford: Oxford University Press.

Rich, A. (1976) *Of Woman Born: Motherhood as Experience and Institution*. New York: Bantam.

Rich, A. (1980) 'Compulsory Heterosexuality and Lesbian Experience' in *Signs*, 5, pp. 631–660.

Robertson, R. (1992) *Globalization: Social Theory and Global Change*. London: Sage.

Rock, P. (1979) *The Making of Symbolic Interactionism*. London: Macmillan.

Rorty, R. (1993) 'Human Rights, Rationality and Sentimentality' in S. Shute and S. Hurley (eds) *On Human Rights*. New York: Basic Books.

Rose, A. (ed.) (1962) *Human Behavior and Social Process: An Interactionist Approach*. London: Routledge & Kegan Paul.

Rose, A.M. (1967) *The Power Structure: Political Process in American Society*. New York: Oxford University Press.

Rostow, W. (1960) *The Stages of Economic Growth: A Non-Communist Manifesto*. Cambridge: Cambridge University Press.

Sacks, H., Schegloff, E. and Jefferson, G. (1974) 'A Simplest Systematics for the Organization of Turn-Taking in Conversation' in *Language*, 50, 4, 1, pp. 696–735.

Sahlins, M. (1976) *Culture and Practical Reason*. Chicago: University of Chicago Press.

Said, E. (1978) *Orientalism*. New York: Random House.

Saussure, Ferdinand de (1916) *Course in General Linguistics*. New York: McGraw-Hill.

Schegloff, E. (1979) 'Identification and Recognition in Telephone Conversation Openings' in G. Psathas (ed.) *Everyday Language: Studies in Ethnomethodology*. New York: Irvington.

Schegloff, E. (1992) 'Repair after Next Turn: The Last Structurally Provided Defense of Intersubjectivity in Conversation' in *American Journal of Sociology*, 97, pp. 1295–1345.

Schegloff, E., Jefferson, G. and Sacks, H. (1977) 'The Preference of Self-Correction in the Organization of Repair in Conversation' in *Language*, 53, pp. 361–382.

Sklair, L. (2002) *Globalization: Capitalism and Its Alternatives*. Oxford: Oxford University Press.

Skocpol, T. (1979) *States and Social Revolutions*. Cambridge: Cambridge University Press.

Smart, C. (1976) *Women, Crime and Criminology*. London: Routledge & Kegan Paul.

Smart, C. (1989) *Feminism and the Power of Law*. London: Routledge.

Smelser, N. (1973; original 1967) 'Processes of Social Change' in N. Smelser (ed.) *Sociology: An Introduction*. New York: Wiley.

Smith, D.E. (1987) *The Everyday World as Problematic: A Feminist Sociology*. Boston, MA: Northeastern University Press.

Smith, D.E. (1990a) *Texts, Facts and Femininity: Exploring the Relations of Ruling*. London: Routledge.

Smith, D.E. (1990b) *The Conceptual Practices of Power: A Feminist Sociology of Knowledge*. Boston, MA: Northeastern University Press.

Snow, D.A., Zurcher, L.A. and Peters, R. (1984) 'Victory Celebrations as Theater: A Dramaturgical Approach to Crowd Behaviour' in *Symbolic Interaction*, 8, pp. 21–42.

Sztompka, P. (1993) *The Sociology of Social Change*. Oxford: Basil Blackwell.

Ten Have, P. (1995) 'Medical Ethnomethodology: An Overview' in *Human Studies*, 18, pp. 245–261.

Thomas, W.I. (1923) *The Unadjusted Girl*. Boston: Little Brown.

Tickner, J.A. (1992) *Gender in International Relations*. New York: Columbia University Press.

Tiryakian, E. (1968) 'The Existential Self and the Person' in C. Gordon and K. Gergen (eds) *The Self in Social Interaction*. New York: Wiley.

Tuchman, G. (1981) 'The Symbolic Annihilation of Women by the Mass Media' in S. Cohen and J. Young (eds) *The Manufacture of News*. London: Constable.

Turner, R. (ed.) (1974) *Ethnomethodology*. Harmondsworth: Penguin.

Turner, V. (1969) *The Ritual Process: Structure and Antistructure*. New York: Aldine de Gruyter.

Vogel, E. and Bell, N. (1968) 'The Emotionally Disturbed Child as the Family Scapegoat' in N. Bell and E. Vogel (eds) *A Modern Introduction to the Family*. New York: Free Press.

Vold, G. (1958) *Theoretical Criminology*. New York: Oxford University Press.

Von Neumann, J. and Morgenstern, O. (1944) *The Theory of Games and Economic Behaviour*. New York: Wiley.

Walby, S. (1990) *Theorizing Patriarchy*. Oxford: Basil Blackwell.

Waltz, K. (1979) *The Theory of International Politics*. Reading, MA: Addison-Wesley.

Warner, W.L. (1936) 'American Caste and Class' in *American Journal of Sociology*, 42.

Weber, M. (1949) *The Methodology of the Social Sciences*. Glencoe, IL: Free Press.

Weber, M. (1968) *Economy and Society*, 3 vols. New York: Bedminster Press.

Wendt, A. (1999) *Social Theory of International Politics*. New York: Cambridge University Press.

West, C. (1984) *Routine Complications: Troubles with Talk Between Doctors and Patients*. Indiana: Indiana University Press.

West, C. and Fenstermaker, S. (1993) 'Power, Inequality and the Accomplishment of Gender: An Ethnomethodological View' in P. England (ed.) *Theory on Gender/Feminism on Theory*. New York: Aldine de Gruyter.

West, C. and Zimmerman, D. (1977) 'Women's Place in Everyday Talk: Reflections on Parent–Child Interaction' in *Social Problems*, 24, pp. 521–529.

West, C. and Zimmerman, D. (1983) 'Small Insults: A Study of Interruptions in Cross-Sex Conversations with Unacquainted Persons' in B. Thorne, C. Kramerae and N. Henley (eds) *Language, Gender and Society*. Rowley, MA: Newbury House.

West, C. and Zimmerman, D. (1987) 'Doing Gender' in *Gender & Society*, 2, pp. 125–151.

Willis, P. (1977) *Learning to Labour: How Working Class Kids Get Working Class Jobs*. Farnborough: Saxon House.

Winch, P. (1958) *The Idea of a Social Science and Its Relation to Philosophy*. London: Routledge & Kegan Paul.

Wittig, M. (1982) *The Straight Mind and Other Essays*. London: Harvester Wheatsheaf.

Woolf, V. (1929) *A Room of One's Own*. London: Hogarth Press.

Wright, W. (1975) *Six-Guns and Society*. Berkeley: University of California Press.

Zimmerman, D. (1971) 'The Practicalities of Rule Use' in J. Douglas (ed.) *Understanding Everyday Life*. London: Routledge & Kegan Paul.

# Index

Entries in bold also appear in the glossary and biographies

# Index

# Index

Mead, Margaret 54
media, portrayal of women 104–5, 109
mental illness 195
**Merton, Robert** 245–6
  anomie 36, 37
  dysfunctions and non-functions 33–4
  functionalism 14, 26, 27, 31, 33, 33–4,
    36–7
  means-end relationship 36
meta-theories 214
**methodological individualism** 118, 233
Miliband, Ralph 73, 83
Mill, James 120, 126, 144
Mill, John Stuart 120
Miller, Walter 38, 54–5
**Millett, Kate** 15, 101–4, 246
  *Sexual Politics* 101–4
**Mills, C. Wright** 15, 51, 53, 62, 225, 246
Mitchell, Juliet 94, 108
**modernisation** 40–2, 43, 213, 233–4
**modernism** 213, 234
**modernity** 234
  characteristics – summary 214
  meaning of 213
  and post-modernity 211–18
Moore, Barrington Jnr 52, 63–4
Moore, Wilbert E. 25, 26, 32, 33, 41–2
moral consciousness 191–2
moral philosophy 120
Morgenstern, O. 129, 131
motivations 121
Mulvey, Laura 94–5
Murdoch, George Peter 31, 99
**mythology** 197, 234

neo-functionalism 17, 205
neo-liberalism, and rational choice theory
  137
neo-Marxism 74
neutralisation techniques 174
New Right 137

**Oakley, Ann** 94, 103, 246
Oedipus complex 107
operant behaviour 122–3, 125–6
order of things 183
ordinary language philosophy 176–7
Ortner, Sherry B. 106
Oxford School of linguistic philosophy
  176–7

**Park, Robert Ezra** 13, 142, 246
**Parsons, Talcott** 1, 14, 118, 224, 246–7
  critics 35
  education 31
  functional prerequisites 29

functionalism 14–15, 25–6, 27
  influence of Weber 14, 26
  modernisation 41
  religion 32
  system integration 33, 34
  *The Social System* 26, 29–31
  *The Structure of Social Action* 26, 34–5
  voluntaristic theory of action 14
party 47, 229
**patriarchy** 94–5, 113, 206, 235
  criticisms of concept 108
  description 100–1
  dynamics of 100–10
  and politics 105–6
  and pornography 105
  reproduction 101–4
    biological 102, 109
    educational 102, 109
    ideological 101–2
    psychological 104, 109
    sociological 102
    use of force 103–4, 109
  role of female body in sustaining 106–7
  and social class 103
  sources, summary 109
Pavlov, Ivan 120, 122
**Perkins-Gilman, Charlotte** 13, 96, 102, 103,
  247
**phenomenology** 161, 166–8, 235
Piaget, Jean 191–2
Piaget, John 183
Pierce, Charles Sanders 142, 143, 187
pig as dirty animal 193–4, 195
**plural society** 235
pluralists 59
polarisation 194, 220
political ideology 137–8
political sociology 59
politics, and patriarchy 105–6
pornography, and patriarchy 105
positive discrimination 114
**positivism** 7, 136, 235
post-modern feminism 96–7, 97, 98
**post-modernism** 17, 96, 185, 214–15, 217,
  235–6
**post-modernity** 73, 205, 211–18, 235–6
post-structuralism 16–17, 184–5, 190, 203,
  205
Poulantzas, Nicos 83
poverty, sociology of 54
power
  exchange theory 134
  instrumentalist theory 134
  and interest groups 57–62, 64
  and knowledge 201, 236
  and structuralism 198–9